BACKYARD GIANTS

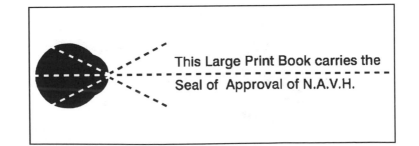

This Large Print Book carries the
Seal of Approval of N.A.V.H.

BACKYARD GIANTS

THE PASSIONATE, HEARTBREAKING, AND GLORIOUS QUEST TO GROW THE BIGGEST PUMPKIN EVER

SUSAN WARREN

THORNDIKE PRESS

An imprint of Thomson Gale, a part of The Thomson Corporation

Detroit • New York • San Francisco • New Haven, Conn. • Waterville, Maine • London

THOMSON

GALE ™

LIBRARY OF CONGRESS CATALOGING-IN-PUBLICATION DATA

Warren, Susan, 1959–
    Backyard giants : the passionate, heartbreaking, and glorious quest to grow the biggest pumpkin ever / By Susan Warren.
        p. cm.
    Includes bibliographical references.
    ISBN-13: 978-0-7862-9950-8 (large print : alk. paper)
    ISBN-10: 0-7862-9950-9 (large print : alk. paper)
    1. Pumpkin. 2. Pumpkin — Competitions. 3. Pumpkin growers. 4. Large type books. I. Title.
    SB347.W137 2007
    635'.62—dc22   2007032100

Published in 2007 by arrangement with Bloomsbury USA, a division of Diana Publishing Inc.

Printed in the United States of America on permanent paper
10 9 8 7 6 5 4 3 2 1

Early to bed,
Early to rise,
Work like hell and fertilize.
— Emily Whaley

CONTENTS

PROLOGUE

Ron and Dick Wallace leaned over the sides of a wood-slatted cart parked at the edge of their concrete driveway south of Providence, Rhode Island. Both men stared intently at the assortment of pumpkin seedlings inside, their eyes resting on each small plant in its turn. There it was: The 2006 growing season, all laid out before them in the flat bottom of a four-by-four-foot, two-wheeled wagon. If the months ahead held a world-champion pumpkin for the Wallaces, it would come from one of these 20 plants. But which one? Ron's eyes drilled into each seedling, trying to see its future. He studied their color, their shape, their size. They were bright-green splashes in dirt-filled peat pots. Some of the week-old seedlings were only about three inches tall, others nearly five inches. But those tiny plants held extraordinary expectations.

For the past 15 years, Ron, a 40-year-old

country club manager, and his father, Dick, a retired factory superintendent, had run a race with hundreds of other growers around the world trying to grow a pumpkin big enough to set a new world record. Competitive growers were on a mission to create steadily bigger monster pumpkins, finding new ways to stretch the limits of Mother Nature. Between 1988 and 2005, the world record was broken 14 times.

Pumpkins were growing so freakishly large, even the growers were beginning to wonder if they were nearing a limit. Surely, at some point, Mother Nature would put her foot down. Progress already seemed to be slowing. The bigger the pumpkins got, the more they seemed to be splitting wide open or rotting on the vine before they could get to a weigh-off. Then again, many people had thought a 1,000-pound fruit was beyond the reach of mankind until a New York grower shattered that barrier in 1996. Now the next breakthrough loomed: 1,500 pounds, a three-quarter-ton fruit. The thought consumed the daydreams of every grower who fantasized about walking to the podium at the annual growers' convention to claim the orange blazer awarded for the biggest pumpkin of the year. Every grower hoped to be the one to crash through that

1,500-pound barrier. And if a grower could manage that, then anything was possible. Even, maybe, one day, a one-ton pumpkin.

So each year, growers wage a battle of good and evil on an epic scale, fighting off disease, voracious insects, and four-legged vermin that could reduce their colossus to compost fodder literally overnight. They invest hundreds and sometimes thousands of dollars, and spend long hours in hard physical labor, pruning and weeding and feeding and watering. They cut down trees that block the sun. They dig up their dirt and send it to laboratories for scientific analysis. Vacations are postponed, marriages are strained, and friends neglected as growers devote every spare moment to their pumpkin patch during the peak season. The dream is that by the time the harvest moon rises in the late-September sky, all that sacrifice will have produced at least one giant pumpkin with a chance to set a new world record, or at least to win a local weigh-off. But every year, the competition gets stiffer as more growers discover the hobby and the secrets of giant-pumpkin growing spread around the world from the United States to Europe to Australia and Japan.

■ ■ ■ ■

What makes a man spend half his year busting his guts to grow a giant pumpkin, and the other half dreaming about it? It's just a hobby, after all. And, Ron didn't kid himself, a somewhat ridiculous hobby. "You've got to remember, you're growing a pumpkin here, not curing cancer," he often reminded his fellow Rhode Island growers — and himself. But like any other obsession, there's something else going on. A need to break barriers, to defy the odds, to test the limits of one's own abilities. Giant-pumpkin growers are on a quest for satisfaction, distinction, respect; they're not much different from athletes who compete for an Olympic gold medal to prove they've reached the pinnacle of their sport. Ron wanted more than just to grow big pumpkins; he wanted to grow the biggest pumpkin the world had ever seen.

In the realm of giant-pumpkin growers, the Wallaces were as skilled and knowledgeable as anyone. But they weren't perfect. They made mistakes. And luck had never been on their side. Over the years they'd grown respectable contenders, sometimes even potential world-record-beaters, but victory had been snatched away by a succession of villains: hungry insects and rodents, nasty microbes, blistering heat, and early cold snaps. Those were bitter disappointments. But the nice thing about life in the garden is that every year you get a new chance.

The pumpkin seedlings spread out now before Ron and Dick Wallace represented prime genetic stock from some of the world's best growers: Checkon, Jutras, Davies, Rose, and of course, Wallace. Each one had the potential to grow a champion pumpkin. And in just a few minutes, Ron and Dick would be planting some of them into the ground to launch the race for the 2006 world record. Ron had been watching the seedlings grow all week. He already had ideas about a few of them. But now he had to make his final choice.

He reached into the wagon and gently turned one of the pots, appraising the plant from every angle. He moved it to one side and reached for another. There was just one thing he needed to know from each seedling: What can you do for me? Which one would grow into the biggest and healthiest plant? Which one would pour enough energy into a pumpkin to push it over 1,300, 1,400 — maybe even 1,500 pounds? Which one?

13

Ultimately, giant-pumpkin genetics are a crapshoot, and Ron was staring down at the gaming table. It was time to place his bets.

1
A LOOK BACK

The year before, like every other year the Wallaces had been growing, had started out with infinite optimism. Ron and his dad had that charged-up feeling you get when you think — you *know* — "This is it. It's my turn." Two thousand and five was going to be the Wallaces' big year.

Except it wasn't. Out of eight giant pumpkins the Wallaces grew in 2005, six never made it to the weigh-off scale. The biggest one that did was puny by competitive standards — only about 840 pounds. A pumpkin that size would have blown the socks off the gardening world just 15 years ago. But now any pumpkin less than 1,000 pounds was a candidate for the compost pile.

So it goes in the world of competitive pumpkin growing. Not only do you risk losing at the weigh-off after months of hard work, there's a good chance you won't even make it to the contest. When pumpkins are pushed to grow so big so fast, swelling up like water balloons on the end of a garden hose, a lot more can go wrong than right. As Ron liked to put it, "Just imagine if *you* were putting on thirty or forty pounds a day."

Ron and Dick belong to a special breed of gardeners that compete to grow the largest flowers, fruits, and vegetables they possibly can. At the end of every season, special events are held where the botanical marvels are weighed and measured and prizes handed out. Thus, the world had been gifted with its first 269-pound watermelon, a 124-pound cabbage, a 24-pound tomato, and a carrot nearly 17 feet long. It is pumpkins, though, that have taken center stage. No other vegetable or fruit grows that big, that fast. Only pumpkins, with their timeless link to fairy tales and family holidays, attract so much wonder and attention. For gardeners seeking the thrill of competition, pumpkins are the tallest mountain in the range, the fastest car on the block.

And yet, clearly, Mother Nature never intended pumpkins to grow as big as hot tubs. These giants are bred to be freaks. They are cultivated from an elite seed stock, then coaxed into an enormous size with special pruning techniques, relentless fertilization, and copious amounts of pesticide and fungicide. The result is not pretty. Gravity pulls on these behemoths as they grow, shaping them into lopsided lumps. The finished fruit often look less like the traditional, orange, Halloween jack-o'-lanterns than like semi-deflated balloons from the Macy's Thanksgiving Day Parade that have drifted into the garden. Many aren't even orange. Genetic tinkering has created monsters with mottled gray, white, and pink skin. As they mature, rough, cantaloupe-like veining spreads across the shell. The effect can be disturbing, as if a huge, cancerous tumor has sprouted in the garden.

The Wallaces had grown a lot of big pumpkins. They just hadn't managed to get one big enough to win a championship. In 2000, Martha Stewart's television show called and asked to follow Ron around for part of the growing season. It was a good year for the Wallaces, and they thought they had finally grown a winner. The camera was rolling at the Topsfield Fair, where Ron had taken his biggest pumpkin hoping not only to win, but to claim the $10,000 in prize money offered to the first grower who brought in a 1,000-pounder. But shortly before the weigh-off began, rival grower Steve Connolly drove up with a bigger pumpkin and snatched victory away. Ron's pumpkin weighed only 885 pounds, while Connolly's tipped over the 1,000-pound mark and won the big money. Ron was a gentleman about it. He squared his shoulders and sucked in his disappointment as he looked into Martha's cameras and offered congratulations to the winner. "He's a nice guy," Ron said. And then he made the same vow he'd made every other year. "That's not the best that we can do," he said. "We can do a lot better than that. We'll be back next year."

But the next year and the year after that all brought the same thing: another six months of gut-wrenching effort followed by gut-wrenching disappointment. The years rolled on and the seasons piled up and still the Wallaces couldn't claim a big win. Ron prided himself on being an expert grower. He'd put in the hours, done the research, spent a lot of money, and made a lot of sacrifices. He'd earned a reputation as one of the most skilled and serious competitors in the game. Yet every year, he and his father had pitted themselves against the greatest growers in the world, and every year they'd come up short. Ron still talked up his game. But deep in his heart, he was beginning to doubt himself. What if he really didn't have what it takes? What if all his time and effort came to nothing?

Rhode Island's small pumpkin-growing club had been in danger of falling apart when its longtime president stepped down in 2004. Already, club members had begun drifting over to the larger, more-established New England Pumpkin Growers Association in neighboring Massachusetts, which hosted the highest-profile giant-pumpkin contest in the nation at Topsfield Fair. It would have been easy just to let the club fade away and transfer loyalties to New England. Except that Dick Wallace and some of the other core members weren't ready to give up on Rhode Island.

Dick turned to his son. Ron's work as a hard-driving, super-organized, no-nonsense business manager gave him just the kind of experience the Rhodies needed. Dick urged him to take charge of the club and build it back up. It was the last thing Ron had time for. He nearly killed himself already fitting in his pumpkin growing on top of the 50 to 60 hours he spent every week at the country club. But Ron also saw an opportunity.

"Rhode Island — smallest state, smallest pumpkins." It was just a wisecrack by another

New England grower that Ron had overheard at one of the weigh-offs a few years before. But the words still stung, and Ron itched to prove how wrong they were. At a birthday party for one of the club members, fellow grower Joe Jutras had given what Ron now calls his Knute Rockne speech — a rousing battle cry to the Rhode Island brothers. Joe, a 50-year-old woodworker with a freckled complexion and red hair fading to gray, was usually the gentle voice in a loud crowd. But that day he was fired up and eager to show the world that tiny Rhode Island shouldn't be underestimated. "We can beat those guys!" Joe declared. Their smallness, he said, would be their strength. Many of the Rhode Island growers lived within just a few miles of each other. The whole state was only about 1,200 square miles, smaller than the city metro area of Miami. If the Rhodies shared their knowledge and experience, they could not only increase the expertise of the whole group, but also bring newer growers up to competitive speed faster.

In a world without giant pumpkins, the Rhode Island growers probably would never have found themselves in the same room together. They were all men, but other than that, they had little in common. They were young, old, and middle-aged. Scott Palmer was a welder; Joe Jutras owned a custom-cabinetry business with his two brothers; Ron Wallace ran a country club; Dick was a retired factory manager; Peter Rondeau ran a business in safety-training for chemical-plant workers. But their lives shared a common thread even before pumpkins: gardening. Not a sunbonnet-and-canvas-gloves, puttering-about-in-the-flowers kind of gardening, but testosterone-charged muscle gardening. These men grew things you could eat — tomatoes and eggplant and asparagus — and they grew them big. They cultivated fruit trees laden with apples and peaches and pears. They produced showcase plants like towering sunflowers and dahlias. But at some point in the past 15 years, each one had drifted into the world of giant-pumpkin growing, and pumpkins had quickly consumed everything else.

Ron agreed to take over as president of the club on one condition: Every member had to pitch in and do his part to make it work. No secrets. No bullshitting. No back-stabbing. Everyone had to help each other. Then, let the best grower win. At the start of the 2005 season, the club renamed itself the Southern New England Giant Pumpkin Growers (SNGPG) to include growers from neighboring Massachusetts and Connecticut. And then the seeds went in the ground and the work began.

Mother Nature didn't make it easy. The season started cold and wet and then turned hot and dry. But by weigh-off time at the beginning of October, several of the club's growers had pumpkins on track to weigh well over 1,000 pounds. Ron and Dick Wallace had two they estimated to be in the 1,300-pound range — easily the biggest pumpkins they'd ever grown.

The Wallaces were counting on those pumpkins to help boost Rhode Island into the top ranks of growing clubs that year. So it was a huge blow when they lost both their pumpkins just days before the weigh-off. Giant pumpkins are vulnerable to bacteria and fungi that can rot them from the inside out. Sometimes, a grower doesn't even know what happened. Something just goes wrong somewhere in some invisible way. Then a soft spot appears, like a bruise on an apple. By the time a grower sees it, it's usually too late.

Ron had noticed just such a soft spot near the base of his pumpkin as he made his daily patch inspection three days before the weigh-off. The bathtub-sized pumpkins were sitting there in his garden, huge and orange and beautiful. But the soft spot — rot — spread fast. Ron stood with his feet planted in the rich, black earth and his heart sinking, staring down at the monster that had consumed his life for the past six months. A thick orangey soup had begun to seep from beneath. A sweet stench filled his nostrils. There was no room for hope anymore. It was over. His giant pumpkin was going down.

Ron's disappointment was sharp and deep, and all too familiar. He cracked the rotting skin open in hopes of recovering some seeds. But the seeds, swimming in a fetid pool of neon-orange slime, were limp and lifeless. Disgusted, he left the broken shards of giant pumpkin lying in the grass next to the garden, an organic monument to disappointment.

The Wallaces were thankful they at least had another big one left — their biggest. It was a huge, flattish beast shaped like a giant beanbag chair. The pumpkin was so heavy it had sunk several inches into the deeply tilled earth of the garden. But early on the morning before the weigh-off, as the harvesting crew of fellow growers arrived to help pick and load the pumpkin, Ron and Dick noticed a wet spot in the dirt. Dick dipped his fingers into the muddy soil, lifted it to his nose, and sniffed the unmistakable perfume of rotten fruit. The pumpkin was finished — probably from the same fungal infection that took down the other one.

The ugly collapse of a year's work was hard to bear. Ron stalked away scowling. But Dick, a 65-year-old former marine, just laughed. "If you can't take defeat," he shrugged, "this isn't the hobby for you." He used a small saw to cut into the pumpkin and reached inside to look for seeds. As he stirred his hand through the stinking soup, the smell billowed into the air, making the growers standing nearby gag and laugh in revulsion. There were no seeds worth saving, so Dick posed for pictures beside the putrid corpse, the saw held across his chest like a warrior's sword.

By then, a cool drizzle had begun to fall, and the harvesting crew moved on to the next grower's house. More rain was in the forecast, and there were still a half-dozen pumpkins to load up before the day's end. Ron and Dick swallowed their disappointment and pitched in to help the others.

It was dark by the time all the pumpkins had been loaded into the growers' pickups. The huge orange- and cream-colored lumps loomed high above the truck beds as the growers followed each other to Frerich's Farm, where the weigh-off was to be held the next day. Farm owner David Frerich used a forklift to carry the pumpkins from the trucks to a grassy field. It was a delicate operation that involved spearing the wooden pallet beneath the pumpkin with the forklift's tines, backing away carefully, and then gently lowering the pumpkin to the ground without breaking its tender shell.

Club members Scott Palmer and Fred Macari were thought to have the best shot at winning that year's weigh-off. Fred was a longtime grower who had won the Rhode Island championship the year before and was hoping for a repeat. Scott was one of the club's newest growers. He and his wife, Shelley, had surprised everyone with the boulder that had sprouted in their patch. Scott and Shelley could hardly believe it themselves. They hadn't even managed to grow a 1,000-pound pumpkin before, but this one was estimated to be over 1,300 pounds. It was a bomb, as the big ones were called. The other growers started calling Scott "Palmer the Bomber," which in their broad Rhode Island accents became "Pahma da Bomma."

Each grower, in his turn, clucked and hovered like a nervous hen as the forklift lifted his pumpkin for the move from truck to ground. They worked in the dark in the wet grass by the headlights of the pickup trucks. Scott Palmer went last. As the forklift backed away with Palmer's bomb of a pumpkin raised high on its pallet, there was a grinding noise and the lift gave way, sending the fork and the pumpkin into free fall. An eternity passed in that fraction of a second, and then the lift shuddered to a stop with a jarring crunch, only inches from the ground. The growers froze in horror. In the shocked silence, the same thought raced through everyone's mind: Had the pumpkin cracked? If it had, it was finished. No cracked pumpkins were allowed at the weigh-off. Scott rushed up to exam it, running his hands across the ribs and leaning over to check it underneath. It was still sound. No cracks. As Scott's worried face broke into a relieved smile, the other growers slapped him on the back in glee. It was a good omen. "You broke the truck!" they whooped.

Scott's pumpkin was added to the row of giants lined up in the field to wait their turn at the scale the next day. In the cool, wet night, the pumpkins glowed white and orange and pink, floating in a sea of grass, illuminated by the headlights of the pickup trucks as the growers headed home. It had been a long day, and they were supposed to get started early the next morning.

A heavy rain began later that night and delayed the weigh-off from Saturday to Sunday, and then again to Monday. A cold, light rain was still falling as the competition got underway, dampening the festival atmosphere and cutting the crowd of spectators to less than a quarter of its usual size. Dick still managed to be jovial, but Ron's mood that morning was as gray as the clouds overhead. He was still mourning the loss of his pumpkins, and he was worried about the club. He had been so sure, as the season wrapped up, that they were going to show the world that Rhode Island had been underestimated. Their lineup gave them a better-than-even chance of racking up the highest average weight for the top-10 pumpkins of any club in the world. But losing the Wallaces' two 1,300-pound contenders was devastating. Nothing was sure anymore.

Ron did his best to fight off the gloom. He had no time to feel sorry for himself — there was too much to do getting people registered and organized for the weigh-off. Despite the rain delays, 52 growers had brought pumpkins to be weighed. A forklift carried the giant pumpkins to the scale one by one. Ron's spirits rallied with the excitement. As club president, he emceed the weigh-off from a platform stage behind the scale. Dressed in a red sweatshirt and faded blue jeans, with a khaki baseball cap pulled low over his eyes, he held a microphone in one hand, engaging the crowd with the easy banter of a game show host and calling out the weights as the growers came forward with each pumpkin.

As the last entries were brought to the scale, Rhode Island grower Steve Sperry surprised everyone with a pumpkin weighing 1,312 pounds. That was almost 150 pounds more than he'd expected, and it was the heaviest he'd ever managed. Then it was Fred Macari's turn. His high, fat, orange pumpkin was bigger than Sperry's, but the digital scale stopped ticking at 1,310.5 pounds. Fred's pumpkin was bigger, but it wasn't heavier.

Massachusetts grower Steve Connolly had created a stir by arriving late, just as he had in 2000 at Topsfield, hauling a small open-bed trailer behind his car. He appeared only moments before the weigh-off began, explaining that his trailer, weighed down by the massive pumpkin, had blown a tire on the road to Frerich's Farm. Whispers swept through the crowd. This could be the winner. The Connolly pumpkin was rumored to weigh more than 1,400 pounds — more than anything the Rhodies had produced.

There is a saying in the giant-pumpkin world that is repeated throughout the year, and especially often at weigh-off time: "The bullshit stops when the tailgate drops." No matter what you think your pumpkin weighs, the scales always have the final word.

The crowd was on edge as Steve Connolly's pumpkin came to the scale. The numbers ticked up . . . past Fred's 1,310.5, past Sperry's 1312 . . . and stopped at 1,333 pounds. That put him in first place, with only Pahma da Bomma's pumpkin left to weigh.

For an instant on that rainy Monday morning of October 10, 2005, in Warren, Rhode Island, as Scott Palmer's pumpkin bomb hit the electronic scale and all eyes were fixed on the red digital numbers zooming upward, past 1,300, past 1,400, some dared to hope Rhode Island might claim the new world record. Why not? Here stood some of the finest growers with some of the biggest pumpkins anywhere. The new world record, set just the week before at 1,469 pounds, seemed within reach. But the red digital numbers slowed, then stopped, at

1,443 pounds. Scott Palmer's pumpkin was bigger than anything else grown in New England that year, big enough to win the Southern New England weigh-off, but it was still 26 pounds shy of the world record.

A quick calculation of the top 10 pumpkins weighed that day revealed an unprecedented club average of 1,173.9 pounds. Even without a contribution from the Wallaces, the Southern New England Giant Pumpkin Growers had seized the title of most successful growing club of all time. The Ohio Valley growers placed second, with their top 10 weighing an average 1,162.2 pounds. And the Massachusetts-based New England club came in third, with a 1,154.6-pound average.

Ron was ecstatic. "That makes us king of the pumpkin world!" he exulted. But the triumph was bittersweet. The club had won without pumpkins from Ron and Dick Wallace. Ron's mind already was racing ahead. The 1,500-pound mark was still hanging out there, waiting to be broken. And once again, with the new year before them, the world record would be anybody's to claim.

Ron and his father had been having too many problems for too long. Ron was tired of the disappointments. Tired of losing pumpkins. It was time for things to change at the Wallace patch. Drastic measures were required to shake themselves out of their losing rut.

What Ron Wallace wanted was really pretty simple. He wanted his name, just once, in that record book. "I know that sometime, before I take that big dirt nap, I'll be a world champion," he said as he looked ahead to the next growing season.

Two thousand and six. A new year. A new chance.

2
DICK AND RON

Ron sat inside the cab of the borrowed dump truck, the engine idling in the farmer's driveway, doing what he usually did when he had time on his hands: he ran the numbers. His mind clicked through them automatically, calculating, measuring, planning. His pumpkin patch was about 60 feet by 125 feet, or about 7,500 square feet. He figured he needed about 20 cubic yards of cow manure, and another 10 cubic yards of chicken manure. The dump truck could carry 8 cubic yards of manure, which would mean at least four or five trips.

He had to work fast. It was December 3, and already temperatures were dropping to freezing in the middle of the day. Soon the ground would be frozen and there wouldn't be a chance until spring to fix the dirt in their new pumpkin patch — the Quarter-Million-Dollar Pumpkin Patch, as his dad called it.

The new garden had been Ron's bold solution. He and his father had made too many mistakes in the old patch. They had poured too many supplements and fertilizers into it, made it too fat and too ripe, a happy breeding ground for giant pumpkins, yes, but also for every bacteria and fungus that might wander in. And plenty had wandered in over the years. So now there was nothing to do but make a fresh start. The problem was, even though Ron's house sat on a five-acre tract of land, there was no convenient place for another patch. The 4,800-square-foot house was heavily landscaped with decks and porches and flower beds. The old patch had sat only about 100 feet from the front door, just a few steps from the sidewalk off the driveway. There was a carriage house next to the main house, and a large red barn near the back of the property with pens for the pony, goats, and rabbits that Ron kept. The lawn was dotted with pine trees and fruit trees. Much of the rest of the property was covered with a large pond and wetlands that meandered through the back. It was beautiful, but it was limiting. There was no place to move a giant-pumpkin patch.

But a plot of seven acres was for sale right next door to his house. Ron had been tempted to buy it when he first learned it was for sale earlier that year, and not just because of the pumpkins. He liked the seclusion in the semirural piece of Rhode Island where he lived. His house was set back perpendicular to the road, shielded by a stand of pine trees. The windows at the front of his house looked straight out over the old pumpkin patch to the property next door, a wooded piece of land filled with scrub brush and pines and crisscrossed with dirt bike trails. If someone else bought the property, they could clear it and build a house smack in his face, ruining his view and his privacy.

The asking price was no bargain, though, and Ron wavered. He wavered right up until they lost their two biggest pumpkins to disease in the old patch. That was the last straw. Ron swallowed hard and plunked down $225,000 for the land, even though he figured he was overpaying. Ron prided himself on being a shrewd businessman, but this wasn't just business. "That's the first time in my life I ever overpaid for something. But how often do you get a chance to buy the land next to your house?" he reasoned.

His dad didn't dispute the logic. Though Ron could rationalize it any way he wanted,

Dick said, "I knew better." The truth was, they both wanted that land for a new pumpkin patch. It wasn't a real estate investment; it was a new lease on the Wallace dream of a world record.

Preparations for the 2006 growing season had started as soon as the last 2005 pumpkin rolled off the scale in October. But the deal on the land didn't close until the end of November, leaving the Wallaces precious little time to prepare a new garden. Giant pumpkins are hungry beasts, sucking up vast amounts of soil nutrients each year to fuel their rapid growth. Growers spend most of October and November shoveling in new loads of compost, manure, and other soil supplements to replace the nutrients devoured during the year. The winter gives it all time to break down and blend together before the next spring planting.

Even established gardens demand a lot of work in the fall. But Ron and Dick were starting from scratch. Worse than scratch — three acres of the land Ron bought would need to be cleared and leveled before they could even think about improving the dirt for a new garden. Rome wasn't built in a day, and a world-champion pumpkin patch wouldn't be either. But the Wallaces figured they had at least two weekends.

Early on November 26, a few days after Ron had celebrated his 40th birthday, a horde of Rhode Island pumpkin growers descended on the Wallace place with pickup trucks and tractors and chain saws and axes. It was a chance to pay back all the help and advice and supplies Dick and Ron had handed out to other growers over the years. Like an Amish barn-raising, it also was the rule of the close-knit community. "Everybody helps each other," Ron said. "That's the way it is. We've helped them over the years, and they help us." But, as Dick noted, the gang of growers was tackling something never before attempted in pumpkindom: To get a 7,500-square-foot patch cleared, leveled, amended, and plowed in two weekends of full-blast, all-out, physically exhausting labor.

Temperatures had risen only slightly that morning from the 20-degree predawn chill, but the men warmed up quickly as they set to work. The chain saws roared and buzzed and 80-foot-tall pines began crashing to the ground. Ron had hired an excavator to help with the heavier work. It rolled across the property, its long-armed trowel dipping down and ripping up stumps, shrubs, and other small trees from the ground, then piling them up for burning. While Dick and some of the other growers tended the bonfire, Ron headed out in the dump truck to a nearby chicken farm to get the first load of manure. Others in the group worked on clearing brush and prying large stones from the dirt. Hot coffee warmed their bellies in the morning, and in the afternoon beer warmed their spirits. By the end of that first day, two acres of tumbled raw land, dotted with great piles of manure, stood ready and waiting at the edge of the Wallace compound.

"This hobby doesn't build character; it reveals it," Ron said once. To view a person through a pumpkin prism seems a strange idea at first. But Ron had a point. Growing giant pumpkins, and growing them competitively, is a test of strength, integrity, commitment, and generosity. It asks certain questions: How hard are you able to work? How flexible can you be? Are you willing to share your knowledge and experience to help others — others who will perhaps then go on to beat you? How do you handle disappointment? Are you a quitter?

The Wallaces, perhaps, were better equipped than most to handle the kind of disappointment and hard luck doled out in the pumpkin patch. The family had gone through its share of tough times. Dick Wallace had it tough almost from the time he was born in upstate New York in 1940. His parents were divorced, and Dick had butted heads with more than one stepfather as he grew up. If he had any happy memories from his childhood, he owed them to his grandparents. Dick admired his grandfather, a World War I veteran, lifelong foundry worker, and volunteer firefighter. But he'd had a special bond with his grandmother. "When I was sick, she always took care of me, and when I got into scrapes, as all kids will, Gram used to say, 'Leave him alone. He's just a kid.' "

Dick never used his bumpy start in life as an excuse. Rather, it gave him a sense of confidence and pride. "I did everything on my own," he recalled. "I never depended on my family for anything. I had my rough spots, you bet your life. But I turned out all right."

Dick quit school when he was 17 and joined the U.S. Marine Corps, where he got his first tattoo — a dagger on his forearm. "I thought it made me look tough," he said. To impress the ladies, he got a second one: a wolf wearing a Marine Corps hat that leered from his bicep when he rolled up his sleeve. He met his wife, Cathy, an Italian-

American beauty, while on furlough visiting a friend in Rhode Island. They married after he got out of the service in 1963. On their first anniversary, Dick got his third tattoo: two intertwined hearts with "Cathy and Dick" inscribed across them. "If I had it to do over again," he said, "that's the only one I'd keep."

Their sons, Richard and then Ron, were born while Cathy was still finishing nursing school. Dick found a job selling frozen foods door-to-door. As a young man, he was tall and lean and handsome, with neatly groomed jet-black hair and a desire to prove to the world that he could make something of himself. He had an unpretentious charm; he was sincere and cheerful and enthusiastic. Sales took off, but Dick grew to dislike his job. He found himself pulled over a line he wasn't willing to cross: convincing people to buy things he knew they couldn't afford or didn't need. "The problem with sales," he explained, "is that the sale gets to be more important than honesty." So he quit in 1983 and went to work for a local manufacturer of electrical components, where his talent for leadership quickly led to a job as production superintendent.

Dick made his entry into the world of giant pumpkins — a tale etched in Wallace family lore — with the wide-eyed innocence of a consummate greenhorn. Times were good for Dick and Cathy as they eased into middle age. The kids had grown up and moved out, and they had bought a new house south of Providence with a big backyard. At long last, Dick had room for the big vegetable garden he'd always wanted. As he poked around in a local garden center, he found a packet of seeds for a pumpkin called the Atlantic Giant. He liked the sound of that, and decided to grow a few pumpkin plants along with his tomatoes, bell peppers, and eggplants. He worked diligently on his garden through that summer of 1989. To his delight, his pumpkin plant grew like a demon, sprouting leaves the size of turkey platters and sending thick tendrils branching out across the grass. He'd never seen anything like it. It filled the whole end of Dick's vegetable patch and spawned several pumpkins that swelled as big as beach balls in the heart of his garden.

When the biggest pumpkin finished growing near the end of August, Dick cut it from the vine and carried it to his garage, where he perched it on top of a tire for safekeeping. He'd heard about a pumpkin contest held in October in the town of Collins, New York, 400 miles away, and couldn't resist thinking about his chances at a weigh-off. He didn't really think he could be so lucky as to have a prizewinner his first year . . . but still. It was a big pumpkin.

His grandmother made up his mind. She was living in a nursing home only a few miles from Collins. Going to the weigh-off would give Dick a chance to stop by for a visit. It tickled him to imagine what his gram would say when he showed her the huge pumpkin he'd grown. So six weeks later Dick borrowed the company van and loaded his pumpkin into the back, and he and Cathy set out for what Dick remembers as "four hundred miles of expectations."

They arrived before anyone else at the weigh-off. Dick spotted a few pumpkins lined up against the side of a building, and his heart beat faster. The pumpkins were about the same size as his. Maybe, he thought, he had a chance after all. But then he found out those were just for decoration. Soon, the real competitors began to arrive, true giants hauled in trailers or the backs of pickups that made Dick's entry look downright puny. Dick thought about leaving. But then his bolder nature took over. He'd traveled too far to just bail out like that. Why not at least find out what his pumpkin weighed? So he set his pumpkin in line for

41

the scale. And when it was weighed, he slunk to the back of the crowd, pretending it was someone else's.

Dick's turn for glory came later, when he stopped by the nursing home to show his pumpkin to his gram. Her excitement was all it took to make the trip worthwhile. She died not long after that, and Dick lost interest in big pumpkins for the next few years. Then one Christmas a coworker gave him a book called *How-to-Grow World Class Giant Pumpkins,* written by a Massachusetts man, Don Langevin. Dick showed the book to Ron, who shared his father's love of growing things. Ron was in his mid-20s then. He read the book cover to cover on Christmas Day, fascinated by the effort and strategy that went into growing the massive fruit. And he was intrigued by the challenge. Ron proposed a father-and-son growing contest. They'd each try growing a giant pumpkin in their backyard the next summer and take their biggest to a local weigh-off.

That first year was 1994, and Ron grew a 250-pounder. Dick's best was 235 pounds. The next year, they pooled their efforts and borrowed a field from Ron's neighbor to dig a bigger garden. Father and son split the labor and expenses and ended the year with a 366-pound entry. They were hooked.

Giant pumpkins began sucking them in a little more, year after year. They made friends at the weigh-offs, asked questions, and sought advice from the best growers. They learned about the importance of having the right seeds. But it wasn't easy. Many of the competitive growers in those days guarded their secrets — and their seeds — jealously. Ron and Dick had to search out the rare grower who was willing to share knowledge and experience with newcomers. Very quickly, father and son were introduced to the giant-sized frustrations of the hobby.

The next few years brought trouble of a different kind to the Wallaces. Dick's health failed him, and occasional, unexplained seizures forced him to take an early retirement. Ron, looking for a bigger place with enough land for a nice pumpkin patch, bought a large new home in Greene, Rhode Island, south of Providence. Ron and his father worked together to renovate the in-law suite on the bottom floor of the sprawling split-level house, and in 2001, Dick and Cathy moved in.

But the troubles kept piling up. Ron's brief marriage to a longtime girlfriend collapsed. Then his mother was severely injured in a car accident and had to quit work. Cathy Wallace already had been battling lupus for years, but now she began having more flare-ups, which affected her lungs and required trips to the hospital to battle a series of infections.

The Wallaces soldiered on through the hard times. Dick threw his heart and soul into the pumpkin patch, spending hours studying seed genetics and growing techniques, fired up with the spirit of competition. Every new season brought the excitement of new possibilities. Now that he and Ron shared a home, the two men collaborated even more closely on each year's pumpkin crop.

Dick and Ron Wallace, father and son, were the perfect partners. Both were sticklers for integrity. Both had soft hearts and an eagerness to help other people and do good in the world. But they also shared the same drive, a burning competitive instinct, and an obsession with excellence. For Ron, especially, growing giant pumpkins scratched an itch that had been bred into him since his childhood Little League days. From those earliest baseball games, he'd been a fierce competitor, rooted on by his equally competitive father, who was his mentor, adviser, trainer, and sometimes, his coach.

While Dick had mellowed with age, Ron

still burned. He favored his mother's dark looks and spoke with an impatient, machine-gun briskness. For Ron, there was no point in doing something if he couldn't give it everything he had. He'd been disillusioned over the years by a world where most people didn't make the same effort, so his temper was a little jagged at times, his patience frayed. It went against his nature to ask less or expect less of himself or of other people.

Ron had acquired a love of cooking growing up in the Italian-American kitchens of his mother and grandmother, where sauces always seemed to be bubbling on the stove and family meals were a source of pride. He graduated from Johnson and Wales University in Providence with a degree in culinary arts and went to work in the kitchen of Quidnessett Country Club, an exclusive resort on the edge of Narragansett Bay. But even in his early 20s, Ron wanted more from life. "I always wanted to be wealthy enough that I didn't have to worry about money," he explained. His salary was under $20,000 in those days as a bottom-rung chef's assistant. So at the age of 24, Ron bought a book called *Sonny Bloch's 171 Ways to Make Money in Real Estate.* "Mr. Bloch ended up in jail for bilking some of his investors," Ron said. "But his book was very, very good."

Inspired by the book's advice, Ron took his first big leap, paying $32,000 for a house at a Housing and Urban Development foreclosure auction. His friends told him he was nuts to risk his money. But Ron was determined to at least try. He invested a couple thousand to spruce up the property, then sold it for a $16,000 profit. He used the money to buy another property, and made another profit. Ron slowly built his real estate investment portfolio. He kept some properties for rental income, but mostly he bought, repaired, and sold quickly to pocket his profits. Ron had the nerve to take the risks, the discipline to stick to his investment rules ("I never flipped a property unless I could make fifteen thousand dollars"), and the drive to do the hard physical work of maintaining and renovating the properties. He progressed to buying condominiums and apartments around New England and in Florida. He made a lot of money. "But it didn't happen by accident," Ron said. "While everyone else was driving to the beach, I was driving to a house with a crew of guys, turning on the lights and sanding floors and papering walls every weekend."

He still kept his job at the country club.

"I'm a food-service person. I love what I do. And it's there for you every week," he said. Thanks to the same work ethic and drive that had made him successful in real estate, he quickly climbed the ladder from kitchen assistant to sous chef to executive chef, and finally, to general manager. The job meant overseeing the operations of the entire club, including the pool, golf course, and restaurant, and private bookings such as parties and weddings. Above all, he had to keep the club's wealthy members happy. That meant being on call 24/7. Even in the slower winter months it was rare for Ron to have a weekend off.

Fitting giant pumpkins into that world was crazy, but Ron rationalized it in different ways. He and his father used to spend weekends fishing; now they spent them in the pumpkin patch — though pumpkins took up far more time than fishing ever did. Pulling weeds, pruning, fertilizing, spraying — it was a stress reliever. It was hard physical work that Ron could forget himself in. The rest of the world, other troubles, faded away in the garden. In the pumpkin patch, he had a clear-cut goal to work toward: a world record. It was simple and clean and challenging enough to keep him coming back year after year.

Dick, in his graying years, preferred to focus on the fun and camaraderie of pumpkin growing. Over the seasons, he had forged strong friendships with other growers around the country, talking with them on the phone and exchanging e-mails and chatting online through BigPumpkins.com, the Internet home of their community. His willingness to help rookies learn the ropes had earned him the respect and admiration of pumpkin growers across the world, who knew him as the grandfatherly "Pap." Dick spiced things up with a boisterous and sometimes bawdy sense of humor. He indulged his class-clown instincts, finding unapologetic hilarity in the most juvenile pranks. On occasion, he shocked and appalled his fellow growers by dropping his extralarge trousers and mooning them when they least expected it.

But if anyone ever needed help, Dick was usually the first to offer it. And it fell to Ron to put the brakes on his father's sometimes too-generous instincts. Dick's eagerness to help meant the Wallaces could end up spending more time doing for others than they did for themselves. "Mr. Helper Friend," Ron called his dad when he was exasperated by one more promise the older man had made.

Ron, though, was really just a younger, rawer version of his father. He was a little better at saying no, and he had a different way of indulging his inner wild child. As he hit 40, single again with plentiful income, he pushed the throttle down. He devoted 60 hours a week to his job. He drank hard and stayed out with friends late into the night. He dated frequently but avoided settling down.

He had life where he wanted it. Yet success in the pumpkin patch had eluded him. As the years of failure had piled up, the disappointments had become harder to stomach. Ron's fixation on winning gained such a powerful grip on him that setbacks in the pumpkin patch would send him spiraling into a depression or stomping off in a rage.

In that way, life did Ron a favor. There's nothing like seeing your parents through serious illness and having your marriage fall apart to remind you what's really important. It taught Ron to roll with the punches, to quit feeling sorry for himself and appreciate what he had. "Everybody in life takes a few sharp sticks in the eye. I live a very good life, and things have worked out for the better for me," he said.

In the past few years, Ron had been able

49

to get a better grip on his passion for winning. A few years ago, if he had lost his two biggest pumpkins just days before the weigh-off, as he had in 2005, "I'd have been in a coma for weeks," he said. Now, "I really love competing, but I don't live and die by it like I used to," he said. "Pumpkins have been put into perspective."

After buying the new land, Ron and Dick hadn't been able to resist making their new patch bigger than the old 6,000-square-foot one. Where they'd had room for 8 plants before, now they had room for at least 10. And they planned on using every square inch for the coming year, even though it meant more work. Ron thought of it as his final big push. He had decided to go all-out in 2006, give it everything he had, and see what happened. Ten plants didn't seem like so much, actually. Last year he and his father had grown 8, and Ron had helped club member Johnny Nicholas grow 6 more. Johnny, 26 years old with a wife and a baby daughter, had been diagnosed with cancer, and after chemotherapy and radiation treatments, he didn't have much left over for pumpkins. So Ron had pitched in, helping Johnny with the pruning and fertilizing and chemicals. In the end, Johnny got an 1,100-

pound pumpkin out of his patch. So in Ron's mind, 10 pumpkins amounted to 4 fewer than last year, not 2 more.

Still, Ron's work was getting busier, and his dad was getting older. He realized he was going to have to cut himself some slack somewhere if he intended to grow 10 pumpkin plants. So he decided to give up growing his giant dahlias and let his flower beds fend for themselves. And after 2006, no matter what happened, he promised himself he'd cut back to just five plants and try to enjoy life more. Over the years, as the pumpkins consumed more and more of his time, he'd been neglecting the 1965 Pontiac GTO parked under a dustcover in his garage. It was his pride and joy, but there was rarely time to even take it for a spin. On many a broiling summer afternoon as he slaved in the pumpkin patch, sweat and dirt mixing into muddy trails down his brow, he'd think longingly, "I could be driving my GTO down the beach right now."

So this would be his last big year. And here he was, starting from scratch. The main thing he needed to do was enrich his soil with organic supplements like manure and compost. And to do the job right, he needed the best manure he could get. Real world-class manure. And he'd found some just a few miles from his home, where a farmer had been piling up and tending to his cow manure for more than three years so that it was thoroughly and evenly decomposed. "This guy," Ron enthused, "is the number-one compost maker around." A lot of farmers just let their manure piles sit, he noted. "But this guy turns the piles, which keeps the microbial activity stirred up."

Ron sent off some samples of the manure to a soil lab to be tested for disease and nutrient levels. It came back with a straight-A report card. It was cheap too — at eight dollars a cubic yard, it was a third of the cost of commercially produced composts. To a pumpkin grower, manure like that was gold.

After the Rhode Island crew had cleared the land that first weekend, Ron had brought the excavator back to dig up some last remaining stumps and to level and grade the new garden area. Then the Wallaces' farmer neighbor, Donald Salisbury, came over with his tractor and gave the new patch its first plowing.

The next weekend, on December 3, as Ron waited for his last load of cow manure, his friends and fellow growers had gathered again back at his house to begin spreading out the giant piles of manure across the garden. It was bitter cold, but no one complained. "Pumpkin growers are pretty tough workers," Ron observed. "It doesn't matter if it's raining or snowing, if you have stuff to do, you have stuff to do." Joe Jutras had brought over his small tractor to till in the manure. After another long day, the patch was as ready as the band of growers could make it.

That evening, with snow clouds gathering overhead and a cold, damp wind whistling through the pine trees, Ron stood at the edge of his new pumpkin patch, marveling at their accomplishment. Time moved so quickly. The 2006 season was officially underway for the Wallaces. Thanks to their friends, they would be ready when spring came. The rest would be up to Dick and Ron.

3
SEEDS

As Jack learned in the tale of the beanstalk, a seed is never just a seed. It's a promise of something bigger, and it has the power to surprise. Giant-pumpkin seeds are impressive even before they've revealed what's inside them. Most are the size and shape of a large, flat almond, and they come in an array of earthy hues, from brown to gold to creamy white. But no grower cares what the seeds look like. What matters is the genetic programming locked inside the tough shell, which dictates what kind of pumpkin it will grow: how big, how orange, how round, how thick. Growers have been tinkering with those genetics for decades to create steadily bigger and heavier pumpkins. But all seeds are not created equal. Far from it. All have the potential to grow big pumpkins, but not necessarily prizewinning big pumpkins. The most hotly sought-after seeds are those engineered to grow the very biggest and very heaviest pumpkins, and which have proven their pedigrcc by already producing several world-class specimens.

That was what had made the Bobier seeds famous. Seeds from two giant pumpkins grown by New York grower Bill Bobier were considered to be the most reliable producers of prizewinning pumpkins ever seen in the world of competitive pumpkin growing. In 1999, Mr. Bobier had found the magic when he grew a 723-pound pumpkin by blending the genetics from two big and heavy pumpkins. The next year, he made the same genctic cross and grew an 845-pound pumpkin. Nearly every pumpkin that had set a record or won a weigh-off in recent years had one of those two Bobier seeds somewhere in its lineage.

In the competitive pumpkin world, seeds have names so that genetic family trees can be traced through generations, like thoroughbred racehorses. Just as horses with championship lineage are believed to have better odds of becoming champions themselves, pumpkins grown from seeds with world-class genetics are thought to have a better chance of setting the next world record.

Seeds are named by combining the weight of the pumpkin they come from with the name of the grower. All the seeds in a single pumpkin will carry the same name. So the seeds that came from Mr. Bobier's 723-pound pumpkin were known as 723 Bobiers, and seeds from his 845-pound pumpkin were known as 845 Bobiers.

Those two seeds quickly established a track record of growing big and heavy fruit. As more growers planted them, the list of champion pumpkins they produced grew longer, making the Bobier name legendary for supergenetics. The seeds were so renowned that, like "Michael" in basketball, or "Bruce" in rock 'n' roll, they no longer needed a last name. Growers spoke of them reverently as simply "the 723" and "the 845."

As more growers caught on to the hobby, more giant pumpkins were being grown each year with bragging rights to 1,000-pound genetics. Each pumpkin can contain several hundred seeds, and the seeds remain fertile for many years. That was making good seeds not only abundant, but also easily obtainable and often free for the asking. Planting another grower's seed is a kind of compliment, and most growers are eager to share and trade their seeds to encourage the hobby. Protocol requires only that seed requests be mailed with a self-addressed, stamped bubble envelope for easy return.

In the competitive giant-pumpkin world, having your name attached to a prized seed stock is almost as prestigious as growing a record-setting pumpkin — and it requires shrewd gamesmanship. A seed can build a reputation only if it produces big pumpkins. And it can do that only if it's planted by skilled growers. Most serious competitors grow 4 to 10 plants a year, and they want every plant to have world-record potential. That leaves little room to gamble on unproven new seeds. Convincing a top grower to dedicate a precious spot in his or her garden to a dark horse requires a brazen lobbying campaign and more than a little bit of shameless hype.

As 2006 rolled around, Bobier's wave of fame was cresting. After six seasons of planting, there were very few of the legendary 723 and 845 seeds left. While that increased their mystique, at a more practical level, it also meant that there weren't going to be many grown anymore. The seeds had accomplished just about all they were going to — which was quite a lot. By 2005, the 723 Bobier was indisputably the number-one seed for producing big, heavy pumpkins. Based on stats collected by one grower in an Internet database, the five heaviest pumpkins grown with the 723 seed were heavier than the top five grown by any other seed, averaging 1,208.5 pounds. The 723 Bobier also owned the franchise on producing pumpkins over 1,000 pounds. The 845 wasn't far behind, ranking as the fifth-best-producing seed of all time. And the seeds holding second, third, and fourth place were all offspring of one of the Bobier seeds.

The record books were about to close on the 723 and the 845, making way for the next generation of hot seeds. As it happened, one of the most talked-about seeds of the 2006 season was the 1068 Wallace — taken from a 1,068-pound pumpkin grown by Ron and Dick Wallace in 2003. The 1068, a child of the 845 Bobier, already had climbed to the number-two ranking after just two years of planting. And Ron and Dick were determined that 2006 would be the year their 1068 Wallace unseated the 723 Bobier as the greatest pumpkin seed of all time.

On an icy Saturday afternoon in late January, several members of the Southern New England Giant Pumpkin Growers club gathered at the Wallace house to discuss the club's strategy for the new growing season. Giant-pumpkin growing wasn't just a spring and summer hobby anymore — it was a year-round obsession. Across the land, pumpkin patches were shrouded in blankets of snow, sleeping, waiting. But pumpkin growers knew no rest even in the frozen months. This was the time for planning and researching and gathering supplies for spring.

Though the weigh-offs were months away, already Ron's kitchen counter was lined with ribbons, trophies, and plaques that Dick had accumulated as he looked forward to the new season. In the winter, Dick passed the time combing through catalogs and Web sites for colorful ribbons and trophies to award as prizes at the weigh-offs. Some were left over from the year before. More were arriving in the mail every week. Taking advantage of Joe Jutras's custom woodworking shop, Dick tapped Joe to help turn out exquisitely crafted wooden plaques and pumpkin-themed trophies. Dick's wife, Cathy, could only roll her eyes at the excess. "Sometimes it gets ridiculous," she said, eyeing the stacks of gaudy gewgaws filling the counter. She teased her husband: "I hope you don't get any. I don't want to have to put them in the house."

This year brought a new kind of pressure to the Southern New England club. They had a reputation to protect. The Wallaces' personal record might have suffered another blow in 2005, but at least they were part of a club that had established itself as the best. Ron liked being at the top, and he wanted to stay there. Though growers often insisted that they grew giant pumpkins for the fun and satisfaction of the hobby, there was never any question that it was, above all, a competition. Ron was determined that the Rhode Island club wasn't going to be just a flash in the pan. "I want to come back and kick everybody's ass again," he announced to the gathering of pumpkin growers, and they all sounded off in enthusiastic agreement.

The half-dozen growers were sitting in the formal living room on the upper level of Ron's house, where a picture window looked out onto the snow-whitened landscape of the Wallace homestead and pumpkin patch. In the middle of the yard, a six-foot circular indentation in the snow marked the spot where the Wallaces' biggest pumpkin had grown, a reminder of what almost was. But that was history, and the Southern New England growers had come to the Wallace house to talk about the future.

Ron had on a pair of faded jeans and his favorite Buffalo Bills hooded sweatshirt. His devotion to the upstate New York football team was second only to his pumpkins. As they discussed different seed prospects, Ron's excitement began to boil over with the peculiar jargon of giant-pumpkin growers: "pollinators" and "fathers" and "mothers" and "crosses." He rattled off seed names like a math professor expounding on the Poincaré conjecture.

Ron shot a question at Steve Connolly: "Steve, what did you put into your 1333?" That was the pumpkin that had placed second at the club's 2005 weigh-off.

"I used the 1253 Sperry," Steve answered.

"There's power in that pollen," Ron said, nodding approvingly. "The 1333 could be a central player this year. Steve's a good pollinator. That 1253 plant also produced a 1,210 for you this year, didn't it? So that's why we should be excited about that plant. Now you've got heavy on both ends."

Ron believed the club had to give priority to planting its own seeds to assure a deep stable of potential champions. But given that a dozen of the club's growers had produced several world-class pumpkins each, that still left a lot of new seeds to choose from. "You know, Joe's 842 could

61

have been a 1,400-pound pumpkin at some point if it hadn't split," Ron mused. "If anyone asked me what I thought, if I only had one or two to choose from of the unknown stuff, I would take Steve's 1333 and I would take Joe's 1228."

The other growers were mostly silent, listening thoughtfully as Ron tossed out calculations and theories. Steve Sperry, a slender man of 50 wearing a black turtleneck, sank back into a corner of Ron's couch, occasionally running his fingers over his close-cropped salt-and-pepper beard. Steve Connolly sat in a chair across from Sperry. Dick, from his chair in the corner of the room, tried to lighten the mood when he thought Ron was getting too intense. "Ahh, we're all just a bunch of liars," he said, laughing. "We're sitting here together today but really we're all scheming against each other."

But Dick was concerned about the coming year too.

"It's going to be tough for this club to do what we did last year," he observed. Despite their success in 2005, Southern New England was still a small club compared to others in New England, Ohio, California, and Canada.

Joe Jutras, leaning against the picture

window seat, was the only one to occasionally argue a point with Ron. His calming, good-natured voice was the counterpoint to Ron's preacherly zeal.

"I think we've got the upper hand," said Joe, upbeat as ever. "We've got the seeds and we've got the guys who can do it."

"Yeah," Ron agreed. "We're going to start pulling more from Massachusetts this year." The notoriety the club had gained with its 2005 success meant more top growers from Massachusetts and Connecticut would bring their big pumpkins to the Rhode Island weigh-off this year. "We'll be a tough act to catch," Ron said. Especially if the club rallied behind its best seed: the 1068 Wallace. Ron and Dick were convinced the 1068 Wallace was capable of producing the next world-record pumpkin. They were so convinced that out of the 10 plants they planned to grow in their new patch in 2006, half were going to be 1068s.

But if the 1068 was going to unseat the 723 Bobier, the Wallaces had to get other top growers to plant it. That wouldn't be so difficult now that the seed had produced several 1,300-pound-plus pumpkins and sat at number two on the list of all-time best producers.

Ron's confidence had soared over the

winter along with the reputation of the 1068 Wallace seed, thanks to the buzz created by its success at auction. Among the rituals of winter for competitive pumpkin growers are the Internet seed auctions held on Big Pumpkins.com to raise money for the various growing clubs around the country. Connecticut grower Ken Desrosiers, a programmer for a software company, had launched the site as a place to try out new programming applications his company intended to use for its products. It quickly became the preferred cyberspace watering hole for the giant-pumpkin community. Growers used the site to exchange information in discussion forums, to gossip and bellyache in chat rooms, and to keep diaries charting their growing experiences each season.

Using the chat feature, the clubs held seed auctions each winter featuring as many top seeds as they could gather. Each club donated seeds from its growers to other clubs for their auctions — in part out of good sportsmanship, but also as a way to build the reputation of its seeds by getting them into the hands of as many growers as possible.

The Southern New England auction was held late in January. The 1068, the star of the auction, was the last seed offered for bidding. With pumpkin growers around the world perched at their computers to watch the action, the first bid to pop up on the screen was $250, followed quickly by $260. The bidding narrowed to a war between two growers, rising steadily through the $300s. The Rhode Island growers sat at home at their own computers, rooting on the bids to help keep the bidding going. "Many predict this seed will grow the next world record!" typed Ron. Within a few minutes, the 1068 — a single seed, with no guarantee it would even sprout — had sold for a whopping $410. "How do you explain that to your wife?" one grower quipped after the final bid.

The auction results helped beef up the treasury of the Southern New England club and added to the renown of the Wallace seed. At other club auctions that winter, the 1068 sold for prices ranging from $350 to $425.

As the 1068's reputation soared, so did the number of seed requests. By the end of January, more than 100 e-mails jammed Ron's account and he had two garbage bags stuffed full of bubble packs sent by growers asking for a 1068. Some included seeds in trade. Some included money, which Ron always returned to the sender. Never mind the hundreds of dollars the 1068 had fetched at auction — "It's not about money," Ron said. If he wanted a grower to have a seed, he sent it free of charge.

But Ron's generosity had its limits when it came to the 1068. The 1,068-pound pumpkin had produced only 254 seeds — fewer than most giants. There were far too many requests to even think about filling them all. Ron's first priority was to have enough seeds for himself and for his club for years to come. Next were people who had helped Ron and his dad through the years who would never go wanting for a 1068 if they asked. And Ron was more than willing to give the seed to any of the hobby's top growers, who would give the seed its best chance to shine. After that, the remaining 1068s would go to the lucky few who caught Ron in a giving mood.

By now, the pumpkin world knew Dick Wallace was a soft touch. Dick enjoyed the brain game of the genetics as much as any grower — he had studied the matter even more than Ron. But his competitive fervor clashed head-on with his instinct for generosity and his desire to help other growers. He wanted to win too, but publicly, he preferred to put the emphasis on the friendship and mentoring aspects of the hobby. "That's what I hang my hat on. I like to help people," Dick said.

Not surprisingly, growers had begun sending their 1068 requests to Dick instead of Ron, and it was getting to be a problem. Ron had no intention of sending 1068s to just anyone. He was enough like his dad that he hated turning people down, but he could be tough when he needed to be. So Dick was under orders to forward any seed requests he received to Ron. One grower wrote to Ron in an e-mail, "I hope you are as generous as your father." Ron chortled as he wrote back, "I'm not." The requests for the 1068 flowed in so fast over that 2005–2006 winter that Ron started to dread even going to the mailbox. He spread the word that he had only a handful of the seeds left. That way, he hoped, people wouldn't take it personally when he told them no.

4
ALL PUMPKINS AREN'T ORANGE

One key question arises when any reasonable person views a giant pumpkin for the first time: What on earth is it? Giant pumpkins have been bred through the decades with the isolated goal of getting them bigger and heavier. Obsession can be as blind as love, and most competitive growers just don't care how their pumpkins look. They want beasts, not beauties. Beasts are big. Beasts are brawny. Beasts are winners. So what if beasts, usually, are also ugly?

It can be a shocking thing to a parent who brings a child to a giant-pumpkin display at the local county fair, expecting to see jumbo-sized versions of those glorious orange orbs so often mentioned in fairy tales. The word *pumpkin* invokes warm, happy feelings of home and family, and stirs memories of schoolhouse decorations, tasty pumpkin pies, and the ubiquitous jack-o'-lanterns of Halloween.

Their large size and bright color give pumpkins a supernatural quality that perfectly suits the requirements of storytellers. Giant pumpkins have been part of our popular culture since French intellectual Charles Perrault introduced the idea of a magic pumpkin carriage in his 17th-century folktale about a young orphaned girl named Cendrillon, or Cinderella. Literary historians still debate what the nursery rhyme Peter Peter Pumpkin Eater could possibly mean. One interpretation suggests Peter murdered his adulterous wife and disposed of her body inside a giant pumpkin. The mystery inspired cartoonist Gary Larsen to feature Peter in one of his *Far Side* panels: Peter's on trial, and his sister, Jeannie Jeannie Eatszucchini, is about to testify against him.

The most well-known portrayal of a big pumpkin in American culture was provided by another cartoonist, *Peanuts* creator Charles Schulz, who captured the wistful, unrequited yearnings of a young child's imagination with Linus's Halloween ritual. Year after year, the faithful young boy missed trick-or-treating because he was waiting in the pumpkin patch for the arrival of the mythical Great Pumpkin, who was supposed to bring gifts to all the children, but never came.

But the salient question remains, *What are they?* In the botanical sense, pumpkins are found in four species of the genus *Cucurbita.* Both pumpkins and squash populate these four species, and little distinguishes the two other than tradition and color; pumpkins are supposed to be orange. They're also native to North America. Pumpkinlike seeds dating back 7,000 to 8,000 years have been found in Mexico. Native Americans grew pumpkins for food and introduced them to American colonists, who then carried them back overseas to the Old World. But the word *pumpkin* is derived from Greek, not Native American languages. Its roots are in the Greek term for a large melon — *pepōn.* The word evolved as it passed through different languages, from the French *pompon* to the Old English *pumpion* and eventually the American *pumpkin.*

Like cucumbers, bell peppers, and eggplants, pumpkins are technically fruits, not vegetables. Though most people think of fruit as anything that could show up in your basic fruit salad, botanists define fruit as the seed-bearing ovaries of a plant, formed when a plant's flower is fertilized through pollination. Vegetables are the edible, non-fruit parts of a plant, including leaves, stems, and roots. Hence lettuce, celery, and potatoes are regarded indisputably as vegetables.

Horticulturalists have chewed over this distinction for more than a century. The U.S. Supreme Court was even asked to weigh in on the question in 1893 in a tariff dispute over tomatoes. Fruit importer John Nix was outraged when New York Customs agents charged him a 10 percent vegetable tax on a shipment of tomatoes. Nix insisted his tomatoes were fruit, which were duty-free, and sued to recover his money. When the case arrived at the Supreme Court, the justices decided to rely on common sense. Since the tariff law had not spelled out precisely what was and wasn't to be considered a vegetable, the Court ruled that the classification of fruits and vegetables should be determined by "ordinary meaning." And ordinarily, tomatoes are regarded as vegetables.

This conflict between the botanic and "ordinary meaning" of fruits and vegetables has been resolved diplomatically by most horticulturalists by simply viewing the words in their different contexts: botanical and culinary. In the more-common, culinary sense, fruits are generally sweet desserts, while vegetables are part of the main meal, cooked and salted.

To giant-pumpkin growers, there is no confusion. Pumpkins are fruit, and growers will correct anyone who makes the mistake of calling them a vegetable. Giant pumpkins are for competition and exhibition, not to be cooked up and served on a plate. They are spectacle, not food.

And yet, giant-pumpkin growers owe their supersized fruit to humankind's need to eat. Civilization has depended on the ability to cultivate crops. In the United States' largely rural infancy, nearly every home had its own garden to produce food for the household. But as the country became industrialized and most people moved to the cities, agriculture became the domain of big business. Now the closest most people get to a garden is the produce aisle in their local grocery store. Consumers no longer even acknowledge the limitations of the growing season; they expect their fruits and vegetables to be available year-round. Now gardening is just another form of entertainment. Most gardens are merely decorative, filled with carefully tended shrubs and colorful flowers. A beautifully landscaped home is a symbol of luxury and status. Some gardeners still grow plants for food, though usually as a novelty. Home gardens can satisfy a basic human need to connect to the earth, but they are seldom necessary for survival.

Competitive vegetable gardening came into its own in 19th-century England, arising from the trend toward "cottage gardens," small plots of public land allotted to the poor for growing fruits and vegetables. One school of thought viewed the wholesomeness of gardening as a remedy to social plagues such as drunkenness and depression. With so many gardens squeezed side by side, it was inevitable that the humans tending them would begin casting an eye toward their neighbors' to compare. Soon, gardeners were competing over who could grow the biggest and tastiest vegetables. Flower clubs already had emerged as a pastime among tradesmen in the 16th century, with shows and awards for the finest floral specimens. The "allotment gardeners" soon took an interest in blooms, as well, and flower and vegetable competitions became a countryside staple through England in the 1800s.

Competitive growers owe much of their technical knowledge to farmers. Modern food crops have been genetically tuned through decades — sometimes centuries — of crossbreeding to bring out desirable traits such as sweeter, juicier flesh, better color, larger size, and disease resistance. That's how grasses became grain crops and small green berries became plump red tomatoes. By using the same techniques, competitive growers have been able to figure out how to tailor their plants to the demands of the stage. They've bred taller sunflowers, more brilliantly colored roses, and bigger fruits and vegetables.

Pumpkins have always been remarkable in the fruit world for their large size. But as they were cultivated more frequently around the world, and new varieties were developed and planted, even prime specimens still weighed considerably less than 100 pounds. By the mid-1800s, gardening publications began referring to a "Mammoth" variety of squash, which regularly produced pumpkin-like fruit weighing more than 100 pounds. But bigger showcase specimens were few and far between. At an 1857 vegetable show in Devonshire, England, a Mammoth weighing 245 pounds was recorded. Then, in Canada, there were reports of a grower bringing a 292-pound pumpkin to an 1883 exhibition.

A Canadian named William Warnock is given credit for introducing a new age of giant-pumpkin growing at the turn of the

20th century. In the early 1890s, Warnock worked as a sawmill machinist and carriage maker in Goderich, Ontario. He was a passionate, lifelong gardener, and he had taken an interest in growing a Mammoth variety of green pumpkin squash.

Warnock made gardening history when he took a 365-pound pumpkin to the Chicago World's Fair in 1893. Then in 1900 he grew a 400-pound pumpkin, a feat so remarkable that he was invited to travel with it overseas for the Paris World's Fair, where the French government awarded him an honorary bronze medal of recognition. Warnock beat his own record once again with a 403-pound pumpkin he displayed in the 18-acre Palace of Agriculture at the 1904 St. Louis World's Fair — the same fair that introduced ice-cream cones and iced tea to the world. Warnock's 403-pound record would stand for an astonishing 73 years.

In the 1970s, Pennsylvania farmer Bob Ford tinkered with the genetics of the giant squash by crossing different varieties. The result in 1976 was a 451-pound, pale-orange fruit that finally broke Warnock's record and set the world on a climb to bigger and bigger pumpkins. While Ford tinkered, a farmer in Nova Scotia was already in the grip of a lifelong obsession to produce the biggest pumpkins in the world. Howard Dill grew up in the 1930s and '40s watching his father take big pumpkins to compete at local agricultural fairs. Back then, it usually took only a 75- or 80-pound pumpkin to win. Mr. Dill never outgrew his fascination with those pumpkins, and as a young man in the 1950s, he launched a campaign to crank up the weights. Each year he selected seeds from the longest, thickest, tallest pumpkins and crossbred them with each other with the idea of producing a new strain that would consistently produce fruit bigger than anything the world had yet seen.

He also bred for color. Dill believed that the seeds his father had been using were descendants of the Warnock record-setting green squashes, and he needed those squash genes for their big and heavy traits. But he also began to select seeds from orange fruit to crossbreed the classic pumpkin color back into the giants.

By 1977, Dill decided he had stabilized the traits he wanted in a new variety of supersized pumpkin he called Dill's Atlantic Giant. Beginning in 1979, Dill proved the potential of his seeds by growing the biggest pumpkin in the world four years in a row, and setting two new world records: with a

459-pound pumpkin in 1980 and a 493.5-pound pumpkin in 1981.

Dill's high-profile success produced a clamor for his seeds. By then there were other big-pumpkin varieties out there, including Big Mac and Big Moon, but those produced comparative weaklings in the 100–200 pound range. Other growers were doing their own successful breeding to produce giants over 400 pounds. But it was the consistent world-record potential of the Atlantic Giant that gave it superstar appeal, and seed companies took notice. Dill began receiving orders for hundreds of pounds of his seeds. With about 1,200 seeds needed to make up each pound, he soon found himself in commercial production.

Competitive growers seized on the Atlantic Giant Seeds and began their own amateur experiments with crossbreeding. They swapped seeds from their biggest and heaviest Atlantic Giant pumpkins with other growers. With remarkable speed, new world records followed one after the other. In 1984, Norm Gallagher of Chelan, Washington, leaped over the 500-pound mark with a new world record of 612 pounds. In 1989, the 700-pound barrier was crossed, and the following year 800 fell. It took another four years to break through 900 pounds. And then in 1996, Paula and Nathan Zehr of Lowville, New York, became the first in the world to grow a half-ton pumpkin, with a new world record of 1,061 pounds.

By the 1990s, there were still a few rare giant pumpkins that could trace their ancestry directly back to William Warnock's Mammoths, but the vast majority of competitive pumpkins were descendants of Dill's Atlantic Giants. Growers used crossbreeding to reinforce the traits in their Atlantic Giants that produced the heaviest pumpkins: long, strong stems; thick fruit walls; flatter, elongated bodies. To keep track of their results, they adopted the weight-plus-grower naming system that allowed them to trace the ancestry of each seed, and to select new crosses based on the traits they wanted to emphasize. But as the pumpkins got bigger, another thing happened: They got uglier.

Nature had not designed pumpkins for the kind of huge sizes growers began to coax out of their plants. Consider this: A fun gardening trick for children is to slip a square box over a baby field pumpkin. As the pumpkin grows inside the box, it spreads into the corners and flattens against the walls. Voilà — a square pumpkin.

That kind of malleability makes a giant

pumpkin vulnerable to other shape-changing forces, such as gravity. Like a ball of Silly Putty slowly oozing flat on a table, gravity pulls on these behemoths as they grow, causing them to sag and flatten. They spread wide where they sit on the ground, drooping over on themselves like Jabba the Hutt reclining on his divan. Growth spurts produce bumps and bulges. The tiniest scratch or prick on a young pumpkin's skin can stretch into ghastly scars as the fruit expands.

Giant pumpkins are so irregularly shaped, it is too difficult to compare size. The only definitive metric is the weight. Common sense suggests the bigger the pumpkin, the heavier it should weigh. So growers developed a measuring system to estimate the weight of the pumpkin based on its size. They quickly learned that size alone could be deceptive. Giant pumpkins could blow up to massive proportions, but if they had large, hollow seed cavities and thin walls, they could turn out to be lightweights. Before long, growers discovered that the heaviest pumpkins were the ones with more squashlike traits: gray-, green-, and blue-colored skin, with warts and bumps and rough cantaloupe netting on the shell. As growers magnified these heavier traits, the beautiful orange color that Dill had so carefully bred into his pumpkins began to be lost, and the confusion between squash and pumpkins grew.

Growers called these mixed-up fruits "squampkins" and forged ahead. Two camps emerged. The pumpkins-are-orange crowd preferred the traditional color and took pains to breed orange into their pumpkins. But other growers cared only about growing the heaviest pumpkin possible, regardless what it looked like. Ron and Dick Wallace were in the latter camp. "I've never had a really pretty pumpkin," Dick wrote on BigPumpkins.com. "I don't pick a seed for color. I only pick for size or breeding. I'd love big and purdy, but it won't happen in the Wallace patch unless by accident. We grow strictly for competition."

As the hobby of competitive pumpkin growing took off in the 1980s, national growing groups were organized to establish standards for the weigh-offs. The color issue became more controversial as clubs struggled to define the difference between a squash and a pumpkin. Three national organizations emerged, each with different guidelines. The largest, most influential group, the Great Pumpkin Commonwealth, sought to establish percentage guidelines for color, decreeing a pumpkin had to be at least 70 percent orange. Anything less and it went into the less-prestigious squash category. This, naturally, spawned bitter disagreements over how to judge the 70 percent rule, since most pumpkins — especially squampkins — were a mottled mix of colors. Grids to count off squares of color were devised, but did little to resolve the disputes.

The question widened the divide between East Coast and West Coast as growing clubs in California and the Pacific Northwest snubbed the GPC and its color rules. Poking fun at the whole subject, someone posted a smart-aleck question for veteran Washington state grower Jack LaRue, who dispensed advice on his club's Web site: "Dear Jack, Why are some pumpkins orange and some white and some pink and some yellow and some green?"

To which LaRue whimsically replied:

Some pumpkins are orange because you pollinated early in the morning of a day that ends in 'y,' using your right hand only while facing southeast, right at sunrise, thus capturing the first orange rays of the day.

Some pumpkins are white because you

pollinated well before sunrise. It is so early that the only light you have is moon light, thus the bleached out white color.

Some pumpkins are yellow because the growers are smarter than the rest of us; they do not care which way the sun comes up or goes down because they are not in the garden, they have a real life. The growers of the yellow fruit are smarter, well-rested, and much more alert for the remainder of the day than the growers with the white or orange pumpkins.

Green pumpkins are usually grown by new growers who got a great deal on seeds through eBay. Just be patient and they may turn orange by Christmas. If you like green pumpkins, I have a few seeds for sale.

By 2005, the question had finally been settled. Sort of. The GPC threw out its color rule and decided the heaviest fruit — whether squash or pumpkin — would be declared the overall winner of each weigh-off. Separate prizes were given for the heaviest "true green" squash and pure-orange pumpkin.

Orange fruit, meanwhile, had begun gaining traction as growers became more successful at breeding color back into their massive squampkins without compromising weight. It was a tricky process. Seeds from orange pumpkins weren't guaranteed to grow more orange pumpkins, just as two brown-eyed parents can wind up with a blue-eyed child if each parent transmits a recessive blue-eye gene. So seeds with a reputation for reliably throwing "heavy and orange" were becoming almost as prized as the world-record winners. The orange fruit were crowd-pleasers at the local agricultural fairs, where most of the weigh-offs were held, perhaps because they actually looked like they deserved the name "pumpkins."

Even more vexing for competitive growers than color was the 1,500 question. Late in the 2005 season, rumors had swept the pumpkin world that a monster was growing somewhere on the East Coast that was big enough to smash through the 1,500-pound barrier. It wasn't hard to guess who was growing this colossus. Pennsylvania husband-and-wife team Larry and Gerry Checkon had been setting records and winning prizes since they first turned the dirt in their pumpkin patch in 1998. They were deadly serious competitors, and extraordinarily, consistently successful. Between the two of them, they'd won their state weigh-off five of the past eight years. Gerry Checkon set a world record in 1999, her first year growing. And in 2005, word leaked out that Larry Checkon had a world-record bomb sitting in his northwestern Pennsylvania patch. Based on the measurements pumpkin growers use to estimate weight, the pumpkin was expected to be more than 1,700 pounds — which would not just beat the 1,446-pound record set in 2004, but obliterate it. The news stirred excitement, envy, and some despondency among pumpkin growers. A 1,700-pound pumpkin would be a giant leap toward the one-ton Holy Grail. It would be a tremendous mark to beat, possibly thwarting any chance at setting a new world record for years to come.

But pumpkins have a maddening tendency to surprise. Some are dense as lead, weighing far heavier than they look, while others are corks — pleasingly round and full of air. So it was that the Checkon's 1,700-pound colossus turned out to be "only" 1,469 pounds.

It was still a formidable accomplishment. But some growers also saw it as a sobering sign that the current round of breeding might be reaching its limit. The pumpkin's size had indicated it would weigh more than 1,700 pounds, and yet it hadn't even cracked 1,500. Why?

Theoretically, plant scientists see no reason why giant pumpkins can't grow to 1,500 pounds, or one ton, or beyond. The trick for pumpkin growers is to figure out what is holding their plants back so they can breed improved traits into their seeds. Do the pumpkins need thicker stems to carry more nutrients? Do they need stronger root systems to support the rapid growth? Do growers need to conduct tests to find out which plants are most efficient at using the nutrients siphoned from the soil?

It's the kind of problem farmers and botanists have been tackling for centuries to improve crops. Commercial growers have gotten so good at isolating traits and breeding them into a seed stock that the process can be accomplished in a few years. Biogenetics, in which scientists manipulate plant genes in the laboratory to produce desirable traits, has sped up the process even more.

But a wide gulf separates commercial growers and amateur pumpkin breeders. Commercial operations produce thousands of versions of the same plant each year, giving them more control over the trait-selection process. Most pumpkin growers can barely manage a few plants a year. They pour all their efforts into producing a prizewinner, leaving little room for experimentation. Even when they do experiment, they don't have the precise controls to tell them whether their results are the product of their experiment or some other factor, such as weather or disease.

During the cold winter months of 2006, the question of whether the new growing season might finally yield a 1,500-pound pumpkin, and which seeds were most likely to do it, consumed the community and dominated discussion boards on BigPump kins.com.

When Larry Checkon's pumpkin fell short of the mark in 2005, quiet sighs of relief were heard throughout giant-pumpkin land. Checkon's 1,469-pound pumpkin set a new world record, but not an unbeatable one. It left ample room for a new world record in 2006. And even more tantalizing, growers were able to hold on a little longer to their dream of growing the first 1,500-pound pumpkin. Still, some quietly wondered if the limits of Mother Nature had finally been tested. Perhaps a 1,500-pound pumpkin would never be.

5
DIRT

By the end of March, winter was slowly beginning to release its grip on the North. As temperatures warmed, the whole world seemed to leap into action after the lull enforced by bone-chilling cold. That wasn't necessarily good news for Ron Wallace. Only in the dead of winter did his schedule ease off enough to allow him anything like a regular life. Now work was picking up again. He'd spent March hiring some new managers for the country club and searching for a pool director. Until he found one, he'd have to take charge of the spring pool maintenance himself, getting the pool drained and power-washed and ready to reopen.

As general manager, Ron was responsible for all things great and small. At 9 p.m. he might find himself answering his office phone and helping a club member schedule a wedding, or unlocking the safe to provide a patron with an expensive cigar. Later, at home, he'd settle into bed with a sheaf of financial spreadsheets to lull him to sleep.

The winter covers would be coming off the greens in a few days, and the golf course would be opening back up. Soon, members would be flocking in to kick off their spring season and Ron would be putting in 60-hour weeks to keep up. In the three years Ron had been overseeing club operations as general manager, the peak summer staffing had swelled to about 200 employees. "There's always someone complaining every day when you have two hundred people," he said. Not to mention nearly 500 club members that he needed to keep happy.

Everywhere Ron looked — at home, at the office, in the pumpkin patch — he saw work that needed to be done. At home his mama goat was about to give birth to twins, and he had to decide what to do with the ornery father. He needed to build a new fence for the pony. He needed to sow grass seed over the bare dirt where his old patch had been. The fruit trees needed pruning and spraying. He needed to power-wash the windows on his house and stain the four big decks that surrounded it. He'd set a deadline of Memorial Day weekend to get it all done.

On top of all that was the lengthy to-do list he had for getting the new patch ready for planting the first of May. After settling under the snow all winter, the garden needed to be plowed again. The dirt was still full of rocks that needed to be picked out and thrown aside. And Ron was waiting anxiously for the results of his latest soil analysis. Depending on what it said, he might have to add more of this or more of that to make sure his dirt was as good as he could get it before growing season started. He needed to get an electrical pump rigged up for the new well he'd dug to water the patch. And he needed to lay irrigation lines so he wouldn't have to drag garden hoses 300 feet across the lawn.

He also had to figure out what he was going to do about a deer fence around the garden. Deer were one of the major problems faced by pumpkin growers. The rampant, succulent growth of a pumpkin plant was a magnet for all kinds of plant-chomping animals, and deer were especially difficult to thwart. Fences needed to be at least 8 feet high to keep them out, and a lot of growers installed live electrical wires to repel them. But whatever Ron decided to use, putting up 400 linear feet of fence wasn't going to be cheap. The money just kept adding up.

All of it together, hitting all at once, was

leaving Ron stressed and a little cranky. The pressure of the new season was already beginning to build, with all those familiar feelings boiling up again: anticipation, excitement, and doubts about why he was even putting himself through this.

The Giant Vegetable Growers Conference in Niagara Falls had come and gone in early March. Larry Checkon had been fitted with his new orange blazer for last year's world record, and once again, the Wallaces had to sit and watch from the audience. But it was a nice break from the winter doldrums, and a major partying opportunity for the Rhode Island growers.

The Rhode Island mafia, as they were known throughout the pumpkin world, rented a van to drive to Niagara Falls in what amounted to an eight-hour, rolling fraternity party. They hit the road at 9 a.m. and the first beer was popped by 10. It was a long weekend of late-night drinking — "Bible study," as the growers winkingly put it. Ron stayed out late and then rolled out of bed, bleary-eyed and hungover, for the early-morning conference sessions.

Now, with spring around the corner, everyone was itching to get started on the new growing season. Ron's phone was still ringing and his mailbox was still filling with requests for the 1068 seeds. The closer the growers got to planting time, the more urgent the requests. But Ron was trying to be firm. He had so few left. He'd gotten a bubble pack and a call from a pumpkin grower named Ed Hemphill in New Brunswick, Canada, asking for a 1068. Ron had never heard of the guy. He told him as politely as he could that he just didn't have enough seeds to fill all the requests. That's the way it was, constantly. And every refusal pained him.

Once he was in the garden and had his pumpkin plants started, some of his tension would ease, even though his workload would double. There was no doubt it was going to be tougher than ever this year. The Wallaces were growing more plants and Ron was worried about his parents. "Dad can't go so strong anymore," he said. "He's slowing down." And every day brought new challenges for his mother. "With lupus, there's always things that are happening."

Ron had been handling his stress with late nights of heavy drinking. He'd been going hard over the winter, and brushed off suggestions that he should slow down. "When I hit that coffin, I'm gonna be slammin' into it," he said. "I'm going to be driving in full blast."

But once the pumpkin plants went in the ground, it would be a nonissue: tending the pumpkins would soak up every minute of his spare time. He couldn't wait and he dreaded it at the same time. The thought of the hours of backbreaking work that lay ahead was a little depressing. He was single, after all. But instead of making the most of his bachelorhood in the years since his divorce, Ron had been throwing himself into his pumpkins. His treasured Pontiac GTO was sitting in his garage under a dust-cover while he spent all his time digging in the dirt. And what did he have to show for it? Not a championship, that's for sure. Not a steady girlfriend. "Maybe," Ron grumbled, "maybe in a couple years I'm done with this pumpkin growing. Maybe I take my car out of the garage and go driving on the beach. Maybe I chase women."

Ron marked the first official sign of spring on Monday, March 27: a turtle sunning itself on a rock in his backyard pond. Searching for glimpses of the turtles living in his pond was a soothing ritual for Ron. He loved all his animals, the rabbits and goats and his white pony, named Spirit by his nine-year-old niece, Rene. They were his own little petting zoo. Taking care of the animals was a lot of work, but it was something he did for Rene, who loved to play with them on her frequent visits with her grandparents, and for his friends, who sometimes brought their children over. But the turtles were Ron's alone. Over the years he'd brought home a dozen or more of them — box turtles and snapping turtles and sun turtles — that he'd found on the side of the road or in drainage ditches. He kept his eye out every day on his commutes between home and the country club. Unlike his other animals, the turtles required no extra effort. They minded their own business. Some disappeared; some stuck around. It didn't matter. But the sight of those that stayed, poking their stumpy heads up out of the water or sunning themselves on a rock, always cheered him.

Here on the brink of April, the snow had finally melted and the daytime temperature had risen to 55 degrees for the second day in a row. There was only a month left to make the final preparations in the garden before planting. The first turtle sighting was the second bit of good news that Ron had received that day. The first had come that morning, when Ron checked his mailbox and found that the soil test report for his new pumpkin patch had arrived. As soon as the ground had thawed a couple weeks before, Ron and his dad had taken shovels of dirt from the patch, mixed them together in a wheelbarrow, poured a sample into a clear plastic baggie, and sent it off to the University of Massacchusetts Soil and Plant Tissue Testing Laboratory for analysis. The results would tell them how close they were to getting their dirt in the best possible condition for growing, with the proper balance of nutrients, minerals, and organic matter. As Ron held the lab envelope in his hands, he paused and took a deep breath before opening it. The whole season would hinge on what he found inside.

Pumpkin growers are connoisseurs of animal waste: pig dung, cow dung, chicken dung, bat dung, horse dung — one grower even swears by mink dung from a commercial fur farm. To keep their soil in prime condition and give themselves the best start on each season, one of the basic tasks of growers everywhere is putting back the nutrients their pumpkins siphon out each year. Giant pumpkins are greedy things. They're huge plants that typically cover 500 to 1,200 square feet in a solid leaf canopy, with hundreds of feet of vines and a dense mat of roots spreading out dozens of feet in all directions. Once the vines begin to bear fruit, they suck in nutrients from the soil like a botanical black hole. Manure is one of the richest food sources. So each fall after the pumpkin crop is harvested and the old plants have been ripped up and thrown in the compost pile, growers begin to haul in truckloads of animal waste to renew their garden's vigor.

As long as humans have plowed the earth to grow things, manure has been the gardener's faithful friend. Prehistoric farmers in Peru and Ecuador added seabird droppings to soil to enrich their maize and beans. Ancient Egyptians relied on manure for fertilizing their crops while developing advanced methods of irrigation and crop rotation. And Roman gardeners indulged the Emperor Tiberius's year-round craving for cucumbers by raising them in baskets full of dung. Some garden historians speculate that medieval monks even positioned their monastery latrines close to their kitchen gardens to provide a ready source of human manure. So in that grand tradition, the giant-pumpkin growers' obsession with animal droppings makes a lot of sense.

But it's only one part of a larger obsession with the most basic necessity of gardening: the soil. Growers spend nine months each year working in the dirt. They till it, hoe it, rake it, water it, dig in it, stir it around, crawl in it, squeeze it, smell it, and even taste it. They get so intimately acquainted with their dirt, so attached to it, that it becomes either their best friend or their worst enemy. One West Coast grower admitted to digging up all the tons of carefully tended dirt in his pumpkin patch and taking it with him to his new house when he had to move.

After years of trial and error, Ron and Dick believed they'd finally figured out what they'd been doing wrong with their soil. In the early years, they had poured on the chemical fertilizers. They had hauled in truckloads of fresh manure and compost without bothering to have the contents analyzed. They didn't know then what they knew now: You can bring in a lot of bad stuff with every load of manure if you're not careful, including nasty microbes that weaken plants and cause disease.

The Wallaces' heavy use of chemicals made things worse by killing off much of the good bacteria and fungi that might have helped fight off the bad guys. It was like throwing open the gates of their garden to an invading army. "We thought by doing everything in excess, we'd get excess in return," Dick said. And they did, except it was an excess of disease.

The soil holds the water the plant drinks and is home to a teeming world of microorganisms that work in concert with the plant to help it thrive. But the soil also can contain harmful bacteria and fungi that can turn a pumpkin into mush in the blink of an eye. Organic matter, such as decaying twigs and leaves and bugs, provide nutrients and improve soil structure. Minerals critical to a plant's growth also reside in the dirt, including nitrogen, potassium, calcium, and sulphur. Well-balanced soil with plenty of organic matter offers better drainage while making essential oxygen, water, and minerals more available to the plant.

In short, if you've got good dirt, your plant will be healthy and vigorous, capable of supporting the explosive growth of a giant pumpkin. If you've got bad dirt, your plant will be weak, disease-ridden, and prone to insect damage — if it grows at all. No world-record pumpkin had ever come from bad dirt.

That's why Ron had been so excited about the new source of cow manure compost he'd found last November. He'd spent more than $100 testing several different composts, including ones made from worm castings and fish by-products. But none held a candle to the cow manure pile in that farmer's pasture.

He needed more than manure though. Ron had first tested the raw dirt in the new patch last fall, before he'd even started clearing it, and the results were better than he'd expected. The Wallaces had a sandy loam soil in their yard, and they were starting with 5.8 percent organic matter, which wasn't bad; the desirable range for vegetables is 4 to 10 percent organic matter. But the Wallace dirt still needed a lot of work before it would be capable of supporting a world-class pumpkin. Its levels of phosphorus, potassium, calcium, and magnesium — all key nutrients for plant growth — were low, as were the pH levels, which measure the acidity of the soil. Acidity affects how well a plant is able to absorb nutrients, and since 14 of the 17 critical nutrients for plant growth are found in the soil, growers have to get their pH levels right to get the most out of their plants. Pumpkins like slightly acidic to neutral soil. A pH of about 6.5 to 6.8 — about the same as human saliva — is usually considered ideal.

In the Southern New England Giant Pumpkin Growers' spring newsletter, Ron had published a comparison of soil reports from the patches that grew the two biggest pumpkins in 2005: Larry Checkon's record-setting 1,469-pounder and Scott Palmer's 1,443-pounder. Over the years, Ron had studied the soil tests of about 25 top growers and formed his own ideas about what worked best for giant pumpkins. "I looked at who's growing in clay, sandy loam, who's organic," he said. "What someone is using in their soil may not work with yours. But if you look at them all, you've got to be in that ballpark."

Larry's and Scott's results looked similar. Larry's pH was 6.1; Scott's was 6.5. Larry had 13.8 percent organic matter; Scott had 9.4 percent. Mineral levels varied slightly, but there was nothing dramatic separating the two plots of dirt, even though they were located almost 500 miles apart.

From his years of research, Ron knew what he was looking for, and he also knew how hard it would be to get his soil perfectly balanced in just a few months. He hadn't even had the full benefit of the fall. Growers start working on their soil the minute their old plants come out of the ground in October so the newly mixed dirt has as much time as possible to "cook" over the winter. No matter how perfect you get the soil chemistry — and getting that right is hard enough — Mother Nature still needs to lend a hand to break down the components, meld them together, and work a little alchemy to make all the nutrients accessible to the plants in the spring. The Wallaces hadn't been able to get into their new patch until the end of November, so they had started out behind the rest of the competitive community. And they knew the odds of getting the soil balanced just right in the first year weren't high. But Ron was determined to give it his best shot. Surely all those years of research and advising others how to do it right would pay off for him now. "I'm not giving up," he said.

The first test results last fall had shown that the dirt in Ron's new patch was too acidic, with a pH rating of 5.5. The easiest way to remedy that was to add lots of alkaline lime to the dirt. Manure would provide an abundance of the other nutrients and organic matter and improve the soil structure so that it would absorb water more efficiently. So as soon as they plowed their patch that freezing day in December, Ron and Dick had heaped on tons of cow and chicken manure and tilled in 1,000 pounds of lime, which also is rich in calcium and magnesium. But Ron had stopped there.

He wasn't about to forget how overdoing

it had cost him and his father all those years. So he held back, adding even less than he thought it really needed. "We always thought we had to be adding something and doing something. And we were adding nothing but trouble," he said. He was determined to wait and see how the compost and lime worked for him over the winter. When he got the soil analysis in the spring, he'd know exactly how much more needed to be done.

And on March 27, that moment had finally arrived. Ron tore open the envelope from the soil lab and quickly scanned the typewritten sheet of paper filled with charts and figures. His heart leaped. The numbers looked good. In fact, they looked great. The pH was up to 6.3; the basic nutrient levels had all jumped into the high range. His soil wasn't too far off from that of Scott Palmer's championship patch. But it wasn't quite perfect. There was a little more fine-tuning that needed to be done. He wanted to boost the soil's pH a little more, increase the level of basic minerals like calcium and magnesium, and add more organic material.

The soil report arrived at the perfect time. That Monday was the first day of Ron's two-week vacation — the first vacation he'd taken in more than a year. He hoped to get down to Florida with a friend later in the week, but first, he had work to do in his patch. Over the next few days, Ron and his dad tilled in 400 pounds of lime, 400 pounds of gypsum, 160 pounds of kelp seaweed meal and 15 cubic yards of the farmer's cow manure. The Wallaces again called on Donald Salisbury, the farmer down the road who was always willing to help out his eccentric neighbors with their pumpkin patch. Salisbury brought over his tractor with a backhoe attachment to help spread the manure. Later that week, Joe Jutras came by with his smaller tractor and tilled the remaining big dirt clods into the soft, fine soil of a garden ready for planting. With those additions, "I'm right in that golden range where I like to be," Ron said with satisfaction.

But there was another problem to be solved: Drainage in the patch was terrible. Ron dug a foot-deep hole, filled it with water, and timed how long it took to drain: three hours. All the heavy equipment running over the land had compacted the topsoil into a dense layer. If he left it like that, a few days of rain could drown his plants. So Ron spent another couple hundred dollars on a piece of equipment called a subsoiler, a long bar with a narrow plow blade bolted on it that's dragged behind a tractor. The contraption dug down 18 inches to break up the hard crust and churn up the soil. Donald Salisbury brought his tractor over again to drag the subsoiler through the patch. After that, the test hole drained in about 25 minutes.

By now, the weather was beautiful, with temperatures climbing into the 70s. But Ron's worries weren't over yet. It had been dry all winter, and they'd had a record dry March. Ron had dug a shallow well next to his patch, counting on there being enough rain to keep it filled. But the water level in the well had dropped three feet over the winter. They needed more rain.

Dick wasn't troubled by any of it. Dick, in fact, was on cloud nine. The patch was primed, and so was the Wallace team. "We're going to make an all-out assault on the world record," Dick declared.

While Ron and Dick went about the huge task of creating a new garden from scratch in just a few months, their friends and rivals in the giant-pumpkin world were also busy tilling and hauling in tons of supplements to prepare their old patches for another season.

Scott Palmer was an exception to the rule. He took a lot of flack each year from his fellow Rhode Island growers for his low-key approach to his garden. He lived just down the road from the Wallaces — about five minutes away, if you drove slow. That made it easy for Scott to drop by any time he needed advice, and for Dick or Ron to drop by and offer help from time to time. This was a mixed blessing. Scott was the first to admit he didn't take pumpkin growing as seriously as the Wallaces. "I don't really have a competitive bone in my body," he said. "I grow pumpkins because I like growing them. And you know, [the Wallaces have] been bustin' my balls for years."

That was the price of membership in the Rhode Island club. Ron and Dick cut no slack for anyone. Their expectations were high, and their teasing was merciless. Not a painless thing to endure even for a low-key, easy-tempered guy like Scott. A welder, Scott grabbed extra jobs whenever he could, seven days a week, to support his wife, Shelley, and Scottie Jr., their nine-year-old son. Scott and Shelley often worked on the pumpkins together, and the fruit that won the 2005 SNGPG weigh-off had been registered in both their names.

No one could figure out how a 1,443-pound pumpkin had come out of Scott's patch. He hadn't even done much to supplement his soil last year; he was too busy, and it was too expensive, but also, he didn't really think it was necessary. And then he'd grown the second-biggest pumpkin in the world. Now Scott was the poster boy for less-is-more.

But the other growers still gave him a hard time about it. And the quieter Scott got, the more they piled on. Scott was there, reliably, at all the club meetings, but he seldom said a word. "I like to be there," he said. "I love those guys. I like listening to them. I love listening to Ronnie and the way he puts things. But I just don't have any input. If they need something, if they need something welded, I can help that way."

Scott lived on two wide-open acres of land, with plenty of room to make his garden as big as he wanted. But he purposely kept it small. He had decided to grow only three plants this year, just as he had last year. Even if he wasn't as obsessed as some of the other growers, Scott still worked hard at growing his pumpkins. "You've got to like being outside. You can't be one of those guys who comes home and is tired and wants to sit on the couch. You've got to come home and work even when you're tired," he said.

Also like last year, Scott had decided not

to add much to his soil this year. No mixing in tons and tons of manure and compost and extra minerals like the other guys. "I don't want to switch anything up because I want to see what works. You need a baseline," he reasoned.

The other growers had started warning Scott that he needed to think about moving his patch to new dirt or he risked developing a disease problem. Anyone who grew several years in one place had to worry about that. But Scott wasn't ready to move yet. His patch had proved lucky for him. "Let's not fix it if it's not broken," he said.

On the West Coast, 2,500 miles away, Jack and Sherry LaRue were taking an entirely different approach to patch preparation. In the spring of 2004, Jack had watched a video called *The Living Soil,* produced by a Japanese agricultural research center. The video promoted the idea of a "no till" growing program. At first, it sounded like gardening heresy. Asking gardeners not to till their soil is a little like telling musicians not to tune their instruments before a concert. After all, humans have been cultivating the earth since we figured out how to drag a branch through the dirt. By 3000 B.C., farmers in Mesopotamia and Egypt were harnessing oxen to their wooden plows to prepare the ground for planting. Plowing and tilling was how pumpkin growers mixed in the tons of manure and other supplements they added each year to their old soil. It aerated the garden and improved drainage.

But Jack LaRue was a man who liked to try different things. He and his wife lived on a secluded hilltop in the lush wooded landscape of the Pacific Northwest, where they'd raised their children and tended a flock of ducks and geese and peacocks and grew their pumpkins. Jack had a curious mind and wasn't afraid to break with tradition if he thought he saw a better way. He charted his own path in seed genetics, following his own instincts and ideas about how best to improve seed lines and bring out more desirable traits for bigger, tougher pumpkins. "Jack," as one grower put it, "is always experimenting with some cockamamie thing." But the growing community took a keen interest in whatever cockamamie thing Jack was trying because he consistently grew some of the biggest pumpkins in the world. He had more 1,000-pounders to his name than any other grower, and he'd missed the 2004 world record by only 26 pounds; his 1,420-pound pumpkin set the U.S. record before losing the world title to Canadian grower Al Eaton's 1,446-pounder.

Jack had become one of the hobby's most deeply admired legends not only for his growing skills, but also for his generosity in sharing information and encouraging new growers. His independent ways were dictated mainly by his firm grip on common sense. If something sounded logical to him, he was willing to give it a try. If it sounded silly, he was the first to say so. It helped that the LaRues gave themselves lots of room for error — they grew more than 20 plants every year on a three-quarter-acre plot at their home in Tenino, Washington, just south of the state capital, Olympia, where Jack worked as a federal grain inspector. Jack, a sturdy, square-built, 54-year-old with the springy vigor of a much younger man, gave all the credit for his energy and fitness to his pumpkin patch: his workout program, he called it.

But there was also much to do on the 10-acre homestead Jack and Sherry had bought in the mid-1990s. Their house was burrowed into the trees near the end of a narrow, one-lane dirt road. "We live on a dead end off a dead end," Sherry liked to tell people when giving directions to their home. They had cleared a couple of acres near the top of the hill for their home site and pumpkin patch. Around the back of the house were pens and a small pond for their ducks and geese and five peacocks. A recently adopted stray dog and 13 cats of various colors and sizes had free run of the property.

Sherry, a tiny woman with black, short-bobbed hair, taught first and second grade at the elementary school in Tenino, population 1,584, and coached volleyball at the local middle school. Jack and Sherry had raised four daughters and now were enjoying two grandbabies. Originally, Jack was the family gardener while Sherry stayed busy raising kids. But now they grew pumpkins together, carefully dividing the garden into his-and-her plots.

Jack still grew the bulk of the pumpkin crop; Sherry selected just a few plants to concentrate on each year. But those were indisputably hers. She did all the work and made all the decisions. When her pumpkins failed, she felt the pain, and when she grew a big one, she got the glory. She had taken the last two growing seasons off to spend time with their youngest daughter, who was graduating from college and about to leave home for the wider world. Now, with their last child gone, Sherry was ready to grow pumpkins again.

Like many long-married couples who have gone through life's uphills and downhills together, Jack and Sherry were reflections of each other. Both were active and industrious, good-natured, and eager to help friends and strangers. There was a joyousness in their pumpkin growing that celebrated the wonders of nature, the ingenuity of mankind, and the spirit of competition. Both could talk a blue streak.

Jack had taken to the theory of no-till gardening promoted in the Japanese video. It was based on a simple back-to-nature concept that appealed to his lifelong love of the outdoors. Forests never needed tilling for plant life to thrive, he reasoned. Each year new organic matter was added to the soil by falling leaves, rotting tree branches, and dying grasses, ferns, and flowers. But none of that was tilled in. It just lay on top, with layer after layer of new organic matter gradually breaking down and releasing a steady supply of nutrients to feed each new generation of plants. Meanwhile, earthworms, insects, moles, ants, and other subterranean creatures did a good job of keeping the soil loose and aerated.

Tilling a garden each fall and spring

destroys all Mother Nature's hard work, the theory argues. The tiller grinds through the tunnels and pathways opened up by subterranean creatures. Earthworms and beneficial bacteria and fungi are destroyed. Tilling does eliminate weeds, and it undoubtedly loosens the soil, but only temporarily. "What happens when you take dust, air and water and mix them?" Jack asked in an essay on no-till gardening he wrote for his growing club, the Pacific Giant Vegetable Growers. "Mud. It's like mixing cement. Mud will dry hard with very little oxygen left in it. The same thing happens when we till our gardens."

After watching the video before the spring of 2004, Jack tilled only lightly, turning the top few inches of old compost to loosen the surface crust and remove weeds. That was the last time he tilled, and he has been pleased with the results. Before 2004, the LaRues had grown only three pumpkins over the 1,000-pound mark, with a top weight of 1,064 pounds. But after adopting the no-till policy, Jack and Sherry grew 18 pumpkins over 1,000 pounds, with their 1,420-pounder still among the top 10 biggest ever grown in the world. That had made the LaRues the hobby's top growers, judged by the average weight of their best

10 pumpkins, which stood at 1,176.3 pounds after the 2005 growing season. That was a better average than Larry and Gerry Checkon, both world champions, or any other world champion. But the LaRues, despite their phenomenal success at growing big pumpkins, had yet to grow the biggest pumpkin of any given year. Jack and Sherry, along with much of the rest of the pumpkin world, believed it was only a matter of time.

"Is the no-till method the next step to the 1,500 pound pumpkin?" Jack asked in his essay. "I do not know. Will this practice continue to work? I do not know. Will problems develop in the future because of this practice? Again, I do not know. All I can tell you is that no till appears to work."

6
PLANTING

Dick Wallace leaned over the wagon cart full of pumpkin seedlings with his forearms resting on the side like a schoolboy peering over the infield wall. He wore a long-sleeved T-shirt with the jumbled black-and-gray pattern of winter camouflage. A white Southern New England Giant Pumpkin Growers cap shaded his eyes from the bright morning sun. His eyes squinted in concentration as he watched his son sort through the 20 plants in the cart.

They had decided to grow five 1068s, plus five other assorted seeds. The extra seedlings would be given away. It was perfect planting weather, and Ron and Dick were eager to get started. But the season's outcome depended on them choosing the best seedlings, and they lingered over the decision. Numbers scrawled on the outside of each pot with a black Magic Marker identified the plants: 500, 1354, 1225, 851, 845, 1068, etc. Ron and Dick didn't need the names of the growers to know which seedlings were which. They knew the seed numbers better than they knew their own social security ID's.

Each baby plant still had the two oval leaves known as "cots" — short for cotyledons — the first leaves to emerge from the seed. These first leaves are the starter engine for the plant, providing energy while it begins to produce a root system. Within a few days, the first "true" leaf sprouts, a tiny, crinkled wad that quickly grows into a mature leaf. A fully grown giant-pumpkin leaf would be big enough to nearly fill the wagon. But on these seedlings, the baby leaves ranged from the size of a pea to the size of Ron's palm.

"I really like this one. That was our 1070," Ron said, thoughtfully tapping the side of one pot.

"What did we grow that from?" asked Dick.

"That was our 500 crossed with the 851 Davies," Ron said. "Now, that 1260 there —"

"Maybe we should put that in instead of one of the 1068s?" Dick suggested. But Ron was still concentrating on the seedlings, not paying much attention to his father. "The

1260 with the 845," he muttered, studying the plants, thinking out loud.

"Maybe we should give that a shot and just go with four 1068s," Dick persisted.

"We've got more 1068s upstairs," Ron said absently, not answering his father but replying to some other question hovering in his mind. He moved another plant to one side. Deep down he knew it was a little pointless. The crummiest seedlings could turn out to be the most robust plants, and vice versa. World-champion lore was full of ugly-duckling stories. But too much was at stake. If he was going to have a chance at winning this year, he had to play every step as if it were the most important step of the season.

"Okay," he said suddenly, straightening up. "We're loaded for bear. Let's just go for it." Ron knew planting five 1068s might be putting too many eggs in one basket. But he believed it was the best seed in the world, and it was theirs so they could afford to plant as many as they wanted. "This is the last year we're going to do ten plants," he reasoned. "We might as well be pigs about it."

Spring was finally taking hold in New England. The part of central Rhode Island

115

where the Wallaces lived was thickly wooded, but the landscape still had the transparency of winter, with houses and sky clearly visible beyond the bare branches of the trees along the road. Though not for much longer. Neon-green buds brought a tinge of new color to the scene, soon the forest would thicken with leaves and transform the winding road to the Wallace house into a lushly forested drive.

As they did every year, the Wallaces had started far more plants than they really needed. Part of it was just good growing strategy: There's no guarantee any given seed would germinate; and even if every seed sprouted, having an abundance of seedlings allowed them to sort through and choose the best-looking ones to plant. But Ron and Dick grew even more than that. They also wanted to have enough extra plants to spread around to other club members who might run into some early bad luck. Ron and Dick had done that numerous times before, as did many other growers. The delicate seedlings were especially prone to disaster just after planting. Killing frosts, high winds, a sneaky fungus, an attack of slugs or cucumber beetles — any number of perils awaited the tender, young plants once they were in the ground.

Ron and Dick liked being able to come to the rescue with replacements. In 2005, Steve Connolly had grown his 1,333-pounder from a 1068 seedling the Wallaces had given him after his entire garden was wiped out by a frost in mid-May. As leaders of the Southern New England pumpkin growers club, Ron and Dick felt a responsibility to look out for fellow club members. Especially this year. If the club was going to repeat its success of the previous season, all the growers needed to be in the game with the best plants they could get.

But there was another factor weighing in this year: the reputation of the 1068 Wallace. Reports were trickling in from growers who were having trouble sprouting their 1068 seeds. That was a very big deal. Some growers had paid hundreds of dollars for a single 1068 seed in club fund-raising auctions. Others had wrangled and begged and traded to get their hands on the hottest seed of the season. Regardless of how it had been obtained, each 1068 hit the dirt that spring with the highest of hopes, often with the prized spot in the garden reserved for it. So when the seed just sat there, a dud, the disappointment was extreme.

It was May 7, and the 2006 growing season was finally off and running. Giant-pumpkin growers across the northern hemisphere were excitedly greeting spring with a trowel, a fistful of pumpkin seeds, and a bag of sterile potting soil. Nothing said you couldn't just plant a pumpkin seed directly into the ground. But few growers did it that way. They wanted as much control as possible over their plants from the very first day. Anyway, in many northern areas, it was still too cold to plant outdoors. A seed might rot in the ground before it had a chance to warm up enough to sprout. And if a grower had to wait a few weeks for the weather to warm up, then the whole season would be thrown off. Growers stick to a very tight schedule. They have only five precious months to turn each seed into a giant pumpkin ready for harvest, and they need every growing day they can get.

That meant pushing the envelope a little. Growers could get a jump on the growing season by starting the seeds in pots indoors a week or two before the weather warmed enough to put the plants into the ground. Just like every other aspect of giant-pumpkin growing, seed-starting invited controversy and debate. There are about as many ways to start a seed as there are seeds to grow. Growers develop their own system, and if it works, they stick with it. Ron and

Dick's system was to use a fingernail file to buff the rounded end of each seed, carefully grinding away part of the shell to allow moisture to seep in more quickly, thus giving the seed a better chance of sprouting before rotting. They prepared the dirt in the peat pots where each seed would be planted, mixing in a little liquid seaweed fertilizer and a "root shield" product to help ward off disease. This season, they added in another special ingredient, a booster that Ron hoped would help push them over the top.

Pumpkin growers, like competitors everywhere, arc always looking for an edge over their opponents. Every year seemed to bring some new theory, product, or practice that promised to lift a grower over his rivals. Often, it was as simple as a new fertilizer formula. Sometimes it was something odd, like the idea of feeding milk to pumpkins.

Many of each season's new theories were acquired in the doldrums of winter, when restless growers fed their pumpkin obsession by turning to the Internet for research. World champion Larry Checkon had decided to try aspirin this year. He'd run across several recent agricultural studies proving that the acetylsalicylic acid contained in aspirin could stimulate a plant's defense systems, making it more disease resistant. The prescription: one to two aspirins dissolved in a couple of gallons of water, then sprinkled over the plants' leaves.

This year, Ron Wallace had been intrigued by the potential of beneficial fungi. His dirt studies over the winter had led him to the work of a scientist named Dr. Robert Linderman at the USDA's Horticultural Crops Research Laboratory in Corvallis, Oregon. A whole world of microbes is present and functioning in the underground root zone of plants. How those microbes work and how they interact with plants to affect their growth and health had become the focus of Linderman's research. His specialty was mycorrhizal fungi, a particular type of fungi that scientists believe existed during the time plants first migrated from water to land about 450 million years ago.

Many fungi live symbiotically with plants and animals. Mycorrhizal fungi specialize in roots. Their spores can remain dormant in earth for years, springing into action only when they bump into the spreading roots of a plant. Then, the fungus infiltrates the roots, branching out in a network of tiny filaments known as hyphae. The fungus feeds off the plant roots, but it also acts as a bridge between the soil and the plant, penetrating into nooks and crannies of the dirt where the bigger roots can't reach and ferrying nutrients and water back to the plant. One cubic centimeter of hyphae webbing — about the size of a sugar cube — could be stretched out over the length of a football field, according to Dr. Linderman.

Plants depend on this fungal relationship to survive — or at least to thrive. The fungi produce stronger, more disease-resistant plants that grow bigger and yield more fruit. With the nutritional boost they get from the fungi, plants can better tolerate hostile growing situations such as drought and high-salt conditions.

After running across Linderman's research on the Internet, Ron Wallace called up the scientist and spent hours picking his brain on how he might use mycorrhizal fungi in his pumpkin patch. "He was an enthusiastic guy, and so am I, so we hit it off pretty quickly," said Linderman, who was amused to think that his life's work might be used to give a competitive edge to giant-pumpkin growers.

Ron wasn't the first pumpkin grower to discover mycorrhizal fungi. It had been used off and on by growers for years, mainly around the roots of seedlings when they were transplanted. But Ron learned from Linderman that growers hadn't been using the fungus in a way that would bring the maximum benefit. Pumpkin plants were so big, with such extensive root systems, that doses of the fungus needed to be added repeatedly as the plant grew bigger throughout the season.

This was a revelation Ron believed might give him a badly needed edge, and he resolved to try it. As he planted his seeds in the peat pots, he added a pinch of the mycorrhizal fungi spores, which looked a little like dried yeast. If all went well, the spores would attach themselves to the roots of the seedling and multiply with the growing plant.

Ron and Dick then placed the seeds into the peat pots, with the pointy tip, where the root emerges, pointing down into the specially prepared dirt. Then the pots were placed inside a homemade germination box. For that, Dick and Ron had taken an ordinary, medium-sized plastic storage container — like the kind sold at Wal-Mart — and drilled one-inch holes all around the base for ventilation and electrical wire access. On the bottom of the box, they laid a board fitted with three lightbulb sockets in a row down the middle, in which they placed 75-watt bulbs to generate just the right amount of heat. They mounted a wire grate about six inches above the bulbs, and on this grate they set the peat pots. They replaced the container's lid with a thick sheet of clear plastic, which trapped the heat and moisture while giving Ron and Dick a view of their seeds' progress.

After hearing that some growers were having problems germinating their 1068s, the Wallaces had started another half-dozen or so seeds to be sure they had enough to share with anyone in their club who needed one. On planting day, the Wallaces had three more 1068s just beginning to break the surface of the soil inside the germination box. Dick had rigged a digital thermometer to monitor the temperature and humidity inside the box. According to the gauges, the temperature hovered at 92.5 degrees, with 32 percent humidity.

Dick and Ron firmly believed their painstaking seed-starting methods increased their rate of germination success. But other methods worked well too. Many growers folded their seeds inside a damp paper towel, placed the towel in a clear plastic baggie, then stowed it in a warm, dark place to germinate. Usually within 36 hours, a crack would appear along the edge of a seed near its point. As it opened wider, like a clamshell, the white tip of a root would begin to poke out. As soon as the seed popped open, the growers would remove it and put it in a dirt-filled pot to finish sprouting.

The advantage of the paper towel method is that growers can see exactly when the seed begins to sprout — a process otherwise hidden beneath the dirt. For growers who hover over their planted seed like expectant parents, it is gratifying to know at the earliest possible moment that a prized seed has successfully germinated. Precious days can be lost waiting for a dud to emerge from the dirt. But Dick and Ron were appalled by this practice. They thought it was too easy to go wrong by making the paper towel too wet or too dry. Many times, seeds would rot before they could sprout. Nature designed seeds to grow in the dirt, and that was, they believed, the most reliable method for producing healthy seedlings.

The weather throughout April had stayed warm and dry, making for a beautiful spring, though Ron was getting a little worried about his well drying up. Still, the weather promised a great start to the new season, and he was optimistic. "I think the weather is going to be good this spring," he said. "I really don't care about not getting rain. If I have to choose between rain or no rain, I'd rather have no rain. That way I can control how much water goes on the plants."

The flood of requests for the 1068 had finally subsided. Ron had handed out all the seeds he was going to hand out. He'd even sent one to a pumpkin grower in Alaska. J. D. Megchelsen had grown a 942-pound pumpkin last year and this year he was determined to be the first person to grow a 1,000-pound pumpkin in Alaska. The ground in his town of Nikiski was still heavy with snow when Megchelsen sowed his 1068 in a heated peat pot on March 25. He needed to get an early start to make the most of Alaska's short, but intense, growing season. On March 30, he posted an entry on his Internet diary: "The tiger is out of its cage." The 1068 had sprouted.

The last 1068 seed dispatched by Ron that spring was to Ed Hemphill, the Canadian grower he'd refused earlier in the year. Though a longtime New Hampshire grower had called and put in a good word for Hemphill, Ron still wasn't convinced. But one day as he was about to walk out of the house, his eye fell on Hemphill's self-addressed bubble pack. On an impulse, Ron tossed in a 1068 and stuck it in the mail. "What the heck," he thought. It was just one more seed.

Ron and Dick couldn't understand why so many people were having trouble with the 1068. They felt bad for anyone who was disappointed. "So maybe the 1068 is a little bit of a tough germinator," Ron acknowledged. But they had planted 13 of the seeds themselves, and 12 had come up. "I'm not Zeus," he said. "It's just basic germination skills and 95 degrees." The Wallaces suspected some of the growers weren't keeping the seeds hot enough. A temperature of 85 degrees was often recommended for seed germination, but Ron and his dad had always had better success with higher temperatures. As they sorted through their seedlings in the wagon cart, they debated what the problem might be.

"My God, these guys don't know how to do nothing, and they beat our ass every year," Dick said.

"Well, there were a lot of good growers that didn't get them to pop," said Ron. "Even some guys in our own club. Maybe it's the kelp we use. Maybe it's —"

"Guess what. Nobody has to worry about planting it if they don't want to," Dick said.

"I look at it totally the other way," Ron countered. "Those are more 1068s that didn't go into the ground that could have helped its average. That's why I'm starting so many more seeds to give to everybody else."

The 1068 germination failures were a worry. This was supposed to be the seed's breakout year. If word got out that it was a dud, it would be a huge setback in their campaign to establish it as the best ever. Ron and Dick were convinced that the 1068 was the surest ticket there was to a world record. Last year had established the seed's potential to grow 1,300-plus-pound behemoths. But every year more world-class pumpkins were being grown and producing more seeds with world-class genetics, increasing the odds that some new hot seed could overtake it. So the game this year was to get as many top growers to put the 1068 in the ground as possible. The more 1068s grown by the best growers in the world, the better its chances of racking up even more 1,300- and 1,400-pounders to secure its place in the history books.

But no one could grow a pumpkin if they couldn't even get the seed to sprout. Even Dave Stelts, a former world champion, hadn't been able to get his 1068 to pop. No matter why it was happening, Ron felt a personal responsibility for the unsprouted seeds. He'd even decided to box up a 1068 seedling and mail it to Dave in western Pennsylvania. Dave was one of the Wallaces' archrivals, and also one of their best friends. Ron wanted to make sure Dave had a 1068 to grow this year. Sending the plant by overnight freight was a little risky, but if it made it intact, it could save Dave a week of growing time. If it didn't make it, Ron could always send him another seed.

Before Ron and Dick headed out to the garden for planting, Ron ran to make a quick check on his newest batch of seedlings. He left his father at the wagon and trotted through the garage, past his shrouded GTO, and up the back stairs into the house. In an office cubbyhole off his bedroom, Ron had rigged up a sunning system for his just-sprouted seeds. He kept a computer and a small desk against one wood-paneled wall of the office nook. A fold-up table was set against another wall. Underneath was the cat's litterbox. On top was a tent of glittering aluminum foil.

Ron pulled a rolling office chair away from his computer and sat down in front of the table. He carefully peeled away a couple of wide strips of the crinkled aluminum foil, revealing a three-foot-long fluorescent light stretching the length of the table, suspended about eight inches above the tabletop. Five peat pots with just-sprouted seedlings were lined up beneath the light.

Ron was proud of his incubation chamber. Left outside, the seedlings might get set back by a cloudy day. But under the grow lights, which mimic the sun's rays, they got a steady dose of energizing warmth that gave them a solid head start. The aluminum foil trapped the heat and reflected the light back onto the seedlings. It was a trick he had learned, he said, from a buddy who had learned it from someone who had read about it in *High Times,* the magazine for marijuana growers. "You ever notice that when they bust marijuana people, the whole place is covered in tinfoil?" Ron said.

Ron tapped the dirt on top of each seedling, checking for moisture. "Here's one my father watered way too heavy last night," he said. Ron was always fussing at his dad for overwatering the seedlings. That's what had gotten them into trouble — doing too much instead of letting well enough alone. He picked up another peat pot with a 1068 seedling just poking above the dirt. Its two cot leaves were wrinkled and yellow, still clasped together like hands in prayer. "I don't know if that one's going to make it," Ron frowned. The seedling had emerged from the dirt with its cot leaves still trapped inside the seed shell. The leaves usually open and throw off the shell, but sometimes, they need a little help. Dick had tried to take the seed shell off the cots the night before, but ended up pulling the entire seedling out of the dirt. He called Ron at work to confess.

"I said, 'How did that happen?' And he said, 'I dunno. It just came out. It didn't have any roots,' " Ron recalled. Dick had stuck it back in the dirt and they'd left it alone to give the roots a chance to grow. It might still be fine.

Satisfied that the seedlings were okay, Ron dashed back down to the cart to finish sorting out their plants. His father had fetched a wheelbarrow to load the plants they would choose to put in the ground that day. Ron looked over the seedlings one last time. "I'm going to take these three," he said, pointing to a group of 1068s he'd pushed to the side. "This one might be the one I mail out to Stelts." He pointed to a sturdy 1068 with slightly smaller leaves. Of course, Ron was keeping the best seedlings for himself. But he felt a little guilty about being selfish.

"Hey, Ronnie. It is what it is," said Dick.

"The ones in the germinating box we'll keep for Steve Sperry and Peter Rondeau,"

Ron calculated. He pointed to another one of the punier plants. They needed that one to give away to somebody, but it wasn't much of a prize. One of the leaves looked slightly deformed. "It's a little yellow, but that doesn't mean anything these first two weeks," Ron said.

"Hey, you know the seedling we gave to Steve Connolly last year," Dick reminded him. "We weren't going to give it to anybody because it was so awful-looking. It was maybe a couple weeks old. A leftover. And he grew his 1,333 on that plant."

The morning sun was bright in a cloudless sky. Ron squinted out across the yard to the garden. It was a neat, dark rectangle of earth carved out of new lime-green grass, surrounded on three sides by tall pine trees. Ron and his dad had already set up miniature greenhouses over the places where they would put each plant. The hutches, covered in translucent plastic, were called "cold-frames" by some growers because they protected the plants in the cool weather of spring.

Ron and Dick had seven premium cold-frames that Joe Jutras had helped them build with sturdy two-by-two and two-by-four lumber. They were completely enclosed, about the size of a pup tent, though

131

half of one side was hinged so that it could be opened for access to the plants or to ventilate the greenhouse on warmer days. These greenhouses were ideal for the pumpkin plants, but a lot of trouble to build. Since they only had 7, and needed 10, Ron had gone to a local hardware store to pick up 3 more. They were much smaller, made of PVC pipe and green plastic, but they were inexpensive and ready to go. Ron and Dick had set all the greenhouses out a week ago. As the sun shone through the plastic, it heated the air inside the greenhouse like a car in summer, warming the soil where the seedling would take root. Cold soil would slow the plants growth. Some growers went so far as to bury heating cables in their garden to warm up the dirt before planting time.

Dick rolled a wheelbarrow with their seedlings and planting supplies out to the edge of the garden. The dirt in the newly tilled garden was a rich, dark brown, crumbly and soft. Walking in it would pack it down with every footstep. But it needed to stay loose — with plenty of air pockets to give the plant roots oxygen and room to spread — the Wallaces had laid long planks through the garden. Walking on the boards distributed their weight so that the soil was less compacted, and limited damage to a single path.

Ron walked down a plank to the first greenhouse, one of the smaller ones. He carried an industrial-sized aluminum cookie sheet, which he tossed on the ground. He flipped his beige baseball cap around on his head, then kneeled down on top of the metal sheet. He zipped open the tentlike coldframe, rolled up the flap, and bent his head inside. The new greenhouses were only about two feet tall, and Ron had to hunch over to lean in.

"Okay, Dad. I need you to get me some mycorrhizae," Ron said. As Dick went to fetch the bucket of fungi, Ron began digging a hole for the seedling inside the greenhouse. The dirt was so soft, he scooped out a bucket-sized hole with his hand. As he dug, he pulled out large clumps of semirotted grass and shook his head. The clumps were left over from last fall, when they had first plowed the new patch, turning under leaves and grass that had been growing in the woodland. He had hoped they would be chopped up enough to rot over the winter. But no such luck. "That's not good," he said, holding up a chunk of semidecomposed grass to show his dad. "It ties up nitrogen." But so far, that was the only major problem he'd detected. Not too bad, really.

"Dad," Ron said as he finished digging the hole. "What do you want to do here, a 1354 Checkon or a 1370 Rose?"

"I think the 1354," Dick said. He picked up a flat wooden paint-stirring stick and a black marker and wrote "1354" on the stick, then he added a big, bold checkmark underneath — shorthand for "Checkon." They'd use the sticks to label the plants once they were in the ground. The 1354 Checkon was the same seed that had grown Larry Checkon's 2005 world record. It had very different genetics from the 1068 Wallace. They wanted to grow it to see what kind of pumpkin it would produce for them, and also they wanted to mix it into their 1068 line as way of diversifying their seed stock.

"Okay, Dad, you know what you can do?" Ron said. "Drop two tablespoons of kelp into the sprinkler can."

Dick reached down and peeled the lid off the plastic tub of liquid seaweed. A powerful stink, like a badly neglected outhouse, wafted up. "Aaaaaaahh. That's a nice aroma," Dick joked. The kelp looked as bad as it smelled — a dark brown sludge dripping down the side of the container. Dick stirred some mycorrhizae fungi into the mixture, which began to bubble and foam like some foul witches' brew. He mixed a few tablespoons into the full watering can and then carried it across the plank to Ron, who sprinkled the newly planted seedling.

Efficient and businesslike, Ron moved on to the next greenhouse. "The 1370," he called to his dad. The 1370 Rose was renowned for producing bright-orange pumpkins. "If we can have orange and heavy, we're going to have it," Ron said. "A lot of people think the 1068 needs color, and it does. The number-one cross made by anyone who has it this year is going to be the 1370 and the 1068 Wallace."

Dick scrawled "1370" on another paint stick and drew a flower, a rose, underneath it. He was amusing himself now. Ron dug a hole, carefully peeled away the peat pot from the velvety leaves of the seedling, and cupping it in both hands, gently settled it into its new home. He scraped the dirt back to fill in the hole, then patted it softly in place around the stem of the plant. "Dad! Water!" he called. He sprinkled the plant, then moved on to the next greenhouse. The old, handmade coldframes were big enough for Ron to crawl inside. He tossed in his cookie sheet and stepped in on top of it. This spot was for a 1068. Dick pulled out another painter stick and wrote "1068." Underneath it, he drew two curving lines cupped around a vertical slash — a naked butt, the Dick Wallace trademark. He grinned devilishly.

Ron dug, planted, and watered, moving down the line of greenhouses until all the plants were in the ground. Since it was a sunny day, he propped the greenhouse doors open a bit to make sure the newly planted seedlings didn't overheat. They were still very young and tender, and it wouldn't take much to fry them. But he also wanted to create a warm, humid microclimate inside the greenhouses to jump-start the plants. It was a delicate but all-important balance. They had to stay on schedule. Ron ran the numbers as he worked — if the plants were in the ground by the end of the first week in May, then some would be ready to pollinate by the end of June. If he could get all the pumpkins pollinated by the second week of July, he should be close to 400 pounds come August 1.

But no, that was the old days. If he pollinated as late as July 14 or 15, he'd lose 10 days of his best growing weather. Now, if he was shooting for 1,500, he would probably need to be at 500 pounds by the end of July. That meant pollinating by the end of June or the first few days of July. To reach 1,500 pounds, Ron figured his pumpkin would need to put on another 800 pounds during the peak growth phase in August. Then, if he was lucky, he could add another 200 pounds in September.

That was the trickiest part. In September, when the pumpkins were maturing and the weather started to cool as the days got shorter, the plants' growth slowed down dramatically and often stopped completely. But that's where Rhode Island had an advantage over some other states up north. It was nearly surrounded by water. The Atlantic Ocean to the south and Narragansett Bay to the east helped stabilize its weather, moderating some of the dramatic temperature swings other places could see in the early fall. It was often several degrees warmer than northern Massachusetts or New Hampshire in September. "I always thought that if we could just figure out what to do, we could beat other clubs," Ron said. "Because our weather is a hell of a lot better."

7

A Change in the Weather

With the day's planting finished, Dick had put on fresh clothes — a bright blue-and-white Hawaiian shirt with palm trees, a pair of long khaki shorts, white socks, and suede ankle boots. His hair was neatly brushed straight back from his receding hairline. His wife, Cathy, wore jeans and a light-blue denim jacket over a black blouse. A pink glass heart dangled from a blue and aqua beaded necklace. They were ready for their Saturday-night date.

Dick and Cathy made it a point to go out to dinner at least once a week, just the two of them. Especially during pumpkin-growing season, when Dick spent so much time in the garden and Cathy felt neglected. The year had been a rough one for Cathy so far. She'd just gotten out of the hospital the week before, after suffering another lung infection — the third that year. She'd been coughing and feeling weak and having trouble breathing. It had been bothering Ron especially. "It's the worst I've ever seen her," he said. Ron was beginning to worry more about his dad too. His lungs had been damaged by a lifetime of smoking, and heart problems had cropped up recently.

While Cathy waited in the car, Dick ran up for another quick look at the three seedlings still in their germination box. He lifted the Plexiglas lid and doused each emerging seedling with a drink of water. "Ron says I water too much," he confessed. "But they were looking a little dry."

Before dinner, Dick wanted to stop by and see how Joe Jutras was doing with his seedlings. Dick and Joe were kindred spirits. They both never hesitated to share their time or resources with other growers, and they had bonded over the years as they collaborated on making trophies for the club's weigh-off prizes. The Jutras house sat on a rise at the bottom of a valley, with several acres of wooded land sloping down in the back. The house was encircled by a green lawn bordered by deep flower beds and dotted with fruit trees and neatly pruned shrubs. On one side of the house, Joe's wife, Sue, kept a vegetable garden. Farther back, Joe grew two rows of grape vines. In the middle of the backyard, well away from the shade of the trees, was Joe's pumpkin patch.

When people asked Joe what he did for a living, he replied humbly, "I'm a wood-worker." In fact, he and his two brothers ran a very successful high-end custom woodworking business, Jutras Woodwork-ing, Inc., in Smithfield, Rhode Island. Joe inherited his love of carpentry from his father, a cabinetmaker. He and his brother Paul started their own residential-remodeling business in 1980, and later were joined by a third brother, Rick. Now they manufactured dramatic ceiling moldings and custom cabinetry for multimillion-dollar mansions. They designed and manu-factured custom furniture, like tables, wardrobes, and entertainment centers, and made built-in wood furnishings and wall paneling for yachts. The three brothers divided the duties of the business according to their particular strengths and interests. One brother was in charge of the adminis-trative side. Another was in charge of sales and customer service. And Joe ran the back of the shop, where he spent his days breath-ing in the smell of fresh sawdust as the wood took shape beneath his hands.

As Joe led Dick and Cathy back to his pumpkin patch, they passed by his cool-weather vegetable garden. He reached down into a bushy-leafed plant, snapped off a stalk of rhubarb, and munched as he walked, savoring the grassy, sweet-tart taste. Joe was 50, and he'd been growing giant pumpkins for 10 years. But now that his kids were older — he had a 19-year-old daughter and a 22-year-old son, who was following him into the family business — he had more time for his pumpkins.

In the pumpkin patch, Joe could match the Wallaces hard-luck story for hard-luck story. In 2005, he'd grown eight plants. He lost one to deer and one to woodchucks munching on the vines. He had to pull out one that was crowding too close to his other plants. He lost one when the stem split. He had one amazing pumpkin that had wowed him by growing 35 pounds a day for a week, then 37.5 pounds a day for two weeks. It put on 770 pounds in three weeks, and reached nearly 1,300 pounds before it split open on August 18. "It was growing so fast, and it was so heavy, I knew something had to go wrong," Joe said. "It was headed on a world-record pace. I could easily have broken the fifteen hundred mark if it had kept going."

But Joe was philosophical about it. "You expect them to break. When you go to these weigh-offs, you hear nothing but horror stories. It's just one heartache after another."

Joe wanted the world record as much as any other competitive pumpkin grower. But he rarely talked about it. He just grew his pumpkins. This year he was growing eight again, and he was trying some new ideas. He was going to let the vines grow longer, which would make bigger plants — he expected each plant to fill 900 to 1,100 square feet of space, compared to about 600 square feet apiece last year. To make room, he had plowed up more lawn to expand his main pumpkin patch and plowed another small patch farther back on the property.

Tons of manure and compost later, Joe was ready to start the season. "But the soil here isn't that good," he told Dick as he showed off his handiwork. "I had to till this thing about fifteen times to break it up. I beat the shit out of it with the tiller. So I don't know what's going to happen."

Joe and Dick toured the pumpkin patch while Sue and Cathy stayed behind at the house to visit. Joe was eager to explain a new pruning technique he planned to try this year. He crouched down on the grass next to the patch and leaned over to draw in the dirt with a stick. "I'm going to grow 'em like this," he said, tracing several straight lines in the soft soil to represent pumpkin vines. "They're all going to meet in the middle, and I'm going to grow 'em backward." He traced several more curving lines. "The main will go this way," he said, the stick scraping a trough in the dirt. "This side vine I'm going to grow out this way" — another line — "this one I'll grow back this way, and then back this way."

Dick looked down at what Joe had traced in the dirt, which looked roughly like an upside-down pitchfork. "So you're going to have a lot more in back of the plant?" Dick asked.

"Yeah," said Joe. "I want to change it up. Try something new." He stood up and followed Dick, who wobbled out along the single-plank walkway to a greenhouse sitting in the middle of the patch. Dick propped open the lid and looked inside. Ten four-inch-square plastic pots sat on a white warming plate. The seedlings were barely out of the dirt, and most had just two cot leaves bracketing the stem. Joe leaned over and peeked in. "I'm in trouble with a couple of them," he told Dick. "This one I put out this morning. I don't know if it's going to work." He pointed to a 1068 seedling with a puckered and curled leaf. "Aww, what's the harm of a friggin' curled leaf," said

Dick. "Half the guys can't even get theirs to germinate, and you're worried about a curled leaf?"

The two men leaned against the side of the small greenhouse, looking down as Joe assessed his seedlings. He wasn't thrilled with how his season was starting. He pointed to another plant, saying, "Look at how crazy that one is; it came up all twisted." The seedling leaned drunkenly against the edge of the pot, one leaf curled under.

"If you could have seen the 1068 we gave Steve Connolly last year, you would have thrown up," Dick offered. He meant this as encouragement.

"See that 1372?" Joe went on. "It's a goner too. I took that out of the shell today and there's no root on it."

"Yeah, but it's starting to turn green."

"Naw. There's nothing there." Joe leaned over to pick up the pot, then plucked the seedling out of the dirt to show Dick. The stem ended bluntly — like a broken toothpick stuck in the dirt. "See, there's nothing there. No root."

"We had one 1068 that that happened to," Dick said, thinking of his own experience plucking a seedling out of its pot.

"Now look at this here, that 842," Joe said,

getting worked up, happy to have someone to sympathize with him. "I looked at that seed and I thought it was a great seed. Great lookin'. But it didn't do anything. I can usually tell in thirty-two hours if the seed is starting to pop and develop a root. That thing didn't do anything, Dick. I put it back up on top of my refrigerator. Next day, still nothing. I took it, put it back in some water, squeezed it, put some more water in there, put it back on top of the fridge. But I wouldn't be surprised if that doesn't make it either."

Dick was incredulous. "You germinated all these on top of the refrigerator?"

"Well," Joe said, sensing Dick's disapproval, "in a paper towel. And I've got a heating pad."

"Boy, you know, I hate that paper towel thing," said Dick.

"I like the paper towel thing," said Joe, rallying to his own defense. "Because you know if it's going to take. I knew right away that this one isn't going to take."

"But that's where a lot of guys screw up, because they leave it too long in there and it rots," Dick insisted.

Joe, ever the diplomat, agreed. "Yeah. And you can damage your root if you don't take it out in time," he said, closing the subject.

Talk turned to Joe's 1225 Jutras seed, which had come from one of the most beautiful orange giant pumpkins ever grown. Dick told Joe that he and Ron had decided to grow the plant, but they weren't going to grow a pumpkin on it. Instead, they would just use the pollen from its male flowers to fertilize other pumpkins in their garden, transferring the orange genetics into their 1068 line. After that, they'd pull the 1225 plant out. Joe's eyes crinkled in a bemused smile. This was an insult to his prized beauty.

"What?" he said. "You're not going to grow it?"

"No," said Dick. "We're being piggish on the 1068s this year."

"Well, the 1225 isn't exactly shabby."

"I know it ain't," said Dick. "It ain't shabby. But we just want the pollen out of it right now because we want to give enough space to the 1068s this year. We've got to get off the shag somehow. You know, last year we had to sit and just watch you guys, and that hurt. And the year before I had to sit and watch you guys all weigh heavier than me. I'm sick of this shit!"

Joe laughed. Dick grinned. "And this year we'll probably have it even worse, and I'll just quit," Dick concluded.

They walked the planks back to the edge of the patch. Before Dick left, Joe steered him over to his compost pile near the tree line. Joe picked up a stout stick and dug into the huge, slightly slimy mound of rotting vegetation, turning over a big chunk. Hundreds of slithering earthworms boiled up. Joe beamed. "They're in there by the thousands." he said. "But you can't put 'em in the garden yet. If you till 'em, you kill 'em. So what I'm going to do is just sprinkle them on top, maybe in July when the soil is warmer." Dick nodded appreciatively. Every grower knows that nothing aerates the garden better than a good batch of earthworms.

The men wandered back up to the house where Sue and Cathy stood talking on the concrete driveway in front of the garage. Sue was telling Cathy about a cruise she was planning to go on with her daughter and her daughter's fiancé. The two couples chatted pleasantly, exchanging tidbits of their lives. Joe mentioned he was working with a beautiful butternut wood at the shop, making a dressing room for a new house. "It's a very soft wood that we don't use that often," he said.

That gave Dick an idea. "When I go, Joe — that's the last thing I want to ask you —

when I go, I want you to build me a casket shaped like a pumpkin, and I'll curl up in there and you can bury me in there."

"Roots up or down, Dick?"

"Bury me in a fetal position."

Cathy rolled her eyes. She'd endured 15 years of pumpkin jokes. The charm had worn off long ago. "There will be no pumpkins at my funeral," she said firmly.

The evening light was fading. Black mayflies had emerged from the grass and were swarming thickly in the air, flitting around their heads in dark clouds. Breathing became hazardous. Dick and Cathy headed for their car.

Early the next morning in southern Massachusetts, Steve Connolly paused at the edge of his sun-flooded pumpkin patch. He turned to walk away, hesitated, then turned back, staring at the garden. "It's like this every year," he said, with a little, self-conscious laugh. "What's the right thing to do? The worries never end."

Steve had been up since 5 a.m., taking his daily run down the winding road along the wooded edge of Borderland State Park in southeastern Massachusetts, and back again to the piece of ground that had been in his family for more than 100 years. Jogging was one of the things that kept Steve wiry thin at the age of 51. That, and moving 90 miles per hour through the rest of his life. He worked as a plastics engineer for a company that manufactures medical implants like knee joints and heart valves. At home he was a husband to Nancy, and a father to their 15-year-old son, Scotty.

Steve was soft-spoken, drifting silently in the background while the more-gregarious pumpkin growers hogged the spotlight with their pranks and tall tales. But he was always intense, always focused, a deadly serious competitor. Steve Connolly was that kid everybody remembers from kindergarten who would go off quietly into a corner and build a giant castle, complete with drawbridge and gun turrets, while the other kids were still arguing over who got the green blocks and who got the blue blocks. Before he joined the Southern New England club, the Rhodies had viewed Steve as a little aloof, a little secretive. But after being named a club director in 2006, he was proving himself invaluable by recruiting sponsors, contributing long, well-researched articles to the club newsletter, and documenting events with digital photos that he promptly e-mailed around to members.

Steve had seen his first Atlantic Giant during a family outing to the Topsfield Fair in 1992. About 70 of the giant pumpkins were lined up for the annual competition, and he was astounded by the sight. For 20 years, Steve had been tending a kitchen garden that was carved into the sloping lawn at the side of his house. The land once served as an apple orchard and cow farm, and was covered in rich, 12-inch-deep topsoil. After seeing the giants at the Topsfield Fair, pumpkins took over his life.

Now, on this morning, Steve was preoccupied with questions. He had been planning to put his second pumpkin plant in the ground, but he was concerned about the weather. The forecast was predicting frost that night, so he'd decided to wait another day. But then he was worried that he was getting a later start than other growers. Of course, a late start hadn't stopped him from growing a 1,333-pounder last year — the second-place winner in the Frerich's Farm weigh-off and the fifth-biggest pumpkin grown in the world in 2005. That season had started off disastrously, with a mid-May frost wiping out his fledgling pumpkin brood. He had to go begging for plants to rescue his season and had snagged a 1068 from Ron and Dick Wallace. The plant, which had been sitting in its pot nearly a month, looked terrible — he would have thought it hopeless if it had not been his best hope. So he put it in the ground and tended it, and it flourished. The 1,333-pounder he produced from the 1068 had helped propel the seed's fame.

Steve wasn't looking for another miracle turnaround this year. He'd much prefer things to go smoothly from the start. And the forecast of frost, so reminiscent of last year, was not a welcome development. But he'd prepared extra fortifications. He'd rigged a makeshift heater inside his greenhouses by cutting a hole in the bottom of a Styrofoam cooler and fitting it with a grow light. He tipped the cooler upside down over the seedling so the lamp hung from the top and bathed the plant in warm light all night long.

That would take care of the frost problem. But the morning's brisk wind was also giving Steve pause. He had brought the tray of seedlings outside earlier to begin acclimating them to outdoor conditions — an important step that would help reduce the transplant shock when he put them in the ground in another day or two. He'd set the tray in the middle of his garden for the day and then placed a greenhouse on top of them.

Already, though, at 8 a.m., the sun was

glaring down from a clear blue sky, threatening to cook the plants under the clear plastic. So back into the garden he went, propping up one end of the greenhouse about a foot off the ground to allow more ventilation. From the edge of the patch, he surveyed his work, but the wind was kicking up, beating on the side of the greenhouse and whip-snapping the loose plastic tacked onto the frame. Not good. One year a strong gust of wind had actually lifted one of his greenhouses over the 15-foot-tall cedar trees at the edge of his yard and sent it sailing over to a neighbor's property. He didn't want that to happen again, so he made one more trip into the pumpkin patch, hopscotching over the boards laid across the soft dirt, to anchor the greenhouse frame down with a large paving stone.

By the second week in May, when most growers around the country should have already had their plants in the ground, complaints about the 1068 Wallace seed were still on the rise. The phone at the Wallace household began to ring as people sought advice on how to rescue their seed or begged for a replacement. Ron and Dick felt bad about anyone who had paid for a 1068 and was unable to sprout it. Ron mailed out several replacements, even though he found it painful to part with his dwindling stock. But, he figured, if the seed didn't break through the top rank this year, then they might not be worth hanging on to, anyway.

The reputation of the Wallace seed seemed to be going downhill fast as a litany of complaints erupted into a public discussion on the BigPumpkins.com message board. In a string of messages titled "Problems with the 1068," several growers groused that the seed was a dud. "It sounds like there have been a lot of failures at germinating it this year," wrote one Utah grower who'd had trouble with it. "I know that I didn't do anything wrong." Another grower called the seed "a finicky bugger," noting his own difficulties. "The 1068 was worst seed I've germinated so far," wrote a California grower — out of 20 seeds he started, it was the only one that wouldn't sprout.

Ron read the complaints on the board and silently steamed. He and his dad believed the growers were having problems because they were trying to germinate the 1068 at lower temperatures. Worse, they suspected some were trying to sprout the seed with the despised paper towel method. "For the 1068, it won't work," Ron said. In any case, the criticism didn't seem fair. There were always going to be some seeds that didn't pop — there's a natural and expected failure rate. But a few disappointments were being exaggerated because of all the attention focused on the seed. A lot of top growers had banked on putting a 1068 in the ground that year. Ron estimated there were 1068s in the hands of more than 50 growers in 2006, most of whom would be trying to grow it. But some were unlucky, and some just weren't careful enough.

Ron was willing to try to help anybody who called or e-mailed him privately about a problem. But he resisted posting a defense on the message board. He'd had bad experiences there in the past when other growers — strangers — had taken his comments the wrong way. And he was appalled at some of the pettiness and backbiting he occasionally saw breaking out. "On the computer, everybody's ten feet tall," he observed. "Whenever you put something in writing, it can be interpreted fifteen different ways." But Big Pumpkins.com was the official grapevine for pumpkin growers, and Ron worried about the effect all the chatter might have on the reputation of the 1068.

So Dick tackled the problem. Dick's view of the Internet was entirely different from his son's. He saw it as a chance to reach out to growers across the country and to make a big impact with just a few words. He logged on to the message boards regularly, mostly to dispense advice, respond to questions, and offer encouragement spiced with heavy doses of his cornball humor.

Dick sprang to the defense of the 1068, reminding the growers that the seed had been responsible for an impressive slate of monster pumpkins in 2005, and had been a big contributor to the Southern New England growers' success that year. He rattled off some of its proud progeny: the 1333 Connolly, the 1312 Sperry, the 1253 Sperry (the 2004 Topsfield Fair champion), and the 1201.5 LaRue (2005 winner of the "Terminator" weigh-off in Oregon). Not to mention, he added, the two pumpkins he and Ron had lost to rot just before the 2005 weigh-off, both estimated to be more than 1,300 pounds at the time of their demise.

But with many more growers planting the 1068 in 2006, Dick acknowledged a higher failure rate than he would have liked. "I have no real hard evidence as to why this is happening," he wrote. Dick offered the Wallaces' prescription for successfully germinating a 1068, including higher-than-normal heat and a good dose of patience. Even under perfect conditions, the 1068 could be a slow starter, Dick warned, sometimes taking four or five days to emerge, compared to a three-day average for other seeds.

The seed's critics didn't hold the floor for long. Several growers chimed in with 1068 success stories. "Mine came up quickly and in good shape," said a grower in the Appalachian Mountains. A New York grower declared he would pick "a slow, wimpy, sad-looking 1068" over any other healthy seedling. One Ohio grower received a replacement seed from Ron when his first seed failed to germinate, but had to call for help again when the second seed came up looking pale and puny. Ron advised him to give it a shot of seaweed solution, put it under a grow light, then step back and watch it take off. "I'll tell ya, that's exactly what it did," the grower vouched.

Then, Dave Stelts in Pennsylvania called the Wallaces to announce, "The Eagle has landed!" The 1068 seedling Ron had sent via Federal Express had arrived safe and sound. Dave had put it straight into the ground the same day. The Wallaces had handed out all their other spare plants to club members in need. Their own five 1068s were in the ground and growing. Despite the 1068's germination problems, the season looked like it was off to a good start for the Southern New England pumpkin growers.

And then the weather, as weather is prone to do, changed.

On May 15, the day after Mother's Day, the National Weather Service flashed emergency bulletins across New England warning that the region was in for one of the worst flooding events in its history. A four-day deluge already had dropped nearly 15 inches of rain on Massachusetts and New Hampshire, pushing rivers over their banks and swamping neighborhoods. Schools were closed, roads washed out, homes submerged. The governors of Massachusetts, New Hampshire, and Maine declared states of emergency. Farther south, Rhode Island and Connecticut were also poised for flooding. Though they were spared the heaviest rains, the five to seven inches they got in four days was close to setting records there too.

The early spring had been so dry that growers had been worried about the prospect of a drought. And then the clouds gathered and the skies darkened and the rain came down. And down. And down. In New Hampshire, which got the brunt of the storm system, some growers were completely wiped out. One grower's pumpkin patch was under two feet of water. Another grower sat in his house and watched the loose dirt of his freshly tilled garden sluice away inch by inch down a hill.

In Rhode Island, water drained off quickly from most patches, doing less harm. The newly planted seedlings were protected inside their greenhouses, safe from the pounding rain, shrieking wind, and sopping mud. But still, there were worries. No one could remember a spring that had been this wet, this long. And the timing couldn't have been worse for the plants. Most growers had just gotten their seedlings in the ground when the rains began rolling through. Even though the plants were dry beneath their covers, they still needed sun to grow.

In a good year, the plants would have been exploding about now, with new leaves bursting forth every day. But the cloudy skies and cool temperatures that came with the storm acted like a brake on growth, putting the plants into slow motion. Growers had difficulty getting into their patches — now quagmires of sucking sludge — to check on their plants. "I stepped into a corner of my garden last night and sunk down one foot into the mud," Steve Connolly wrote to Ron

Wallace in an e-mail. "That's never happened before."

In fact, according to the National Weather Service, the New England region hadn't seen torrential rains this severe since 1936. Worse, there was no sign of it being over yet. The forecast called for more rain through the rest of the week, with daily chances ranging from 30 to 90 percent, and only one day showing a possibility of the sun breaking through.

As the storms raged in southern Massachusetts that Mother's Day night, Steve Connolly stepped outside his house in his rubber boots and snapped some pictures of his garden. The lights he had rigged inside each greenhouse to keep his plants warm blazed through the black night, turning the greenhouses into great, glowing lanterns in the darkness. The wind whipped at the plastic covers and the rain beat down in a relentless rhythm.

Growers were glued to television and Internet weather reports, desperate for news of a break in the weather. Every day without the sun was hurting their chances of growing a championship pumpkin, and already, they were running behind. "New England is off to a horrible start," worried Ron. "We're like a prize fighter that got slugged in the face in the first round. We're staggering a bit."

As Ron watched the rain fall, he passed the time calculating the damage. And it wasn't just his pumpkin patch he was worried about. At the country club, the rain was keeping away the golfers who produced a hefty chunk of the club's income during the warm season. In the past 10 days, the club was running 250 rounds below normal. And if the golfers weren't golfing, they weren't drinking at the bar or eating at the restaurant either.

At home, the pumpkin plants were growing, but very slowly. They were a pale green — paler than they should be. Normally, the seedlings already would be lengthening into a long main vine, getting ready to start a blistering pace of growth, which would cause them to outgrow their greenhouses before the second week of June. But by the looks of the plants now, there was no way they'd hit that mark this year. And that was cause for worry.

Everything depended on the growing schedule, and the schedule depended on the weather. If the plants were slow to vine, that could throw off the timing of pollination. Ron figured he had to have a pumpkin started no later than the end of the first week in July to have any kind of shot at a world record. But at this rate, it could be a week or two later than usual before the vines matured enough to produce fruit. If that was so, Ron could kiss his world record good-bye. The whole club would be hurt. Maybe, he began to think, it wasn't going to be their year to shine. While New England drowned, the West Coast had been having glorious weather: warm, sunny days mixed with occasional gentle showers. "The good rain," as Ron called it.

For as much time as they spend researching fertilizer and soil chemistry and pruning techniques, giant-pumpkin growers are ultimately at the mercy of the weather. So if it was New England's year to have lousy weather, and it was the West Coast's turn to earn Mother Nature's smile, then so be it. Ron tried to look on the bright side. This was his first year in the new patch, anyway. Next year the soil would be aged and blended and he'd have a better chance at something special. And for now, the rains weren't all bad. When it was so dry, he'd been worrying he would have to dig his new well deeper. But now it was brimming. And the new grass seed Ron and his dad had sowed to cover the bare ground of their old patch was loving the rain. If they could just

161

get one or two sunny days, the seed would explode out of the saturated earth into a thick, green carpet of rye.

Out in the Wallace pumpkin patch, hunkered under the cover of their greenhouses, the new crop of pumpkin seedlings were shielded from the terrible weather. In fact, other than being behind schedule and a little pale, this was the most robust set of young plants the Wallaces had ever grown. Ron was determined not to get carried away over pumpkins — that was a road that led only to disappointment. But he couldn't help but feel excited by his tough-looking new batch of seedlings: their thick, well-shaped leaves, stout stems, firm posture. He ran the dates through his head again, what needed to happen, when it needed to happen, for him to have a shot. They weren't doomed yet. It might still turn out all right. He just needed the weather to give him a break.

8
THE TROUBLES

May had dumped roughly three times the normal rainfall on New England, including a stretch when it rained 10 days straight. June was starting out even worse, with bigger storms, heavier rain, and more ferocious winds. A massive pocket of unstable air was hanging out over the eastern seaboard, generating repeated storms. Such weather patterns can be stubborn; they feed on themselves, creating a cycle of weather that can be difficult to break. The rain had saturated the ground with moisture, and as the moisture evaporated, it saturated the air and then it fell back to the earth. Weather forecasts along the East Coast for June boiled down to two simple words: more rain.

By the beginning of the second week in June, the Wallaces' pumpkin plants were finally beginning to outgrow their greenhouses. Ordinarily, the coldframes would have been removed already, but the plants were lagging more than a week behind the normal pace. At least the shelters warmed up the air and kept the young plants safe from the heavy rains and cold winds that continued to blow through. "It's been just an awful spring," Ron groused. "It's June 8 and this is the second day under sixty degrees. That hasn't happened in fifteen years!"

The day before had been the worst yet, with an unheard-of summer nor'easter barreling in with 50 mile-an-hour winds and five more inches of rain. The storm had begun the night before, and though Ron had checked the weather reports repeatedly throughout the day, the forecasters had predicted only about an inch of rain, and hadn't even hinted at the gale-force winds that had blown all day long. Ron and Dick had staked down the greenhouses securely just in case, tying each corner to steel rods driven deep in the ground, so the plants were protected. But the storm's intensity was a surprise. From his office at the country club, Ron called his father in the middle of the storm to see how the pumpkins were doing, but he didn't go rushing home. He was getting better at letting go. "I can't do a thing about the weather," he said. "What happens, happens."

Ron was more concerned about damage at the country club. "We lost three big tables outside — the umbrellas ripped off and smashed them. That aggravates me because I should have thought of that. And the pool took a ton of leaves and debris. We'll have to work on it for the next two days to clean it out before it can open."

Ron was feeling pessimistic about his plants' world-record chances now. "Once you get off to a slow start, and you're seven to ten days behind, and the weather is still terrible, it's tough to catch up," he said.

If they wanted to reach 1,500 pounds, the hardest part would be getting the pollinations timed just right for maximum growth during July: The plants had to be big enough, and the pollination early enough, for the baby pumpkin to gain 400 to 500 pounds by the end of the month. And the prospects didn't look good. "Maybe if we get a good weather pattern in the next few weeks," Ron said hopefully. "But the way it looks right now, it's going to be very tough for our club to repeat as champs."

By mid-June, most growers had stored away their greenhouses in garages, basements, and barns for another year. Now, the most grueling part of the season was about to begin. Giant-pumpkin plants are high-maintenance creatures, and it requires hours of tedious labor to keep them under control. Pumpkin plants are really ground-crawling vines. From the plant's base, the main vine feels its way forward. During peak growth, a giant-pumpkin vine can grow nearly a foot a day, which is why the vine is said to "run."

Every eight inches or so, on alternating sides, the vine sends up a single leaf, which grows straight up on a stiff, hollow stem. The leaf spreads out horizontally from the top of the stem in a heart shape. When fully grown, a giant-pumpkin leaf can rise three feet from the ground and spread as wide as an elephant's ear. The huge leaves are nature's parasol, shading the roots of the vine to keep them cool and moist, and providing cover to tender new pumpkins as they grow. The vines send down extra roots at every leaf node to anchor the plant more securely and siphon more nutrients from the ground. To encourage even more root growth, many growers bury their vines in the dirt.

"Side vines" branch out opposite each leaf, and more vines sprout from these. As all the vines grow, they put out fingerlike tendrils that grab and coil around anything they can reach — sticks and grass and other leaves. It's the pumpkin's version of a handrail, something to steady itself and support its huge, unwieldy leaves.

Left alone, the plant would turn into a giant, twisting knot of vegetation. The rampant growth drains the plant's energy, reducing the size of its fruit. It's the giant-pumpkin grower's job to prevent that, and to guide the plant into a controlled shape with careful pruning. Growers have developed a number of pruning patterns tailored to their different theories about what will produce the biggest pumpkin. The most common is the "Christmas tree" pattern. The plant is pruned into a triangular shape, with the leading tip of the main vine serving as the pointed top, and the side vines forming branches that spread wider near the base.

Mature pumpkin vines eventually harden into a tough, sinewy rope, but when they're first growing, they are green and brittle. Some vines have an exasperating habit of growing straight up toward the sky. The leading tip of the vine reaches for the sun, curving up from the ground with its cluster of leaf buds pointing forward, looking much like a bright-green dancing cobra. This is a terrifying situation for a pumpkin grower. The slightest puff of wind can blow the vine over and snap it in half. And if the leading tip of the main vine snaps off, it stops growing. A side vine can be trained to be a new main vine, but the chance of it growing a champion is diminished. To safeguard the precious leading tip, growers drive two long sticks into the ground at angles, forming an X over the end of the vine and stabilizing it while gently forcing it closer to the ground.

As the Wallaces' vines began their run across the patch, Ron and Dick spent hours every day pruning and burying and bracing the vines. Though the rains had set them back almost two weeks, Ron was still pleased with the way their 10 plants looked. All the main vines were thick and strong, and the 1068s, which had been slower to get started, now were taking off. "They're coming on like a freight train, leaves as big as a bushel bag," he said.

Though the initial germination problems with the 1068 had faded into history, now Ron was starting to hear complaints from other growers about its seedlings' sluggish behavior. Typically, the 1068 was a tortoise, not a hare. The seed was slow to germinate, the vines slow to run, and the pumpkins slow to take off. But the 1068 had staying power, and it would generally blow past any other plant in the garden by the end of the season. What mattered, after all, was how you finished, not how you started. Even so, Ron was getting e-mails from several growers saying their other plants were outpacing the 1068. And he was getting tired of explaining. "I'm like, 'Okay, if you want to go with an unproven seed from a cross that nobody's heard of, go ahead and pull out the 1068,' " Ron said.

With the garden bursting into its lushest growth of the season, growers weren't the only ones paying attention. The animal kingdom includes a lengthy slate of ravenous varmints with a taste for pumpkin plants. Cucumber beetles devour the leaves and transmit a deadly virus known as bacterial wilt. Squash vine borers, the grublike larvae of moths, burrow into the vines and gorge themselves on the juicy insides. Known among growers as "the dreaded SVBs," dozens of these larvae can infect a single plant, slowly killing it as the vines are hollowed out. And squash beetles, with their gray, shield-shaped armored bodies, suck the juices from the leaves, turning them into crispy shells blackened as if the plant had been burned by a blow torch.

Fortunately, growers had available an assortment of deadly chemicals to dispatch these botanical predators. Competitive pumpkin growers were diligent about spraying their gardens with an array of pesticides tailored to each insect. But there were more difficult pests: furry ones. Mammals were much cleverer than bugs, and they had even bigger appetites.

Rhode Island grower Steve Sperry was worried about deer. His backyard patch was surrounded by woods, and deer often crept into his yard late at night to feast on his landscape plants. He'd recently noticed they had chomped his hosta lilies to a stubble. And deer were also known to have a taste for young pumpkin plants. After getting home from his late shift after 11 p.m. one night, Sperry took a powerful spotlight with him into the backyard and shone it into the woods around his garden. Several pairs of glittering eyes stared back.

But before he could figure out what to do about the deer, another calamity struck. On Father's Day, Sperry was entertaining his brother and nephew on the back deck of his home, when his brother sat up suddenly and pointed toward the patch. He'd just seen a woodchuck run behind one of the cold-frames sheltering the pumpkins near the edge of the woods. Like many other growers that year, Sperry had fallen behind because of germination problems and the cold, rainy weather. He still had his cold-frames over his plants, but he'd opened one side to let in the sun and fresh air. Unfortunately, it let in woodchucks too.

A rotund member of the rat family, and also known as groundhogs or "whistle pigs," woodchucks were notorious for nipping off the succulent new growth at the end of a pumpkin vine, terminating the vine's growth. Sperry had noticed a woodchuck sniffing around his garden a few weeks earlier, but his plants were closed up in their coldframes so he hadn't been too worried. He set a trap, didn't catch anything, and then forgot about it. Now the woodchuck was back, and within snacking distance of his exposed plants.

"I looked down and saw it standing up halfway hidden behind the box, with one eye focused on us," Sperry said. He leaped from his chair and ran down to the garden. The woodchuck sprinted away, and Sperry went after it, running between the cold-frame and the woods, and then circling around. If he could catch it, he aimed to give it a swift kick into oblivion. But the woodchuck had vanished. And in those few seconds, it had bitten off the tip of the plant's main vine.

Sperry went into combat mode. He borrowed another trap from a friend. It was time for the coldframes to come off the plants, so after removing them, Sperry dashed to the hardware store for some wood fencing to keep out the woodchuck. He was gone 20 minutes, but that was enough time for the animal to pay another visit to the garden and eat a side vine and several leaves off his 1068 plant. Sperry's frustration boiled over. "I thought about purchasing a gun," he said. Instead, he put the fences around his plants and then searched the woods until he found the entrance to the animal's den. He set a trap next to the hole, and two days later he had the woodchuck. His first thought, he confessed, "was to put the pitchfork to it." But his wife convinced him not to kill it. Instead, she put it in her car, drove it several miles away, and let it go.

Animal lovers will cringe, but many pumpkin growers don't hesitate to kill any creature that dares to mess with their plants. They have too much time and money and work invested in their garden to have any sympathy for a giant rodent foraging for lunch. Growers develop a fierce maternal instinct while tending to their plants day and night — nursing them when they're sick, fussing over them when they're slow, bragging about them when they're doing well. And like a she-bear protecting her cubs, growers can reveal a vicious streak when it comes to defending their botanical babies.

Even the soft-hearted Wallaces had been known to shoot the woodchucks in their pumpkin patch. But generally Ron tried to avoid it. A few days before they'd taken off the greenhouses this year, Ron had noticed a woodchuck meandering through his garden early one morning. He had immediately set out a trap baited with peanut butter. But he hadn't seen the animal since. "He was kind of cute," Ron said. "He waddled around out there underneath the deer fence."

"Cute" isn't the word most gardeners would use to describe a woodchuck. They can erect high fences to fend off deer. But woodchucks and their cousins, gophers, are harder to keep out — they can crawl right under a fence or tunnel under other barriers — so most growers prefer to just kill them. The more gentle-natured growers tried to trap them and then relocate them miles away. One year Steve Connolly trapped 14 of the animals at his southern

Massachusetts home.

At the same time the Rhode Island growers were battling woodchucks, a grower in San Diego was on the hunt for a gopher that had moved into his pumpkin patch and was chowing down on one of his plants. The grower, who kept a diary on BigPumpkins .com under the screen name "Duster," already had dispatched one gopher that was plaguing his patch in May. A neighbor had poisoned it for him, and Duster posted a picture in his online diary of the gopher's stiffened carcass with the caption "Ding dong the wicked gopher is dead!!!!!!!!"

But in June, another, more-persistent gopher arrived. Duster labeled it "the unkillable gopher" after he had made several unsuccessful assassination attempts that included running a hose into the burrow to flood it with water, then laying in wait with a rifle outside its den in hopes of shooting it when it poked out its head. Finally, Duster announced jubilantly on BigPumpkins.com that his seven-day war with the gopher was over. "He survived 4 floodings, two days of trappings, two poison days, one assassination attempt with my gun and today, finally, he was nailed in the last flooding attempt. The hardest gopher I have ever come up against," Duster wrote, brimming with satisfaction over the kill.

Any pumpkin grower whose patch has borne the brunt of an animal's appetite could sympathize with Duster's homicidal fury at the rodent. When a deer jumped over Jack LaRue's six-foot barrier into his pumpkin patch, Jack said, "I wailed him a couple times on the butt with a fence post. I left a lasting impression. He has not been back."

Ron was worried about one of his plants. The leaves were splotched bright yellow, and he couldn't figure out why. At first he thought maybe there was something wrong with the dirt in the new patch — a nutrient deficiency, maybe — but then the problem wouldn't be on just one plant, right in the middle of the garden. He watched it closely every day, and by the end of June, it hadn't gotten any better. Then another mystery cropped up. Ron discovered tiny spiderwebs spreading across the top of some of his leaves. He'd picked up the webs and looked closely at them. They were white and gossamer-fine. He let them drift away in the air, sailing on an almost imperceptible breeze. Weird.

A few days later, Ron noticed sap bubbling up on top of a few leaves, like tiny amber blisters. That was strange too. But he'd just sprayed some fungicide on the plants. Maybe it was condensation beading up and then drying out. Then, it started raining again and it was difficult to do much of anything in the garden for three days. When the rain stopped long enough for Ron to get a good look at his plants, a jolt of panic shot up his spine. The leaves in part of the garden were turning a reddish brown, as if they were covered in rust, old before their time. "My leaves went from looking buff to what-the-hell's-going-on-here!" Ron said.

From his office at work, he called Steve Jepsen, a fellow grower who also happened to sell pesticide. Jepsen had become the chief chemicals guru of the giant-pumpkin community because of his expertise and his willingness to patiently and promptly address an endless stream of questions from panicky growers. Steve immediately had a suspect in mind. Go home and hold a white sheet of paper underneath one of the rusty leaves, he instructed Ron. Then tap on the top of the leaf and look at the paper. If you see black dots crawling around, you've got spider mites.

Spider mites are minuscule insects the size of a dust speck that congregate on the bottom of leaves and multiply with dizzying speed, spreading from leaf to leaf until the whole garden is infested. The webbing Ron had seen two weeks ago was a classic sign of infestation. The rusty color was where the mites had literally sucked the life out of the leaves. Ron rushed home from work that afternoon and did the paper test. Sure enough, the paper crawled with black dots. This was a new disaster for the Wallace patch — and by now there weren't many new ones left. Ron's inner samurai leaped forth. He didn't want the spider mites to draw another breath. He hastily deployed his arsenal of chemicals, filling his sprayer and blasting the plants with a powerful poison.

Ron hoped that if he could just keep the plants healthy and growing, then he might still be able to pollinate on schedule. Already, female flowers were beginning to appear with their cargo of pea-sized baby pumpkins beneath the closed petals. That was good and bad: Good because it meant the plants knew it was time to start producing pumpkins. Bad because he needed his plants to be as big as possible before pollinating the fruit, and the weather had stunted the plants' growth. Ron and his dad wavered between dismay at the rough start to the season, and optimism that they could still recover. They weren't the only ones hurting. The weather had completely knocked out the plants of several growers in New Hampshire and Massachusetts. Others growers were set back weeks, making it unlikely they could turn out a competitive pumpkin.

In their own club, Scott Palmer had to make a trip to the hospital for a hernia operation, which had put him out of commission for a while. Dick and Ron and some of the other growers had gone over to help Scott's wife, Shelley, prune and bury the vines and spray the plants for bugs and fungi. But it was yet another setback on top of the bad weather. Steve Sperry had lost his best plant to the woodchuck. Steve Connolly had a plant damaged by the storm. And now weeds were taking over in the Wallace garden. Ron had used some Roundup weed-killer, but he'd found that some of the chunks of grass sod plowed under in November were taking root with all the rain. He needed to hand-turn the earth, but it was so wet, he couldn't get into the patch.

"We're in trouble, no doubt about it," Ron admitted. There was still no end in sight to the storms moving through the area day after day. "There's just way too much water. You just can't keep that much water on the plants, or you're asking for problems." When he forced himself to be realistic, he knew it wasn't likely they'd be able to grow any world-class specimens this year.

But Ron wasn't admitting defeat. He couldn't do all the backbreaking work that lay ahead without believing they still had a chance. The bad weather was bound to end. And in the meantime, the plants were doing their part. They were getting bigger, and despite everything, they looked good. "They're ready to go," Ron said. "Now we'll see what happens."

In Pennsylvania, Dave Stelts sympathized with the New England growers. But he had his own pumpkins to worry about and so far he was satisfied with the way things were going. His area had suffered some of the same turbulent weather as the Northeast, though nothing as constant or severe. Dave's home was right on the Ohio border northeast of Pittsburgh. Technically, he lived in Pennsylvania, but he had grown up in Ohio and had only recently moved over the state line, so he still considered the Ohio Valley Giant Pumpkin Growers his home club. He hung out with the growers from Ohio, and that's where he took his pumpkins for the weigh-off.

Dave Stelts made no bones about why he grew giant pumpkins: He grew because his life depended on it. Dave was a burly 47-year-old tractor salesman, with a head of thick, brown hair and bushy eyebrows that stretched seamlessly over hazel-brown eyes — inspiring Dick Wallace to nickname him "the Uni-Brow." He had a slightly manic personality, a ferocious competitive instinct, and a sense of humor that cut straight to the harsh reality of a matter. He also was a recovering alcoholic who had stopped drinking when he scraped rock bottom in the early 1990s.

Dave's interest in gardening dated back to his childhood, when he'd helped his father in the family vegetable garden. Back then, Dave and his dad grew what he now disdains as "small, tedious vegetables" — tomatoes and green beans and such. When he was 13 or 14 years old, he saw a picture of a great big orange pumpkin in a Burpee Seeds catalog and decided that was what he wanted to grow. "I wanted the 'Wow' factor — the biggest, orangest pumpkin I could get. And that's still the way I am today," he said. With his father's help, Dave grew two pumpkins over 100 pounds when he was still in high school.

But then he grew up, went to college, and

moved to Florida on his own, where he proceeded to live life as fast as possible, which included a lot of hard drinking. He married and then divorced. He moved back to Ohio in his 30s and, with a partner, opened up a bar and restaurant. It was a bad idea. "I was my best customer," Dave said.

Dave gave up the business and checked himself into rehab. His last drink was October 13, 1993. Dave's therapist suggested he find a hobby to concentrate on to help him stay sober. So he went back to growing pumpkins with his father. They joined the Ohio Valley pumpkin-growing club, and with the advice and guidance of more-expert growers, he and his father managed to grow a 447-pounder their second year. "I am still dry to this day," Dave said. "Because I focus all my obsessive-compulsive tendencies on my pumpkins."

Dave married his wife, Carol in 2004. They had dated for five years, "so she knew what she was getting into," he said. "She indulges me, and she gets out there and helps." Carol had become an expert at pruning and burying vines — she called it "manicuring" the plants. "In the summertime, if she wants to spend time with me, she knows that's where she has to go," Dave said.

Dave and Carol built a house on a steep hillside in Edinburg, Pennsylvania. A spare bedroom serves as Dave's pumpkin headquarters, filled with weigh-off ribbons and plaques. Two pieces of dried pumpkin vine tied with a red-and-gold-plaid ribbon are mounted high on one wall. They're from the 1,140-pound pumpkin that won Dave his world record in 2000. That win gave him bragging rights to having grown the biggest pumpkin of the 20th century. But it hadn't dulled his competitive drive one bit. Dave still grew to win every time, and he was banking on 2006 being his best year yet.

Dave had launched the 2006 season with his usual proficiency. He breezed through germination, and his plants had gone into the ground right on schedule, the first week of May — all except his 1068, which hadn't sprouted. But the plant Ron sent by FedEx arrived in pristine shape. Dave's Ohio-Pennsylvania region was notorious for its roller-coaster weather — highs in the 50s one day and in the 90s the next. The dramatic temperature swings were hard on the pumpkins. But Dave would take his weather any day over what he saw happening in New England that year. "I feel bad for them. But

182

it's just their turn to have crappy weather," he said. "If they're gonna get to thirteen or fourteen hundred pounds this year, somebody's going to need a rabbit foot."

Dave reckoned the West Coast was having the best weather. "They have a leg up on everybody." But the Ohio Valley growers were doing well too. They'd had their share of spring storms and rain, but most of the growers had come through without much damage. Everyone was still on track. If fortune smiled, Dave believed his Ohio club was primed to snatch the top growing award away from Rhode Island this year.

In the Pacific Northwest, rain had cooled things down in late May, but Jack and Sherry LaRue hadn't minded a bit. The rain fell at night and then the clouds cleared away during the day, warming the air and giving the plants plenty of sunshine. "The weather has been just about perfect," Jack said. "The way it's setting up right now, we're in great shape."

The LaRues had spent most of the spring in their pumpkin patch. Their no-till method had minimized the weeds they had to deal with, but they still had plenty of work laying down manure and compost and putting up some more permanent greenhouses to replace the temporary ones they'd been using. Jack had decided to grow 20 plants, and Sherry 4. Most of Jack's lineup was made up of his own seeds, all 1,000-plus-pounders, but he also was growing a selection of East Coast genetics, including a 1469 Checkon, a 1333 Connolly, a 1370 Rose, and a 1225 Jutras. He and Sherry each were growing a 1068 Wallace.

They'd had no trouble germinating their seeds, which were in the greenhouses and growing by early May. There'd been just one hitch so far that spring. "I'm not exactly sure what I had going on," Jack said. Some of his plants had a puzzling affliction that resembled salt burn — a leaf-browning that occurs when the plant gets too much salt, usually from some kind of fertilizer or soil supplement. "Basically, the plants stopped growing," he said. "The leaves turned yellow and the leaf margins started to rot off." The same thing had happened in 2002, and though it wasn't as bad this time, it still worried him. He suspected the magnesium supplement he'd put on the plants had too much salt in it, so he flooded the patch with water, hoping to flush any excess out of the soil. The plants did better after that, especially his 1157 LaRue. "My 1157 came out of that salt burn and it was pissed!" Jack said. "I can't believe how much growth it's put on in the last couple of days." In fact, now the 1157 was probably the best plant in his patch. "Sometimes a little stress on these things just makes them try harder," Jack said. Last year he'd almost pulled out one plant — his 1068, in fact — because it looked so puny and pathetic. Then it wound up growing his biggest pumpkin.

The covers came off their greenhouses the first week in June. Sherry's 1068 had been the first to grow long enough to hit the greenhouse wall. Jack's 1068s were coming along more slowly. He had two now. A nearby grower had decided his 1068 seedling was too small and puny to plant, so he'd offered it to Jack. "Since Mr. Obsessive Pumpkin Grower can never turn down a needy seed, Jack took it," Sherry said.

For much of June, Sherry had battled a flat-vine problem on two of her plants, including her 1354 Checkon — the seed that had grown the current world-record winner. Flat vines, one of the many botanical riddles growers face, are basically a plant deformity. Instead of a single main vine, the plant grows two, which fuse together into a flat, ridged shape. The flattened vines are sometimes called "ribbon vines," and plant scientists know the problem as "fasciation."

At the leaf nodes, the plant grows twice the number of leaves, twice the number of side vines, and twice the number of tendrils. Growers weren't exactly sure how flat vines affected the size of their pumpkins, but since it wasn't normal, it didn't seem like a good thing. The cause was also a mystery — growers didn't know whether the mutation was organic or genetic. Sherry had hoped the problem would correct itself on her two plants, and the vines would start growing normally, as they sometimes did. But when it didn't, she cut off the flattened main vines and trained normal-looking side vines to replace them.

Other than that, the LaRues so far were having one of their best seasons. Baby pumpkins had begun showing up on all their plants. Pollination time was right around the corner.

9
THE KILLER CROSS

Ron and Dick spent the afternoon of July 5 working in the pumpkin patch. Summer was in full bloom at the Wallace homestead. The air was filled with the singsong of finches and sparrows and flocks of other birds attracted by the whimsical wooden birdhouses and birdfeeders Dick had made and scattered throughout the trees on the property. The sky was overcast, threatening rain, and the warm air was heavy with humidity. The Wallaces' sandy loam soil had managed to absorb the recent rains, and there were no puddles in sight. The ground was wet and spongy but still firm underfoot.

As Dick walked across the lawn from the house to the garden, the goats caught a glimpse of him and began bleating for attention. The rabbits stirred and thumped in their hutches. They had been multiplying, as rabbits will, so Dick and Ron had more animals to feed than ever. Dick took care of that chore while Ron was busy in the garage, pulling out his Stihl sprayer. His plants were due for a dose of organic fertilizer, and for such a big garden, Ron needed a heavy-duty piece of equipment. The sprayer included a motor and a pump with a 3.7-gallon tank, which could be filled with all of a grower's essential brews, from pesticides and fungicides to liquid fertilizers. Shoulder straps allowed Ron to mount the sprayer unit on his back. A long, black, bazooka-like nozzle curved from the tank and jutted out 2 feet in front. Ron gripped a handle extending up from the nozzle to guide the spray in slow, wide arcs back and forth across the plants. The sprayer made it easy for him to move around the patch unencumbered by garden hoses and without having to return for frequent fillups.

Before filling the sprayer's tank, he rinsed it out with the garden hose to avoid mixing the last application of pesticide with the fertilizer spray. Dick, finished feeding the animals, walked over to a 25-gallon black plastic container labeled "Soil Soup" that was sitting atop a table next to the garden. He flipped a switch and the container rumbled to life with a low, vibrating hum. It was a system for making compost tea — a rank mixture of water, manure, compost, and just about anything else a grower cares to throw in: molasses, seaweed, banana peels. The switch turned on an electric pump that gurgled air through the container, mixing the microbe-rich brew with oxygen and speeding the fermentation of ingredients. Ron filled his sprayer tank with the Soil Soup. The sprayer would atomize the liquid fertilizer and envelop the plants in a nutrient-rich mist.

Before Ron strapped on the sprayer, he bent down to lace up his father's latest invention — a pair of garden walking shoes. The boards they'd laid down between the plants didn't always go where Ron wanted to go, so he had been dragging a plank along with him through the garden, laying it down and walking on it to reach a vine that needed pruning or a pumpkin that needed pollinating. But that was difficult to do when he was spraying the plants and needed to move about more freely. So Dick's inspired solution was to design a snowshoe-style garden shoe for Ron. He'd sawed a piece of plywood into 17-by-6-inch boards and then screwed a pair of Ron's old sneakers into the center of the boards. Then he nailed a shorter, wider board beneath the first. It looked like the shoes had wings, so Dick called his new invention "wingtips."

The shoes distributed Ron's weight over a larger area, making it less damaging to walk in the patch. "They look funny as hell," Dick admitted. They weren't easy to walk in, either: The board stuck out several inches around the shoes, and Ron had to swing his legs wide in a high-stepping gait to keep from tripping. But Ron wore the shoes because they worked, and of course, he wore them because his father made them.

Strapped in, laced up, Ron was ready for action. He stood at the edge of his new pumpkin patch, his sprayer mounted on his back, his wingtips planted firmly in the earth, looking like an astronaut preparing to leave the ship on a space walk. His gaze swept over the patch, making a critical survey of the plants. The patch looked picture-perfect. The plants were huge — each one was 15 to 20 feet long and 25 feet across at the base. They were planted back to back, with the stumps in a row down the middle of the patch, and the plants were growing out in perfect Christmas-tree shapes, their triangular forms pointing toward the edges of the garden like the prows of battleships lined up at a dock.

Despite the record rains, the garden dirt still looked fluffy from the hand-tilling Ron had done around the vines. Ron and his dad kept the dirt weed-free in a five-foot zone around each plant. Small weeds were sprouting in the spaces in-between, but they didn't care about that anymore. Ron and Dick were determined to work smarter, not just harder. That included cutting down on some of the intensive labor, such as weeding every square inch of garden. In their former, more-fanatical days, Ron and Dick had been meticulous about keeping the whole patch weed-free. "But it's not a beauty contest," Ron said. As long as the weeds were kept away from the plants' root zones, the rest didn't matter as much.

Only one large weed was left growing right in the middle of the patch. It was a two-foot-tall Cleome, or spider flower, crowned with delicate clusters of pale-violet blooms. Dick had convinced Ron to leave it alone as long as it was flowering, and it stuck out oddly, though prettily, from the neatly groomed greenery of the surrounding pumpkin plants.

Ron viewed all this with a critical eye. He saw the good — the plants were the healthiest he'd ever grown. But he also saw all the work that still needed to be done. Steady rains had kept him out of the patch for two days, and the vines were already getting out of control.

They'd grown two feet in those two days, and it was crucial to get them covered with dirt as quickly as possible so they could begin forming the root system that would pump more energy into the growing pumpkin. The root system along the vine also acted as a kind of insurance policy. If anything happened to injure the plant farther back toward the base, it could still survive. Ron and his dad had been able to grow pumpkins as big as 1,200 pounds after losing the stump to rot, thanks to the plant's auxiliary root system.

With the brownish-greenish-black compost tea sloshing in the tank on his back, Ron stepped into the pumpkin patch, fired up the sprayer's engine, and blasted a fine, drifting spray that soaked the plant leaves and dripped down into the dirt below. While Ron sprayed the plants, Dick wandered back to the Pumpkin Shack. The Wallace carriage house made the perfect headquarters for the Southern New England growing club. It had been renovated into a simple, one-room cottage with plywood walls and a concrete floor, a small kitchen, a bathroom, and a refrigerator stocked with beer. Pumpkin photographs, dozens of ribbons and plaques, and framed copies of Dick's pumpkin cartoons covered the walls, along with a hot-pink poster of the rock band KISS. "It's a seventies thing," Dick explained.

On the kitchen counter, Dick had laid out a stack of tan T-shirts imprinted with the new club logo he'd drawn. It was a simple map of Rhode Island, Connecticut, and Massachusetts, with a bright-orange giant pumpkin in one corner and the club initials above. Dick was the official club artist. Over the years he'd composed a thick portfolio of one-panel cartoons lampooning the life of giant-pumpkin growers. He called them his "PumpkinToons," and had some printed on T-shirts and caps that were popular among growers.

Dick planned to hand out the T-shirts at the club meeting that would begin shortly, along with large white lapel buttons he'd had made to commemorate the Southern New England Giant Pumpkin Growers 2005 weigh-off championship. The directors and some of the Rhode Island members tried to get together at least once a month to discuss club business, and that night they needed to review prize money for the October weigh-off. Some snacks and paper plates and plastic utensils were already laid out on a table for the meeting.

Assured that all was in order, Dick took a seat in a lawn chair on the porch to rest for a few minutes before the club members arrived. Despite the terrible weather, Dick was well satisfied with the way the season was going. Their plants seemed to have caught up, and they were right on schedule for pollinating. Of the 10 they were growing, Dick felt good about 8. The 2 others, including the 1354 Checkon, were dragging. "But who knows. We could still get our best pumpkins out of them," he said. He was still betting on their 1068s, though. Out of the 5, he felt sure they could get at least 3 competitive-sized pumpkins.

As Dick watched Ron work in the patch, Ken Desrosiers, the BigPumpkins.com Webmaster, arrived for the evening's club meeting. He was one of the club's directors, and he'd come straight from his office in Connecticut. He walked over to talk with Ron, who was finishing spraying the plants, then the two men joined Dick on the porch. Ken drew up a chair and sat down, declining Dick's offer of a beer. "No thanks. I have a long drive home in the dark," he said. Ken had a wife and two young children to pull him back to firm ground whenever the undertow of pumpkins got too strong.

Ron puttered around the porch, not yet able to sit down and relax. He checked the dirt inside the flowerpots arranged along the edge of the porch, then fetched a green plastic watering can to give them a drink. The conversation drifted inevitably to pumpkins and the topic on everyone's mind: pollination.

The time to pollinate the baby pumpkins had finally arrived — a pivotal moment in the growing year. The season started when the plants went into the ground in early May, but pollination was the starting gun for the race that really counted. It was early July, and most of the plants were finally big enough and mature enough to have baby pumpkins nestled beneath their female blooms ready for fertilization. Left unfertilized, the tiny pumpkins would simply shrivel up after a week or so and fall off. So there would be no giant pumpkins without proper pollination, and that meant joining the male and the female flowers together in carefully orchestrated intercourse.

Pumpkin plants have both male flowers, which provide the pollen for fertilization, and female flowers, which grow the pumpkin. So a female (mother) can be pollinated with a male (father) from the same plant. But growers usually like to mix up the genetics by pollinating the female flower with a male flower from another plant — a process called cross-pollination, or "crossing." Every grower hoped to have his name attached to the next "killer cross" — pumpkin jargon for a genetic matchup between pumpkin plants that would take the giants another step up the evolutionary scale. The 1068 Wallace, for instance, was the result of a killer cross between an 845 Bobier female and an 898 Knauss male.

Growers hand-pollinated the female flowers on every plant to control the genetic parentage and to make sure each selected female was thoroughly fertilized. Ultimately, just one pumpkin would be grown on each plant so that all the energy would be poured into blowing up that pumpkin as big as possible. But growers started out by pollinating several females on each plant. Sometimes the pollinations wouldn't "take," and the embryonic pumpkin would abort. Some baby pumpkins would grow faster than others. Some would have a better shape. Some would be in a better position on the vine. All those things were carefully weighed and debated by every grower at pollination time.

"The weirdest thing happened to me on one of my plants," Ken Desrosiers was saying to Dick. He worried that the rainy weather had messed up his pollination chances on one of the two plants he was growing. "I'm twelve feet out on the main,

196

and the females were getting ready to go, and all of a sudden they shriveled up on me. They never even opened. That's the first time that's ever happened."

"Yeah," said Dick, with a knowing nod. "If you look at the flower, and the tip looks like it's kind of burned, like it's glued together . . . that was from all that rain."

"I would have been ready to go on July 1 with that plant," said Ken. "But now I just pollinated one on the other plant, the 1173, yesterday, on July 4." Ken was a fairly new grower, and he was still figuring out what worked best. "I used to pollinate everything. I had two plants and I'd pollinate forty flowers," he mused.

"We were talking about that the other day," Ron said, pausing with his watering can tilted over one of the flowerpots. "I said, 'Dad, remember that year when we did one hundred and twenty pollinations?'"

"Oh yeah. We had like fifteen pumpkins pollinated on each plant," Dick recalled. "We were culling three-hundred-pound pumpkins until we said, 'What the hell are we doing here?' Getting hernias! The thing is, the more you do this hobby, the more you learn that sometimes less work is better."

Soon, the other club members began to

arrive for the meeting, their trucks filling the driveway and spilling over into the grass. Ron had called the meeting to discuss the club's budget and other administrative matters, but in the soap-opera world of giant pumpkins, the only thing the growers gathered in the Pumpkin Shack really wanted to talk about was who was pollinating whom.

Fifteen-year-old Alex Noel, who had been growing pumpkins since he was 11, was dropped off at the meeting by his dad. Ron tried to bring him into the conversation. "Alex, how're your plants doin'?"

"Doing good," Alex answered. "Pollinated the 1068 this morning."

"What did you put into it?"

"The 1058."

"Oh, that's a nice choice," Ron said approvingly. "The 1058 is bomb-proof. It's not known for splits. Long and wide. It's not known for color, but it averages 10 percent over the charts. That's a nice cross."

"I don't care about color at all," said Alex.

"That's like me — I'm not a color guy at all," Ron agreed.

Peter Rondeau, who lived only a few miles from the Wallaces, asked Ron if he could have some male flowers off one of their plants to pollinate one of his females the next morning. "I'll cut them and take them home and put them in the fridge," he told Ron.

Ron snapped to attention. "Why are you putting them in the fridge?"

Peter looked up, startled. "I don't know."

"Those plants you're taking them from aren't in the fridge," Ron pointed out. "Leave 'em at room temperature. Put 'em in a little bit of warm water, that way they open up in the morning. You want something that's fresh and open." Peter nodded, a disciple eager to learn.

Growers decide on the seeds they'll plant each year mainly based on which ones they think will grow the biggest pumpkin. But they're also constantly thinking about the genetic matchmaking game. Seed decisions are sometimes influenced by which plant a grower wants to cross with another. The male doesn't affect the growth of the current season's pumpkin; it only matters for the seeds that will grow inside that pumpkin, which will carry the combined male and female genes into the next generation.

Before the meeting started, Ron and Dick took the club members on a tour of their new patch. The growers strung out in different groups as they walked slowly around the perimeter of the garden. The seaweed-infused compost tea had left behind a slightly fishy odor, like at the beach. Ron and Dick had already pollinated several pumpkins, and two others would be ready to go the next morning. Ron pointed out a leaf stalk crowding one of the baby pumpkins he planned to pollinate the next day. "I don't like that leaf rubbing up against the pumpkin, so I'm going to cut it," he told Joe Jutras.

"I'd leave it," said Joe. "I leave it if it's on top. If it's on the bottom, you have to take it off."

"I'll take it right off," Ron persisted. "I want to be wide open there."

"I don't know," said Joe. "You guys grow a lot of friggin' birdbaths." A birdbath was grower slang for a pumpkin that tipped over on its stem so that the opposite, "blossom end" was pointing up. The blossom end often sank in to form a concave spot, like a birdbath. It wasn't a desirable shape, and Ron didn't much like being reminded of their track record.

"That leaf has nothing to do with birdbaths," he argued. "Why would a leaf have anything to do with a birdbath?"

"I don't know. Maybe it's nothing . . ."

"I don't know" was Joe's polite way of saying, "I think you're wrong." A lifelong gardener, he had more experience and was at least as knowledgeable as the Wallaces when it came to growing the giants, but he was quieter about it. Still, he didn't hesitate to voice his opinion, and when he did, all the growers paid attention, Ron and Dick included.

Ron and Joe carried on discussing the characteristics of each plant as the other growers spread out around the patch. Ron was proud to show off his plants, but he was anything but confident. "I still don't know if this soil is capable of growing a truly world-class pumpkin the first year," he said to Joe. "That's asking an awful lot — to balance it, get it corrected, and get it rolling the first year. I mean, you can grow a plant, and so far the plants haven't suffered or anything, but to grow thirty or forty pounds a day . . . I guess we're going to find out in a couple of weeks."

The growers arrived at the spot where Ron and Dick had planted Joe's 1225 orange beauty. Since they planned to pull it up as soon as they'd used its male flowers, the plant hadn't received the same care as the other plants, and it looked straggly and weak. "There's Joe's 1225," one grower pointed out, teasing Joe about the shabby treatment of his prized pumpkin seed. "They're really taking care of it, I tell you.

Grown for pollen. We get no respect."

Joe's mouth tilted in a good-natured grin. "Prettiest pumpkin I ever grew," he said. "True orange."

"Just strippin' it for parts, like a junk car," the grower said, twisting the knife.

Ken Desrosiers noticed the giant weed growing in the middle of the pumpkin patch. "What's that?" he asked Ron.

"Oh, that's a Cleome. My father found it growing there, so he wanted to keep it. I'll pull it out as soon as the main vine finishes growing."

Joe jumped to the flower's defense. "It won't bother anything," he said.

"It'll be gone," said Ron, closing the subject.

Ron rounded up everyone and hustled them back to the Pumpkin Shack to grab a bite to eat before the meeting started.

Cathy Wallace dropped in to say hello as everyone filled their plates with calzones and spinach pies. She had just come out of the hospital again, after another lung infection, but on this evening she looked fresh and youthful in a white blouse and pale denim overalls. She stood near the door to the club headquarters, greeting the growers, most of them old friends.

"I missed the Fourth of July picnic at

Ronnie's club," she said wistfully. "The first year we've ever missed it." She wasn't complaining, just remarking on it. "There's always next year," she said.

Cathy was feeling weak and tired much of the time lately. Mostly, though, she worried about how her illness was affecting Ron and Dick and their granddaughter, Rene. Whenever Cathy was sick, Dick would get to feeling blue too. Ron was constantly fretting over what he could do for his mom to make her more comfortable. Cathy had accidentally dialed his cell phone the other day when she meant to call someone else. She canceled the connection, but not before her name popped up on Ron's caller ID. He called her right back. "Mom, did you call me?" "No, Ronnie," she said. "I was trying to call someone else." "Okay," he said. "But are you sure you don't need anything? Are you sure there isn't something I can do for you?" Cathy smiled a mother's sad smile as she told the story. She was touched by her son's concern, but hated that she was the cause of his worry. "When Ronnie was a little boy, he was never one for a lot of hugs or kisses," she said. "But now he hugs me and tells me he loves me all the time."

The Southern New England growers were

in high spirits as Ron convened the meeting at 6 p.m. sharp. Most of their plants had made it through the worst of the weather. They were excited to be starting the next phase of the season, and every grower was eager to share stories of what they had going and what they planned to make of it. The growers grabbed lawn chairs off the porch and lined them up against the wooden walls inside the Pumpkin Shack. Scott Palmer showed up late and stood just outside the open door on the porch, smoking a cigarette.

Ron sat in front of the group in a white lawn chair, one bare ankle crossed over his knee as he chewed the end of a pen and ran his eyes down a typewritten agenda he'd prepared. The twittering songbirds had given way to the noises of crickets and frogs living down at the Wallaces' pond. But all that was drowned out by the raucous laughter and numerous one-liners being tossed back and forth. The men talked louder and louder to be heard in a steadily rising tide of noise. This was no orderly business session. It was more like calling a meeting in a saloon full of rowdy cowboys fresh off the Chisolm Trail.

There was much discussion about fundraising and prize money, but little was decided. The club wanted to increase its prize money for the weigh-off — which went up to $3,000 for first place — but first they needed to find out if several sponsors would be coming through with donations. After Ron ran through his agenda and adjourned the meeting, the growers lingered. Talk turned to the ethics of killing animals who invaded their pumpkin patches. As Webmaster, Ken Desrosiers had recently been flooded with complaints after a grower posted a picture in his BigPumpkins.com diary of a pesky gopher he had chopped to pieces with a shovel. Ken slapped a CENSORED banner over the photo to obscure the grisly image. But debate still raged over the incident, with some siding with the grower, and some with the gopher.

"We all know the only good woodchuck is a dead woodchuck," declared Jeff Blais, a fortyish truck driver with lean, muscled arms and sharp eyes that didn't miss much. He had two hobbies: growing pumpkins and drag racing.

"Hey, let's put it this way," said Ron. "Have I killed a woodchuck before? Yes I have. Have I caught them and taken them ten miles away in a trap and let them go? I've done that more times than I've shot 'em. If I had to kill a woodchuck, I'd do it quick and painless with a .22 to the head. I wouldn't have it in me to take a shovel to it. I couldn't do that."

"The world's smallest violin is playing," said Jeff.

"Hey, everybody's got their own way of doing things," Ron acknowledged.

"I would have taken that rat down to the reservoir for a nice trip in a submarine," Jeff noted.

The night was wearing on. Jeff yawned and stretched in his green plastic lawn chair, peering from under the brim of his baseball cap with a wide grin on his face. "Okay, boys," he announced. "I need to get goin'. Gotta get up early in the morning for sex." Pollination inspired a lot of jokes like that.

As the growers pushed back their chairs and rose to their feet to leave, Dick walked over to Scott, who had spent the meeting leaning up against the door jamb of the porch, occasionally tilting his head back to peer in at the raucous goings-on. "You've got to admit," Dick said, "if the average citizen walked into this room and looked around, they'd say, 'What a bunch of weirdos these people are!' "

"Yeah," Scott said, "then they'd shut and lock the door."

■ ■ ■ ■

The next morning, July 6, dawned in Rhode Island with charcoal skies and a light, steady rain. The Wallaces had two female flowers ready to pollinate, but Ron didn't rush out at the crack of dawn to pollinate anymore. Wiser, or maybe just more tired, he had reasoned that waiting a couple hours after sunup might be better; it would give the pollen more time to ripen, developing into a grainy powder that would fly freely off the stamen and maybe even do the job more efficiently.

It's not hard to understand why hand-pollinating giant pumpkins generates so many jokes. The large male and female flowers have prominent reproductive organs that make comparisons to human sex unavoidable. The male flower's sturdy, inch-long stamen juts up aggressively from the center, its rounded tip packed with grains of bright-yellow pollen. The female flower has its corresponding stigma, a nubby, lobed structure with openings designed to receive the pollen.

Even when the petals are closed, the male and female flowers are easy to tell apart. Male blooms are the first to appear on the plant. They are simple flowers, rising up from the vine on long, slender stems. The females are generally closer to the vine, with each bloom sitting atop a baby pumpkin. The females are rarer, emerging at the tip of new vine growth, and first noticeable as a pale-green or yellow bead buried in the leaf buds. As the leaves mature, the bead grows along with the flower bud. By the time the female flower opens for pollination, its pumpkin has swelled to the size of a small egg.

The petals are brilliant orange or yellow and open into a trumpet shape. The blooms are the size of a saucer. Their bright color and sweet fragrance act as a beacon to guide bees into their male or female landing pads. The flowers open early in the morning, and close in the afternoon, providing a window of several hours for pollination. Growers get just one chance to pollinate each female. The flowers close again by the end of the day, then shrivel up to form the blossom end of the growing pumpkins.

The male pollen carries the male's genetic material. When a female flower's stigma receives a grain of pollen, it forms a tube that carries the pollen down inside the baby pumpkin. Each pollen grain fertilizes an ovule, or seed. A successful pollination signals the plant to begin growing its pumpkin, where the seeds will mature along with the fruit.

It doesn't take long for a grower to learn to predict when the male and female flowers are about to open: the five-inch, teardrop-shaped buds suddenly blush a pale orange, and the tips of the petals loosen slightly. During pollination time, growers scour their patch every evening to pinpoint females that would open the next morning. Then they slip ziplock baggies over each ripening female bloom, sealing them as close to the stem as possible to keep out bees and other insects. If a bug gets to the flower first, it could ruin the genetic pedigree of the pumpkin. Who knows where that bee has been? It could be carrying pollen from another, unknown pumpkin plant and that pollen could end up fertilizing the female flower. The resulting pumpkin could still be grown, of course, but with questionable parentage, its seeds would be bastards, and no one wants to plant bastard seeds.

Though Ron wouldn't pollinate until later that morning, he still had roused himself early to get some others chores done in the garden before he had to leave for work. He was hunched over in a drizzling rain by 7 a.m., his red jacket a bright spot of color in

the gray morning. The mellow light intensi-
fied the colors of the garden, making the
grass and pumpkin plants and surrounding
trees glow a deep green. A weather front
that had moved through overnight had
brought cooler temperatures; it felt more
like fall than summer.

Ron was crouched on his hands and
knees, undeterred by the wetness, burying
vines. It had to be done. His right knee, clad
in a knee pad, rested on a two-by-four. His
leather-booted left foot was planted on his
trusty jumbo-sized cookie sheet. A blue
baseball cap shielded his eyes from the rain
as he scraped away wet dirt with his hand,
slowly placed the vine in the shallow trench,
covered it back up, and then staked the end
of the vine down with slender stalks of
bamboo.

Ron stooped over to examine a female
flower crowded next to a leaf, the same leaf
Ron had debated cutting off with Joe the
evening before. The leaf's bristly stem had
rubbed a raw spot into the tender skin of
the baby pumpkin forming beneath the
flower bud. If he ended up keeping that
pumpkin, the raw spot would form a scar
that would grow with the pumpkin, ending
up as a big, ugly rough patch. "That's a
prime example of why I take the leaf," Ron

said, pulling out a pocketknife and creeping in closer to cut the stem off near the vine. "I need to go real slow so that I don't nick the pumpkin," he said. He cut away the leaf and tossed it to one side. Then he went to fetch a lawn chair. The big leaf had been the baby pumpkin's umbrella, and now a chair would have to provide its shade and shelter.

Ron retreated from the rain, which was beginning to fall faster. He was worried about work. He didn't have to leave for the office until 11 a.m. or so, since he usually worked long past dark in the summer. But the rain meant the country club pool wouldn't be able to open. And he didn't want his staff to be standing around getting paid with nothing to do. He pulled his mobile phone out of his pocket as he walked toward the house and called one of his assistants at the country club. "Everything's on hold," he said, issuing instructions for her to call another supervisor. "There's a possibility we'll be open this afternoon, but I won't know until around noontime. I might just have the noontime person come in today. I'll get in touch with them as soon as I can. And please call the snack bar people . . . Thank you."

Ron snapped the phone shut and put it

back in his jacket pocket. He plopped into a chair on the porch of the Pumpkin Shack as the rain dripped steadily from the eaves and splashed on the concrete. A hummingbird with purple wings and streaks of luminescent green flitted up to a feeder Ron had mounted at the edge of the porch. He liked watching the hummingbirds. But now he was thinking about work, getting peeved. "Lifeguards are the most notorious whiners to manage," he groused. "Most of them are kids . . . Talk about whine."

One lifeguard had recently complained about her shift being canceled at the last minute because of the rain. She didn't get paid for the day, and she also hadn't been able to make other plans. That kind of attitude steamed Ron. He didn't control the weather. "The lifeguards want to come in and sit inside the cabana and bullshit and get paid," he said. "No way. I'm not paying people eleven dollars an hour just to sit around. My boss judges me by the numbers. He looks at the rain gauge just like I do. He'd be saying, 'What's going on here? We had fifteen rain days and our labor costs are still the same as last year?' "

Ron's phone rang. "Hello? Yeah. Okay. That's fine. Then have those two come in and have everybody else on hold. And then we'll go from there. Thank you."

Ron pocketed the phone again and continued his rant. "They're kids. They're like motion-activated. They don't do nuthin' until you walk up on 'em. It's just sad."

He cast another worried glance at the rain. The ground was too muddy to finish burying vines. "Part of me is saying, 'Gee, I don't have to do four hours' worth of work today.' But now I'll have to be out there no later than six a.m. tomorrow because those vines have to be buried. I have to be in to work by eleven a.m. There's four hours of work, and then it takes me an hour to get cleaned up and dressed and thirty-five minutes to drive to work. If I had a nine-to-five kind of job, I could do it when I got home. But" — he shrugged — "You work when you can."

Dick had already left to go to the country club early that morning. He had a part-time job there that summer, three days a week, mowing grass on the golf course. The greens had to be mowed rain or shine. Dick had a system: He cut left to right on Wednesday, right to left on Thursday, and then on Friday, when he had to double-cut, because the greens wouldn't be cut again until Monday, he made one round left to right, and then went over the course right to left.

"I have six holes that I cut. And it takes

me four hours," Dick explained. "That ain't bad. That's taking my time to make sure it's done right." Even with a menial task like mowing, Dick took pride in his work. "I look at it as a personal thing," he said. "You always want to do the best job you can. It's only mowing. But it's not just mowing. If you don't do it right, it looks like hell."

With his dad at work, Ron needed to feed the animals. He walked into the big red barn and greeted the goats, who were sticking their heads through the slatted gates of their pens, bleating for food. "I'm careful not to feed them too much. My father always overfeeds them," Ron said. He fussed like that about his dad a lot, but more from affection than real annoyance. Except he was getting more worried about his dad's health. "He's smoking like a chimney. He's a massive accident waiting to happen. He doesn't care. You can't talk to him about it. None of us are perfect, but he's like me, a tad on the stubborn side."

Ron emerged from the barn and squinted up at the sky. The rain had lightened to a spitty mist. It was time to pollinate while he could. He had harvested a bunch of male flowers the night before and left them in a plastic cup of water in the Pumpkin Shack.

The males, too, had to be protected from insects before they opened. Now he grabbed a fistful of the flowers and headed back out to the patch. It would be quick work once he got started.

Ron had pollinated hundreds of females in his pumpkin-growing career, and had developed his own particular way of doing it. With a bouquet of male flowers in one hand, he advanced slowly down a slippery-wet plank toward his target. He laid out his board and kneeled down over the female, slipping the Ziplock bag off the bloom like a bridegroom lifting a veil. It was now a little after 8 a.m., and the petals were all neatly folded back, the looped lobes of the stigma in open view. Ron liked the looks of this one. He liked his pumpkins to be shaped like eggs, not Ping-Pong balls. He believed the lower, longer pumpkins had a smaller seed cavity and would weigh more when mature.

He stripped the petals off one of the male flowers to expose its pollen-laden stamen. Then he gently pushed the female's petals open wider and poised the stamen over the stigma. Many growers use the exposed stamen like a paint brush, gently rubbing its pollen off onto the female's lobes with quick, efficient strokes. But Ron preferred

215

to flick his finger against the stem of the male, knocking the pollen off so that it rained down onto the stigma. "I don't like to mash pollen grains," he said. "I like to get that nice, gentle pollen flying down on there." *Tap tap.* He flicked away for a few seconds and then picked up a second male to repeat the process. "I think more pollen contributes to a higher seed count," he explained. *Tap tap tap.*

The stigma by this time was blanketed thickly in pollen grains. But Ron kept flicking. "I don't want to miss anything," he said. "I make sure I do a real thorough job. I try to get every last bit of pollen. I've had them sometimes looking like Shake 'n Bake on a chicken in there."

Finally satisfied, Ron stood up. The stripped petals of the male flowers lay in a pile next to the plant, a bright-orange splash in the black mud. So much thinking and planning and worry and toil and sweat had led up to that moment. And now there was nothing to do but wait. If fertilization fails, then the pumpkin will wither and fall off, and another pumpkin will have to be pollinated elsewhere on the vine. If fertilization is successful, the bloom will shrivel, but the baby pumpkin will begin to swell and slowly lean over to lay down in the soil, where it will make its bed for the duration of the season.

Ron moved on to the next female. Females flowers with their baby pumpkins emerge at the tip of the growing vine, along with new leaves and side vines. So each new segment of the vine will usually bring another female. By the time he and his dad were finished pollinating for the season, each plant would have two or three baby pumpkins growing on it. And then they'd have to choose which ones to keep. That could be a torturous guessing game. The first pumpkins pollinated would have a head start on the later ones, but they would be on smaller plants. Ron liked his competition pumpkins to be set 12 to 14 feet out on the vine — what he called the "golden zone." And that might not happen until the second or third pumpkin was pollinated.

Ron believed that pollinating a pumpkin on a bigger plant would provide a stronger growth engine. It also would allow the side vines more time to finish growing. He wanted the plant's energy to go into its fruit, not into its leaves. "We're growing pumpkins, not salad," he'd say.

Already, Ron was calculating which newly pollinated pumpkins were in better position. He stood at the edge of the garden and looked back at the bloom he'd just finished pollinating. He'd fertilized another pumpkin on the same plant just a couple days before. "I would rather have this one, growing to the outside over there," he said, pointing to the pumpkin pollinated earlier. He lifted his finger, jabbed it in the air, and counted its nine side vines. "But if *this* one was the one," he pointed to the female he'd just pollinated, "I'd have ten to eleven side vines."

Ron moved down the garden, appraising each plant. He stopped to look at another recently pollinated pumpkin. "If that one underneath the chair takes, I'm going to keep it. You always want farther out, and that one's going to be about fourteen feet."

He spotted a female flower about to bloom in a prime spot on another plant. "That's a good sign. That's about four days away from being ready to pollinate. I've got a good shot there of getting one set within the golden zone."

Ron picked up his board and dragged it to the end of the garden. He was already thinking ahead a couple weeks to when all the pumpkins were pollinated, all the side vines were finished growing, and the work would get a bit easier. But the weather had to ease up first. With the pumpkins growing so fast now, and everything so wet, conditions were ripe for disease. Ron wasn't sure he could stomach another season of losing his best pumpkins to rot.

"Granted, you're always going to lose a pumpkin or two. But you know what? Me and my father deserve a little luck," he said. "Sometimes that's all it is. It just comes down to luck. And we deserve a little luck too." Ron grew pensive, thinking about their long history of misfortune. He plodded back toward the house, staring down at his boots squishing through the wet grass.

"Well," he said, "I guess it's like Clint Eastwood said in the *Unforgiven.* 'Deservin's got nothing to do with it.' All you can really ask for is opportunity. We've got ten plants out there and five of them are from the best seed in the world. You can't get any better than that."

10
CHOICES

By the middle of July, New England was finally enjoying some bright, sunny weather. Temperatures had crawled into the 90s several days, and pumpkin growers were beginning to think fondly on those cool, cloudy weeks of rain. After all those gray days, the sun was a shock to the plants, which reacted much the way humans do when a light is suddenly flipped on in a dark room. Many were getting sunburned, their young leaves crisping under the sun's harsh rays.

The question consuming New England growers now was how much they should water their plants, and when, and how. Sprinkle on top? Drip hoses in the ground? By hand, underneath the leaves? The pumpkins' massive root systems sucked hundreds of gallons of water each week, and could turn wet topsoil into dry, crumbly dirt in 24 hours with the help of a little sun.

But the 18 inches of rainfall they'd had in two months hadn't disappeared completely. The water table was high, keeping the dirt moist deep down. Much of the moisture was still in the air, cranking up the humidity to choking levels and steaming up the pumpkin patches. It made the work of growing even hotter and dirtier.

Early Saturday morning, Dick had rolled out of bed and headed straight for the patch, wearing just a T-shirt and boxer shorts. He picked up the garden hose and began watering. He wasn't worried about anyone driving by and seeing him in his underwear. "What difference does it make? They look just like colored shorts," he pointed out. "And they're nice and thin and cool." It was going to be a big day in the pumpkin patch.

Today Ron and Dick had to make their final choice about which pumpkins to keep on each plant. The keepers would have to be carefully lifted, still on the vine, and placed on a special piece of coated wire mesh fabric designed for use on factory conveyor belts. The material made the perfect foundation for giants to grow on — water drained right through it, and it was a tough barrier to mice and other varmints that liked to tunnel under and eat the fruit from the bottom.

The pumpkins already were growing so fast that soon they would be too heavy to lift. Even now, it was a two-man job: Ron lifted the pumpkin a few inches off the ground, while Dick quickly slid a large piece of the fabric underneath it. Then they covered the pumpkin with a sheet. They'd decided not to build shade tents this year. Instead, they would shield the fruits' tender skins from the sun with a simple white sheet. They had borrowed the technique from other growers who found that the cloth worked just as well as the tent, and also reduced the risk of damage if a windstorm came along and blew the tents down.

All the growers now were putting in long hours in the patch every day just to keep up with the rampant vine growth. At this point, every giant pumpkin plant had at least 10 side vines extending from each side of the main vine. During peak growth in late June and early July, those side vines might grow a foot a day. Add in the main vine, and that's 21 feet a day that need to be inspected and pruned and buried on each plant. Many of the bigger plants could have 30 or 40 side vines, and the top growers were looking after at least 3 or 4 plants. The Wallaces were growing 10. The LaRues were growing 25.

By 8 a.m., Ron was sweating through his T-shirt as he crawled on his hands and knees across a board in the pumpkin patch, searching for stray vines that needed trimming. His faded denim shorts were dark brown in front where he had repeatedly wiped the dirt from his hands. His white socks sagged down around the ankles of his leather boots. The sun was white and hot in a cloudless blue sky. Ron wore his favorite red-and-blue Buffalo Bills baseball cap, the onc he'd had since he was 11, to shield his eyes from the glaring sun.

Ron and Dick followed a strict schedule for fertilizing their patch with compost tea and applying pesticide and fungicide to ward off pests and disease. That meant strapping on the heavy backpack sprayer and moving slowly through the patch to thoroughly coat each plant at least once a week and usually more often. If they slacked off, it would take only a few days for a rampaging fungus or a swarm of hungry insects to damage enough leaves to create a huge hole in the plant, crippling its ability to produce enough energy to feed a giant pumpkin.

Already, the hot weather was bringing the

bugs out in force. As Ron set to work that morning, the orange and black blur of a squash vine borer moth buzzed by, swooping low over the plants and then flitting off into the woods before Ron could catch and kill it. "First squash vine borer of the year," he noted.

"Look here!" Dick hollered from the other side of the patch. He pointed to a female squash bug creeping slowly along the top of a pumpkin leaf, leaving a neat, double-rowed trail of reddish-brown eggs behind. That was definitely not good. An infestation of squash bugs could suck the life out of a plant in a matter of days. Ron did a quick search, spotting another half-dozen bugs and several more clusters of the sesame-seed-sized eggs glued to the tops and bottoms of leaves. It was a full-fledged invasion. Ron would have to haul out the backback sprayer again that afternoon for a liberal dose of pesticide.

The Wallace patch was nearly running out of room. The mature vines had lost their neat, triangular shape and were beginning to fill out the spaces between plants. The baby pumpkins remained hidden beneath the spreading canopy of leaves that covered the garden. The emerald ceiling hid a sanctuary beneath, where the shaded roots of the plant grew less than half an inch beneath the moist soil.

Pollination was finished, and every plant now had one or two or three baby pumpkins growing on the main vine. Most were whitish-yellow, with smooth, polished skins, like a peeled onion. Some had a lovely round shape. Most were elongated, almost oval, like short, fat, albino watermelons. They varied in size, depending on when they had been pollinated. The youngest were about the size of a large lemon. The biggest, about two weeks old, were a little bigger than a basketball, and weighed about 50 to 60 pounds. But Ron and Dick hadn't begun the official measuring yet. It was still too early. The measurements at this point didn't mean much. A strong-growing baby would expand several inches every day.

With the dirt packed deep under his fingernails, his sweat-soaked shirt clinging to his back, his knees black with mud, and every muscle in his body aching from hours of stooping and crawling, Ron had just one sustaining thought as he slaved in his pumpkin patch. After all the setbacks, after all the terrible weather in the spring, he had beautiful plants. He had healthy pumpkins. He had a shot. Maybe his best shot ever.

Down the road from the Wallaces, Scott Palmer was in need of some help. Because of his hernia surgery, he was still barred from any strenuous activity, especially the kind of bending and lifting and reaching required for work in the pumpkin patch. Dick and Ron and Peter Rondeau had spent a recent afternoon in Scott's patch to help prune and bury the vines. Then Dick had appeared one day with the backpack sprayer to give the Palmer plants a dose of compost tea. Scott and Shelley appreciated the help — were grateful for it — but felt guilty. The backpack sprayer was heavy. Dick was getting older, and he wasn't exactly a prime specimen of good health. But he wasn't ready to think of himself as old, even though his body was sending a different message. He'd gotten the job done, but he was red-faced and soaked in sweat when he finished. Shelley was horrified. She fussed at Scott, "Why did you let him do that?"

"You know I can't get him to stop," Scott answered.

"I just feel bad about it," Shelley said. "I told him, 'You're going to go home and

Cathy is going to yell at you. In fact, I'm going to tell her to yell at you.' "

But the extra dose of fertilizer had helped. Scott's plants had caught up. He had pollinated three pumpkins — one on the exact spot where he'd grown his prizewinning 1,443-pounder the year before. Still, things weren't going perfectly. "I've been having to water every single day. My dirt just won't hold any water. I need some more organic matter," he fretted. Scott was beginning to regret that he hadn't done more work on his soil that spring. His experiment in letting well enough alone was beginning to yield some results. And he didn't like what he was seeing.

From the beginning, Ron hadn't liked the looks of one particular pumpkin. The female flower had what growers called "seeds in the blossom." It was a developmental defect that caused some of the teensy ovules, which should be down inside the baby pumpkin fruit, to leak up into the flower itself. Not actual seeds yet, the ovules are tiny white dots, not much bigger than grains of salt. As giant pumpkins became more heavily inbred — siblings crossed with siblings, mothers and fathers crossed with children — growers had been noticing more seeds showing up in the blossoms every year.

The question they endlessly debated was, did it matter? Some felt that, absent some obvious deformity, a few seeds in the blossom didn't make any difference. Others felt strongly that any defect in the bloom would result in a defect in the growing pumpkin, making it stunted or deformed, or more likely to crack halfway through the season.

Ron wasn't sure what to think. He'd gone ahead and pollinated the pumpkin even after he'd noticed a few seeds in the blossom. Everything else about the baby fruit had been perfect — its location on the main vine, its shape, its growth rate — and it had been pollinated at the perfect time during that first week in July. But as always, he'd pollinated a couple more pumpkins on the same plant as insurance. Now he had to decide which one to keep. This was one of competitive growers' most agonizing decisions of the season, which pumpkins to cull and which one to keep?

Often, there were two or three pumpkins on each plant that had good potential, and any one of them might produce a big pumpkin. But not every one would have the potential to be a champion. So many things needed to work together in perfect synchronicity to grow a world-record pumpkin. The fruit needed to be in the right position on the vine to pull the most energy from the plant. It had to be the right shape — some growers believed oval shapes were able to hold up better during the explosive August growth phase, while rounder pumpkins were prone to splitting midway through the season. It had to be growing fast, and it had to be free from deformities (though often those wouldn't show up for several more weeks). And it had to have been pollinated early enough to give it time to put on a world-class weight by harvest time.

When it came to culling time, growers could torture themselves over which pumpkin to keep and which to cut loose. They wanted as much time as possible to evaluate the pumpkins to make the best choice, but for every day the plant had to support more than one pumpkin, the growth of the eventual keeper was slowed. Delaying the cull too long would make it less likely that a pumpkin would make it over 400 pounds by the end of July. Yet every time growers cut a reject off the vine, they were plagued by the thought, "Did I just send the future world record to the compost pile?"

Ron had been wavering for days, and the seeds-in-the-blossom pumpkin was already the size of a human head. Another pumpkin pollinated several days later on the same plant was only the size of a baseball. Keeping the first one was tempting, and Ron hadn't been able to bring himself to cut it off yet. Every day he delayed, though, was stealing energy from the baseball-sized pumpkin on the vine. It would continue to grow slowly as long as the first pumpkin was sucking up all the juice. Today was the day he had to decide.

"It's either one of those two," said Dick. "Just make the decision so it can grow." Dick had changed into a bright-orange T-shirt and gray sweatpants cut off below the knee. He wore a yellow straw cowboy hat with the brim turned up on the sides. His face was rosy from the hot sun and humidity.

"Well, take a look," said Ron, calling his father over to inspect both pumpkins. Dick tottered out on the narrow board behind Ron and crouched down in the leaves, his hands braced on his knees. The seeds-in-the-blossom pumpkin was a beauty: a butter yellow, perfectly symmetrical sphere. He looked closely at the blossom end of the pumpkin, opposite the stem, where the seeds had appeared. There was nothing unusual that he could see. "We could make this plant a test to see what really happens," suggested Dick. "We've got nine others, Ronnie, right?"

Ron still wavered. He stood up and stared at the plant, debating out loud. "You've got this one twelve foot out, and you're about sixteen foot there with the other one, but it had a real late start . . . We could always just leave it for another day. Keep an eye on it until tomorrow maybe."

"You know what, Ronnie, cut the freakin' thing. It's not like we don't have anything else," urged Dick.

That did it. Without another word, Ron bent down with his knife and sliced off the bigger seeds-in-the-blossom pumpkin, then stood up holding it by its stem, executioner style, to give it one last appraising look. "Pumpkin, we hardly knew ye," Ron said, then tossed it to the side of the patch. Now that the deed was done, there was no use second-guessing himself about it. "What are you going to do? You've got to take some risk. That thing could've split on me up around seven hundred or eight hundred pounds, and then I'd be saying, 'Shit, I should have taken it off.' I'd rather take my chances with the baseball."

Dick picked up a shovel and walked over to the cast-off pumpkin. He lifted the shovel blade and jammed it down, cleaving the smooth-skinned orb in half. Maybe, he thought, a pumpkin autopsy would reveal the mystery of the seeds in the blossom. Dick bent down to examine it. Inside was a solid mass of pale-yellow pulp, ringed by the denser, darker border of the rind. Filmy white seeds had begun forming in the pulp, which would begin to hollow out as the pumpkin grew, eventually becoming the stringy, slimy stuff so well known to jack-o'-lantern carvers. Dick aligned the spot on the blossom where the seeds had appeared with the inside of the dissected pumpkin. There was an odd, tubelike growth coming out of the rind at that point. Was that related to the seeds in the blossom? Was it a potential defect? Dick showed Ron the odd growth. "Look at this," Dick said. "See that? That was a split waiting to happen."

"That would have made for a weak point later," Ron agreed.

Dick studied the pumpkin some more. "Smells great," he said, breathing in the sweet, cantaloupey smell of the opened fruit. He turned half of the pumpkin over in his hands. A dirt-blackened line accented the stubs of his closely bitten fingernails. "Lots of seeds, Ronnie. There would have been lots of seeds in this one." A tinge of regret crept into his voice.

"You think it would have made it?" Ron asked, the second thoughts contagious.

"Look at how thick it is at the blossom end," Dick said. "Maybe this one would have been extra heavy. Maybe . . ." But he snapped himself out of it. "Awww, that's all right," he said. "No big deal." He heaved the two halves of the baby pumpkin over the fence to the edge of the woods. It was deer food now.

As July wore on, temperatures continued to tick up across the nation. The heat, especially on the East Coast, began to generate headlines as air conditioners were cranked up and electricity demand spiked through the roof. New York mayor Michael Bloomberg turned off lights at City Hall; power customers across the East Coast set new consumption records. By Tuesday, July 18, the Associated Press reported that the heat had killed 12 people around the country.

The pumpkin plants were wilting in the afternoon heat and the sun was literally cooking tender new leaves. Anyone who hadn't yet successfully pollinated a pumpkin was out of luck. Some desperate growers tried packing their baby pumpkins in ice, but they still aborted within a few days because of the heat stress on the plants.

Relief finally arrived July 18 for the Northeast, though not the kind of relief the pumpkin growers wanted. A cool front descended from the north, sliding in under the warm air and wreaking havoc in the atmosphere. Thunderstorms began boiling up in New England, lighting up the National Weather Service's Doppler radar. About 9:30 p.m., the weather agency issued a severe thunderstorm warning for Rhode Island. A major storm was getting ready to cut right through the center of the state, and forecasters were sounding the alarm for nickel-sized hail and winds gusting up to 70mph.

Tuesdays were Ron's day off, but he'd still rolled out of bed at 5:30 a.m. and was in the patch by 6 a.m. to beat the heat. He spent the next two and a half hours trimming and burying vines and inspecting plants and pumpkins. Things were easier than before. "Two days ago it was four hours," he said. "Next time it might only be two hours. It's getting better. We're getting most of the work behind us now." Temperatures had risen to a miserable 95 that afternoon, but everyone was focused on the cool front due to arrive that evening. Ron watched the 6 p.m. television news, which warned of a few thundershowers as the front moved through. Nothing to really worry about. But a few hours later, as he was puttering around his house, he heard the big-screen television in his den start beeping with an emergency alert signal. He went in to look and saw a message streaming across the bottom of the screen, warning of the approach of a violent thunderstorm with winds that already had begun toppling trees and blowing down power lines across New England. It was almost 9:45 p.m. and the fire-red splotches on the radar showed the storm hovering on the western edge of Coventry, near the Wallace house. "Holy crap," Ron thought. "We're going to be right in the path of the storm. If we get this, we're all done."

Any storm could wipe out a pumpkin grower's months of work in a few short minutes. A burst of wind-driven, pea-sized hail could shred pumpkin leaves into cole slaw. Bigger hail could pound the plants to smithereens, smashing stems, crushing vines, and leaving the tender skin of the growing pumpkins cratered with dents. The plants were huge — 500 to 900 square feet — the size of a one-bedroom apartment. There was no way of sheltering them. Even one gust of 60-mph wind could turn the broad, flapping surface of the pumpkin leaves into sails that could rip the vine from the ground and lift it into the air. Strong winds had been known to snap a plant from its stump and hurl it all the way across the yard.

Outside, the air was dead still. Then the night sky darkened ominously, and the wind began to blow. "Here we go," thought Ron. He dashed outside and started across the yard to make sure the sheets were secured around the baby pumpkins. The cloth covers would at least provide a little protection if hail began to fall. But within seconds, the rain began to pound down and the wind whipped the trees as lightning lit up the sky and thunder crashed so loudly that Ron turned back. Pumpkins weren't worth dying for. There was nothing he could do now except watch the storm blow through, wait for morning, and repair whatever damage he could.

As Ron retreated inside the house to watch the storm from his window, the phone began to ring as the other growers called to check in with him and find out if he was getting hit. They called one after another, beeping in on call-waiting, so that he jumped from one person to the next without ever hanging up the phone. And then, as suddenly as it had started, the wind died down, though the rain continued to fall hard and steady in the dark. The worst of the storm had passed by. Ron woke briefly during the night to hear another thunderstorm blowing through about 2 a.m. "Jesus," he thought, before falling back to sleep. "All that hard work for nuthin'." But when he woke up at first light and went outside to check on the pumpkins, he found no harm done. "I didn't have even one leaf bent over," he said. "We dodged a real big bullet."

The pumpkins, meanwhile, were gathering steam. During the early days, the newly pollinated pumpkin grows so quickly that its progress is visible day to day. The fruit swells from the size of an egg to that of a baseball within a day of, then to the size of a grapefruit, a cantaloupe, a volleyball, a basketball, a beach ball. After a couple weeks, the daily difference in size becomes less obvious, but the weight begins to pile on — 30 to 40 pounds a day or more at peak growth.

By the weekend of July 22, the Wallaces' pumpkins already were beginning to look like giants. It was as if someone had found the air valve and pumped them up several sizes. The green canopy of their pumpkin patch was punctuated with 10 pale-yellow crescents looming moonlike above the leaves. Most of the pumpkins were now 16 to 20 days old, with the largest about two feet tall and approaching 200 pounds.

That was good, and over the next several days, the Wallaces would be getting an idea of whether it was going to be good enough. They would begin measuring and charting the pumpkins every week, starting when each pumpkin reached its 20-day birthday after pollination. They hoped to have pumpkins measuring 210 pounds at the 20-day mark. Then if the pumpkin put on 25 to 30 pounds a day, they'd be right around 420 pounds by the end of July. "If you're going to be world-class, that's the kind of growth you've got to have," Dick said.

The Rhode Island club was hosting visitors that weekend: three pumpkin growers in their early twenties from Ohio, Pennsylvania, and Michigan who had decided on the spur of the moment to drive to Rhode Island to tour the patches of the world-champion pumpkin growing club. Dick had received an e-mail from one of the young growers asking if they could sleep on the floor at his house. It was a little disconcerting to get that kind of request from a total stranger, but the pumpkin growers were a worldwide community with an implicit trust. Criminals would never grow giant pumpkins, growers believed; it was too much hard work with too little payoff. In that world, Dick Wallace, especially, had gained a reputation for hospitality.

Lots of stories about Dick's generosity circulated among pumpkin growers, but a favorite was of the British pumpkin grower who came to the United States one summer a few years before to tour American patches. Another U.S. grower had called Dick to ask if he would mind if the British visitor stayed with him for a day or two as he scouted out New England patches. "Whoa now, wait a minute," Dick answered, "Who is this guy? How long has he been growing pumpkins?"

"He's been growing about eight years," the grower answered.

"Well, what's the biggest pumpkin he's ever grown?" Dick asked.

"About eight hundred pounds."

"Eight hundred pounds?" Dick repeated. "He's been growing eight years and the best he's done is eight hundred pounds?"

"Yeah, that's right," said the other grower, beginning to feel a little put out.

"Well then," Dick roared, "tell him to

come on down. Anybody who grows giant pumpkins for eight years and doesn't give up even though he's never gotten over eight hundred pounds has got to be okay. He's growing for the right reasons."

So Dick naturally said yes to the three young visitors and arranged a patch tour for them that Saturday afternoon. They stopped for lunch at Peter Rondeau's house, where the growers stood around comparing notes. Now that everyone's pumpkins were well underway, the main question was how fast they were growing — and how fast they *needed* to be growing to be a world champion. If a grower was aiming for 1,500 pounds, how big should the pumpkin be at the 30-day mark? How big should it be at 40 and 50 days?

Most of the major weigh-off contests are held around the first week of October, so the growers had about 90 days to grow a world-record pumpkin — July, August, and September. The arc of weight gain for the pumpkins is shaped like a steep hill, curving up in July, peaking in August, and declining in September. Dick and Ron figured that if they were going to have a shot at 1,500 pounds, they had to have a 400- to 500-pound pumpkin by the end of July. Then they'd have to push to add 800 pounds in

August. *Eight hundred pounds in August.* To put that in perspective, the 1990 world title had gone to a pumpkin weighing 816.5 pounds after growing a full season. Now growers were talking about doing that much in just one month. That would mean an average weight gain in August of 26 pounds a day.

The problem with that was the growth curve. At the beginning of August, a world-class pumpkin might start off growing 40 pounds a day, but as the fruit begins to mature, and as the days get shorter, with less sunlight, and the cool nights return toward the end of the month, growth slows dramatically. By September, adding 15 pounds a day is considered good. And by the end of September, most East Coast pumpkins stop growing entirely. Then it's just a matter of holding steady until the weigh-off.

After lunch, Dick shooed the visiting growers into their cars for the next stop, Joe Jutras's house. Dick was trying to keep the group on time. He was irritable and a little anxious. He'd promised Cathy he'd be home by 4 p.m. to take her and their grand-daughter, Rene, shopping for a new pair of running shoes. This was not optional, and he needed the tour to stay on schedule so he could make it home on time. But trying was pointless: By the time they wound up the tour late that afternoon, they were running nearly two hours behind. Dick had to peel off early to make it home by his deadline. The fact of the matter was, it hadn't been the best time for hosting a patch tour. July is the peak work month in the pumpkin patch. It's also the time when the "pumpkin widows" begin to roar.

There are plenty of women who grow giant pumpkins, but by far the biggest faction of competitive growers is made up of middle-aged men, most with wives and children. By mid-July, growers' wives had endured two and a half months of the growing season, with their husbands spending more and more time in the garden tending the plants. It wasn't just the time stolen from their families; it was the obsession that drove the wives crazy. Year-round they had to endure the hours their husbands spent chatting with other growers on the Internet, or researching new fertilizers and pesticides and exchanging seeds. They had to watch as a big chunk of their backyard was dug up and turned into a pile of dirt that smelled like dead fish and manure. Then the junk would start piling up: the 50-gallon plastic barrels and the garden hoses and the buckets and jugs of pesticides and fertilizers and the sheets and towels and long-handled gardening tools.

So it was already bad enough by May, but then as the growing season got underway, the to-do lists around the house would get steadily longer as chores were neglected and even major maintenance was postponed. Growers tend to be workaholics who spend long hours at their day jobs, then come home and head straight into the pumpkin patch, where they often stay until after dark. The faster the vines grow, the more time the plants require. And over the years, as the growers got more hooked on the hobby and more competitive, they'd often want to increase their odds of success by growing more plants.

And so the dirt patches would get bigger and the lawns would get smaller and the hours in the garden would get longer. The obsession didn't stop when they came in the house. The whole family's nerves were frayed from the grower's constant fretting over the plants. Wives had to listen and nod and pretend to be interested as their husbands babbled on about 1068s and 1370s and 1225s and 1354s. They had to listen to endless discussions about pollination and pruning and growth charts. They had to endure snarling moods when things went wrong — as things frequently did. They had to constantly clean up mud and dirt and manure tracked into the house.

And if all that wasn't bad enough, the phone rang constantly as other growers called to compare notes or ask advice. If the growers were out in the garden, the wives would get peppered with questions about the plants.

"Some days," Cathy Wallace admitted, "I think I'm going to go insane if one more pumpkin grower calls."

The wives all had different ways of coping. Some grudgingly endured, with their annoyance occasionally erupting into an argument over the amount of time or money or talk spent on pumpkins. Some laid down the law, setting deadlines, for chores and limiting the hours their husbands could spend in the patch. Most understood that their husbands were pursuing their passion — a passion, happily, that kept them at home. These wives simply demanded a little balance. They insisted their husbands make it to the dinner table at a certain time, or reserve some hours in the day to spend with the family. Steve Daletas, the 2003 world-record holder from Oregon, agreed to take the whole 2006 growing season off to devote to his wife and two children.

Wives who had their own hobbies handled it better. Sue Jutras liked to grow things too, so she understood that part of her husband's obsession. She had her own vegetable garden and took charge of much of the landscaping around the house. In recent years, she had started raising orchids after Joe gave her one of the exotic plants for Valentine's Day. Orchid growers are as passionate as pumpkin growers, so while Joe tended to his giant pumpkins, Sue tended to her flowers. Joe had recently added on a sunroom to the house to give her a better place to keep the orchids.

Tracy Rondeau had found that her husband's pumpkin obsession gave her new leverage around the house. She would agree to nag-free time in the pumpkin patch if Peter finished other household chores first. And she wasn't beyond threatening sabotage. She'd gotten fed up that year with the ugly sight of the 50-gallon drums and gardening equipment piled at the back of the yard. Peter had never gotten around to putting up the fence he'd promised to build to hide it. So one evening Tracy told him that if it wasn't done by the end of the week, she'd see to it that he didn't have a single female flower left on his plants to pollinate.

The fence — cute wood pickets with a wooden pumpkin sitting on top — went right up. "I've discovered the secret," she said, laughing. She confessed she'd even threatened to cut the pumpkins off the vines or pull up all his plants if he didn't take care of his household responsibilities.

"He knows deep down that I wouldn't really do it," she said. "But there's just the tiniest doubt. When I got really mad at him and told him I used his toothbrush to clean out the toilet, he didn't really believe I did that either. But he still threw away his toothbrush."

Her frustration was understandable. Over the years, she'd put up with a lot from Peter and his pumpkins. Unlike most of the other Rhode Island pumpkin growers, with their multiacre expanses of property, the Rondeaus lived on a suburban street and had a modest, suburban-sized backyard. Peter had always used part of the yard for a vegetable garden, but when he got hooked on giant pumpkins, he had expanded the garden to 1,500 square feet, taking up nearly the entire backyard.

This year, he'd cut down several trees on the perimeter of the yard during the winter to bring in more sunlight. He'd had seven cubic yards of cow manure delivered on

Easter Sunday. "Great, Dad. Smells good," his teenage daughter had commented.

Peter tried to do his part to keep the peace. He grew a few decorative gourd plants for his wife each year. And he made sure he came up with at least one nice, big orange pumpkin for his wife and daughters to carve for Halloween. His job conducting safety-training classes for plant workers kept him away during the day, while Tracy, a manicurist, often worked into the evening and on Saturdays. So as soon as Peter got home, he'd go straight outside and get all his work done in the pumpkin patch. That way, he said, "When my wife gets home, it's, 'What would you like to do, honey?' "

Tracy had her own interests and hobbies. She described herself as "Martha Stewart on steroids" and spent much of her free time making crafts and thinking up new decorating projects. So she appreciated that Peter had things he loved to do, too. She looked on the bright side. Lots of men had hobbies like hunting or fishing or golf that took them away from home. Peter already had to travel a lot for his job. "And now he can't wait to get home to his patch," she said.

A few wives made it work by sharing the hobby with their husbands. Gerry Checkon was intrigued by the giant pumpkin her husband, Larry, grew his first year, so she decided to grow her own pumpkin the next season. She not only grew a bigger pumpkin than her husband; she set the 1998 world record. Now the couple divide their pumpkin patch into his-and-her halves. "He goes out and does his stuff, and if I want to be with him, then I'm out there with him. And if I want to be in the house, then I'm in the house. When he's not at work, he's out there, so I always know where my husband is," Gerry reasons.

Sherry LaRue picked up the hobby when she resigned herself to the fact that it was the best way to spend time with her husband, Jack. Their three older daughters had never been very interested in the pumpkins, but their youngest decided to try growing in 1995. She was only 9, but she did all the work with Jack's guidance. At the end of the season, when they lifted the pumpkin to take it to a weigh-off, they discovered it had cracked, which made it ineligible for the contest. That was a keen disappointment, and the next year their daughter went back to more typical 10-year-old stuff like soccer and hanging out with her friends.

As Jack got more caught up in the competitive part of the hobby and started growing more plants, he began spending all his spare time in the patch. "I found that if I wanted to talk to him, I was doing it in the garden," said Sherry. "He would say, 'Could you pull that weed while you're there? Would you hold this? Do that?' " Sherry also helped out by pollinating the plants during the week when Jack had to leave early for the office. "I decided that if I was doing some of the work, then I might as well enter the contest myself. So I started growing my own plants."

Sherry didn't want anyone to think that she was entering a pumpkin that really had been grown by her husband — a perennial complaint at the weigh-off contests that limit entries to one pumpkin per grower. Growers with multiple big pumpkins have been known to enter them under the names of their wives and children, even though they hadn't really done much more than turn on the sprinklers. That wasn't considered fair to the growers who really put in the work. So Sherry demanded her own space in the garden and kept her pumpkins separate from her husband's. She did all the work on her own plants, from picking the seeds to pruning the vines. Though she doesn't grow nearly as many plants as Jack, the hobby has come to unite them, instead of dividing them.

Early on, as they both began spending more time in the garden, they resolved to set aside one day each weekend to do things together as a family — to go hiking in the mountains or take a trip to the beach. As their children grew up and moved out, they continued to set the time aside for themselves. "It might just be dinner and a movie, but it is time away from the pumpkins," Sherry said.

By July 26, Ron and Dick had all the 20-day measurements they needed to give them a better idea how their pumpkins were shaping up. It was looking good. A few even appeared to be — though it made them nervous to say so — on a world-record pace. They'd made separate growth charts for each pumpkin so they could compare the growth rates.

Estimating the weight of a giant, irregular object of unknown density is a tricky matter. But over the years, a few pumpkin growers with a talent for math had boiled down hundreds of pumpkin weights and measurements to come up with a formula for how much a pumpkin weighs based on a combination of three measurements. One is a simple circumference measurement taken roughly parallel to the ground at the pumpkin's fattest point. Charts had been composed using the circumference measurement alone to give growers a rough idea of how much their pumpkins might weigh. As a pumpkin gets bigger, every inch of circumference accounts for exponentially greater mass, and therefore many more pounds. For instance, a 100-inch circumference would translate to about a 273-pound pumpkin, while a 181-inch circumference would yield a 1,300-pound pumpkin.

Giant pumpkins are warped and lumpy objects, though. Some are very tall and narrow, while others are flat and wide. Odd bulges and dips and curves can make a circumference at any given point almost meaningless. So for better accuracy, growers take two other measurements and add them to the circumference. Growers take a second measurement by running the measuring tape laterally over the top of the pumpkin, dropping it straight down to the ground on either side. The pumpkin is then measured the same way back to front, from the ground, over the stem, over the top, and back over the blossom end to the ground. Growers refer to this process as "taping." The three measurements added together are called the over-the-top measurement, or OTT.

Dick made a brief note of some of the 20-day measurements at the Wallace patch:

500 Wallace × 1173 Macari — 195″ OTT = 167 lb. (could surprise.)

1068 Wallace × 887 Orr — 185″ = 145 lbs.?

1228 Jutras × 1225 Jutras — 192″ = 160 lbs.?

1068 Wallace × 1225 Jutras — 209″ = 202 lbs. (world class)

1068 Wallace × 1068 Wallace — 202″ = 184 lbs. (world class)

1068 Wallace × 1354 Checkon — 214″ = 216 lbs. (world class)

The Wallaces still had six days to make it to their 400- to 500-pound goal at the end of the month. Giant pumpkins at this point should be growing 25 to 30 pounds a day. The 500 Wallace, for instance, had been the first pumpkin pollinated, on July 1. On its 20-day birthday, July 21, it weighed 167 pounds. If the pumpkin gained an average of 25 pounds every day, it should weigh almost 420 pounds by the end of the month.

"It's a fantastic start," Dick said hopefully. But every grower knows that at this point, it's only a start. "All of these are better than the twenty-day measurements of our two largest pumpkins last year," Dick noted. "But that's all it means."

The grim odds of giant pumpkins dictated that by the end of the season, more than half the fruit that had started out so beautifully would be in the compost pile, either split open or taken down by disease. Last year the Wallaces had ended up with only two out of the eight they started, and neither of those two were competitive. Joe Jutras had wound up with just one competitive pumpkin out of eight he'd started. Peter Rondeau lost three of his four.

The Wallaces' numbers this year were ahead of most of the other growers in the club. But giant pumpkins can slow down or speed up unpredictably. "So what if somebody's got a pumpkin forty pounds heavier than yours right now?" Joe Jutras noted. "You can make up forty pounds in one day."

The toughest part for the growers was controlling the impulse to measure the pumpkins constantly. It was hard to resist when so much was riding on how fast the pumpkins were growing. For pumpkin growers, who already have proven their compulsive credentials, measuring the pumpkins could become an obsession of its own. Sitting in their houses, they can almost sense the pumpkins expanding in the patch.

They think about it, wonder about it. They need to know. How much? How fast?

It's a weakness, especially, of newer growers, whose hopes have not yet been tempered by years of disappointment. Peter Rondeau admits he's been carried away by this enthusiasm more than once. He unabashedly looks up to some of the other, more-veteran pumpkin growers and feels pressured to try to keep up. He was starstruck at the growers' conference in Niagara Falls that March — his first year to go. He was one of the few growers to religiously attend every conference session. Sitting at the table with the Rhode Island gang was, he said, "like sitting in the dugout with the Boston Red Sox." Everywhere he looked, there was pumpkin royalty, world-record holders and names he knew by the pedigree of their seeds — Bobier and Daletas and LaRue. "We go out to eat for lunch, and Jack LaRue is sitting to my left and I'm talking to this guy like I knew him all my life . . . and he's the guy who grew the 1420, and it's like, 'Wow. These are normal people.' "

The summer before, Peter recalled, Dick Wallace had brought Joe Pukos, another of the hobby's great names, over to Peter's for a visit. "I was like, 'Clean the house! Clean the house!' My wife said, 'What's the matter?' and I said, 'It's Joe Pukos, it's Joe Pukos!' I'm running around like a nut. He's in the driveway and I'm in the backyard working like mad — gotta prune!"

So it was no surprise that Peter fell into the obsessive-measuring trap. In 2005, he'd measured his pumpkins at least once a day, and sometimes twice, meticulously recording every inch in his growing diary. When the pumpkins got bigger, it was difficult to reach all the way around it to get an accurate measurement, so Peter recruited his 14-year-old daughter, Abbey, to help him. By then, Peter's family knew it could get ugly if the pumpkin wasn't growing as fast as he hoped. "You have these expectations," Peter explained. "And then when they're not met, you're kind of mad. You're angry. You get in a bad mood. It kind of drives you nuts."

Peter's daughter quickly figured out that if she slipped her fingers under the measuring tape on the other side of the pumpkin where her father couldn't see, she could add an inch or two to the total, and her dad would come away happy. So whenever it looked like the pumpkin might not be growing fast enough, Abbey pulled her little trick. Just a couple of extra inches and daddy smiled. It worked like a charm.

By the end of the season, though, the numbers weren't adding up, and Abbey had to confess. It was a double gut-punch to Peter. He had to accept that his pumpkin hadn't grown as much as he thought it had, and that was painful. But what was worse was the realization of how much his pumpkin-driven mood swings had been affecting his family. He was ashamed of himself. So this year, Peter had vowed he wouldn't obsess over measuring. "That's how your sanity goes down the tubes," he said. He was determined to restrain himself. He would, of course, check on his pumpkins every day, watch them grow, but he had decided to measure them only on day 10, day 20, and then every five days after that during the peak growing period.

"I'm lowering my expectations this year," Peter said. Or, at least, he was trying to keep them under control. He felt a little like the slacker of the Rhode Island group. He was hanging with a 1,300- to 1,400-pound crowd when his biggest pumpkin last year had been only 1,100 pounds. "I've got a lot I'm going up against," he said. He felt the pressure. He was the guy coming up from behind. But by the end of July, he had two really big pumpkins, including a 1068, growing in his backyard. Growing really fast. He wondered if this might be his year.

Through most of July, the storms had boiled up, blown over, and passed by the Southern New England growers without inflicting any serious damage. The men were marveling at their good fortune right up until Friday, July 28. Joe Jutras had finished up his day at his woodworking shop, come home, eaten dinner, and headed straight out to the patch to tend to his plants. As he waded carefully through the green sea of leaves, examining vines and snipping off unwanted new growth, the skies darkened overhead and the wind picked up slightly. The breeze felt good. It had been so hot and humid that a little thunderstorm would be a relief.

When the rain began to fall, he headed up to the house. He and Sue stood in the shelter of the open garage looking out over the backyard, watching the rain come down in swirling, silvery sheets. The skies had turned even darker, the winds had picked up, and now Joe was beginning to feel a little anxious about his plants. The temperature had been a balmy 90 degrees, but had plunged at least 20 degrees in a few minutes, making the wind-driven rain feel suddenly cold against their skin.

Joe never figured out exactly what it was

— a downdraft? A microburst? — but it was a ferocious wind that swirled around and over the house, churning a path through the rain, bending trees, scattering the lawn chairs on the back deck, and then sweeping across the lawn to the pumpkin patch. In an instant, the pumpkin leaves were smashed flat to the ground in a wide swathe cutting across the garden.

"It came through like a freight train," Joe said. "It was like an elephant stomping on the plants. I've never seen anything like that." His heart sank as he watched part of the deer fence surrounding his patch blow over on top of the plants and shred leaves as it flailed in the wind. He threw on his rain jacket and ran out to the garden, trying to pull the fence off the plants before it did more damage. Then, almost as quickly as it began, the storm passed. The winds died down and the rain quit.

About half an inch of rain had fallen in 20 minutes, Joe estimated. He surveyed his smashed garden. At least 500 pumpkin leaves were lying against the ground, many with broken stems. Three long side vines on one of his most-prized plants had snapped and uprooted. The vines couldn't be saved. Neither could many of the leaves. There wasn't much Joe could do, so he ran back in the house and began dialing up the other Rhode Island pumpkin growers to see how they had fared. The storm had passed harmlessly over everyone else. Only Joe had suffered damage.

Saturday morning, Dick Wallace and Peter Rondeau showed up early to help Joe mend as much of the damage as they could. Joe had gone out that morning and bought dozens of three-foot-long sticks of bamboo at a local Lowe's hardware store. Most of the leaves were a lost cause — he trimmed about 300 whose hollow stems had snapped when the wind blew them over. But another couple hundred leaves looked salvageable. The stalks had bent over and creased, but hadn't broken. Joe figured he could use the bamboo sticks to splint the stems and get them standing back upright until they could heal themselves.

So for hours that morning, the three men worked, moving from leaf to leaf, poking the bamboo down into the dirt next to the vine, then using duct tape to straighten the leaf stem and secure it to the stick. Peter and Joe crouched in the dirt until their knees creaked with the strain and their backs ached from stooping over. It was hot, sweaty, dirty work under a blistering sun that was quickly turning the day into another scorcher. Dick brought his usual light touch to the job, tearing off short strips of tape and sticking them to his belly so that Joe and Pete could reach up and grab one whenever they needed it — the human tape dispenser.

On July 23, Steve Connolly's 1068 pumpkin had weighed an estimated 330 pounds. The next-best pumpkin in his patch weighed only 243 pounds, even though it was five days older. At the end of July, Steve measured again. At just 32 days old, his 1068 was now more than 600 pounds. That was well over the 400- to 500-pound benchmark the Wallaces were shooting for. Steve had never had a pumpkin that had grown anywhere near that fast. It was, without doubt, a world-record pace. And all of August, the peak growing period, loomed ahead. Steve thought the 1068 would easily be able to put on another 1,000 pounds by the end of September. And that would give him a 1,600-pound pumpkin at weigh-off time.

11
GROW 'EM BIG

Larry Checkon's pale feet padded silently across the grass as he headed out of the house, around the back of the garage, and down to pumpkin patch No. 1. His toes gripped the blades of grass as his feet rose and fell, his footprints quickly disappearing in the resilient sod. There was nothing, except maybe a slight low trail in the green grass, to betray how often Larry had walked this path.

Every summer day he woke up with first light, jumped from bed, put on a pot of coffee, and headed out to see how his garden had fared through the night. This morning, on the way to the pumpkins, Larry stopped first at another part of the garden, where a tall corn plant was leaning slightly to one side. Using his bare foot as a hoe, he scooped up some dirt, piled it around the base of the plant, and then gently tamped it down to straighten up the plant and give it more support. Bare feet were Larry's antennae in the garden. Just by walking around, he could sense how warm or cool the dirt was and whether the patch needed water. He could even feel the earthworms squirming underfoot in the fresh-tilled soil. Standing on the edge of the garden, he stretched out a foot and used his toes to pluck a weed. "You can do a lot with toes," he said.

It was a clear morning, the last weekend in July, and a cool mist still rested lightly across the wooded hills surrounding the Checkons' 2.5-acre homestead. This was not just a piece of property here on the outskirts of Spangler, Pennsylvania; this was a piece of Larry's soul.

The land, tucked into a valley in northwestern Pennsylvania, had been in his family more than 100 years. Larry had lived there all his life. He stayed on after his mother died when he was 19 years old. And when he married, his wife moved in and together they cared for Larry's aging father, George, until he died. George Checkon had lived a long, productive life on that land. He was a coal miner for 37 years, breathing in the black dust and straining to see through the darkness underground. But when he'd come home, he'd work in the sunlight, in the garden, growing things.

When Larry got older, Larry grew things too.

Now there were gardens carved out all across the Checkon backyard, which stretched around in an L shape behind the house. In these gardens Larry grew onions and red potatoes and asparagus and sweet corn, tomatoes and broccoli and cauliflower and horseradish, carrots and rosemary and peppers. The plants were huge, healthy, and lush, growing in neatly tended rows. Flowers bloomed along the edges of the gardens. Larry's dad had liked to grow flowers around the vegetable patch, and they still popped up faithfully year after year. "Every time I go to pull one, I can hear him say, 'Don't pull that out.' So I leave it," Larry said. "You know, he's been gone for three years now, but I still talk to him every day. So I just leave a few poppies for him."

If giant pumpkins went to heaven, it would be a place like this, where every molecule of air invited things to grow. Small wonder, then, that the Checkons had won two world titles in the past seven years. Larry and his wife, Gerry, were the only husband-and-wife team ever to have achieved the singular and slightly obnoxious feat of growing one world-record pumpkin each. Gerry had set her record with the first pumpkin she ever grew, a 1,311-pounder in 1999. Larry was now the reigning world champion for his 1,469-pound pumpkin. The his-and-her titles made them the indisputable king and queen of the giant-pumpkin world. But the twin triumph hadn't dulled their desire to win one whit. "After growing two world records here, I guess anything else would just be gravy," he acknowledged. "But we would like to break the fifteen-hundred-pound mark."

Larry and Gerry, both 54 years old, were born the same year in the same town and graduated from the same high school together, but they married later in life, in 1993. It was Gerry's second marriage and Larry's first, and they'd found an easy equilibrium together. Gerry worked as the marketing coordinator for a county-owned long-term care facility for the elderly, and Larry was an electronics technician, building and repairing radios for fire trucks, police cars, and other commercial vehicles.

Originally, Larry's father had been the giant-pumpkin grower. In 1997, he was 87 years old and growing frail. He knew it was the last year he'd be able to grow pumpkins, and he wanted to give it everything he had. So it was a very big deal when he produced his biggest pumpkin ever: 700 pounds. The pumpkin, unfortunately, cracked open before they could get it to the weigh-off. But according to competition rules in years past, that didn't matter. Larry helped his dad seal up the crack with some caulking putty, and, to make it look nicer, they touched it up with a little orange paint.

When they got to the weigh-off in Altoona, about 30 miles away, George's pumpkin was weighed and it looked like he would win second place and $500. "He was so excited," Larry recalled. But then the judges came over and told him he was disqualified. The Pennsylvania club running the weigh-off had joined the Great Pumpkin Commonwealth that year and was following new GPC rules that disqualified damaged pumpkins. Larry's father was crushed. Larry was mad. Larry was *very* mad. "Something just sort of snapped in me," he said. "I told Gerry right on the spot, I said, 'Next year I'm going to grow a pumpkin and I'm going to come down here and win this thing.' "

The next morning at 6 a.m., Larry grabbed a shovel from the garage and walked out into the middle of the lawn and started digging. He worked through the day until it was dark, and then he kept on working late into the night. Gerry asked him, "How can you see anything out there in the dark?" And Larry answered, "I can see perfect. There's a streetlight out front and a full moon in the sky."

It took him two weeks to finish digging and tilling the new patch. And then he spent the whole winter researching how to grow giant pumpkins. Come springtime, he got a soil test and added in some more compost and manure. His father thought he'd gone nuts. But Larry told Gerry, "If I'm going to do this, I might as well do it right." The next fall, Larry took an 815-pound pumpkin to Altoona and won first place in the weigh-off.

George Checkon was a stern man, not one for showing emotion. "But I saw tears in his eyes that day," said Gerry. "That was the happiest I ever saw Dad."

Until then, Gerry had always left the gardening to Larry. But there was something about the fun of watching those giants grow, and the thrill of the competition, that drew her in. She told Larry she'd like to try growing a giant pumpkin the next year. So two giant pumpkins swelled in the Checkon patch in 1999. There was Gerry's, named Moonie because of its round shape and white color, and there was Larry's, named Womper.

Womper zoomed to over 1,000 pounds by

the middle of August with no sign of slowing down. The current world record was 1,092 pounds. If his pumpkin would just hold together until the weigh-off, he would have a new record in his hands. Larry got grower's fever: sleepless nights, churning stomach. He checked on the pumpkin as soon as his eyes opened every morning. "It gets to the point where you're half afraid to look," he said.

Sure enough, one morning in the third week of August, Larry saw a black line running across the skin of his pumpkin. He picked up a piece of straw and poked at it. It went in. He pushed the straw in slowly, an inch at a time. It went all the way through the shell. His world-record contender had split. Larry was devastated. "You put all that work into it. Hundreds and hundreds of hours of time, and all at once, it's over. All that effort and work is for nothing. Plus, this pumpkin wasn't just a pumpkin; it was a world record for sure," said Larry. "It just made me sick. I was sick for a whole week."

"Three weeks," Gerry corrected him.

But all was not lost. Gerry's pumpkin, Moonie, was a big pumpkin too. They figured they'd at least win the local weigh-off. "I was hoping for a thousand pounds," said Gerry. Her pumpkin came in at 1,131 pounds, and the Checkons set the new world record after all. "We were just so surprised," Larry said. "Everybody started yelling, 'New world record!' and stuff, and my dad was there too."

"Yeah, Dad cried again that day," Gerry said.

Larry finally got his own world record in 2005, though victory was bittersweet. He was convinced he'd broken through the 1,500-pound mark, the 1,600-pound mark, and even the 1,700-pound mark, all in one fell swoop. His pumpkin was a true giant among giants — by far the biggest thing anyone had ever heard of, much less grown. The over-the-top measurements totaled 441 inches, which suggested a weight of more than 1,770 pounds. But in the end, it was a balloon, weighing nearly 300 pounds lighter than expected. That is the puzzle of giant-pumpkin growing, and a supreme frustration of growers. It is a contest of weight, not size. And the OTT measurements only provide an estimate of how heavy a pumpkin is. The bigger giant pumpkins were getting, the more variability there seemed to be, leading to more surprising wins and crushing disappointments.

Larry kept painstaking records of every

growing season, recording daily weather conditions such as temperature, rainfall, and sunshine. He made a note whenever he did anything in the patch, from watering to fertilizing or applying fungicide. He measured his pumpkins daily and compared the growth rates to the other conditions he recorded. It was interesting to see how a cold snap slowed growth, a warm spell speeded it up, and a heavy rain sent the pumpkin into overdrive. That's when he realized that pumpkins put on most of their growth at night as they poured the energy they accumulated during the day into the fruit.

"This is a science," Larry said. "I like to make all sorts of observations. I like to know exactly what's happening."

The Checkons had plenty of room to grow as many pumpkin plants as they wanted — 8 or 10 like many of the big growers, or even 20-something like the LaRues. But they believed they were better off taking meticulous care of just a few plants. "We believe in quality, not quantity," Larry said.

So he and Gerry grew only two plants apiece. They rarely used sprinklers, preferring to water by hand, spraying a hose beneath the leaves to keep the foliage dry and reduce the chance of fungal infections.

They shunned the rigorous fertilizing and pesticide routines other growers followed. When they saw the plants looking a little pale, they fertilized; if bugs showed up, they sprayed. "It's like a tire," Larry said. "If it looks a little flat, you put some air in it. If not, you don't put air in it."

To protect the pumpkin patches from deer and vandals, Larry used his technical skills to rig motion-activated alarms. If the alarm was triggered, an alert would sound over a speaker in their bedroom, and he would jump out of bed and run to the patch to scare away any intruders. This happened a lot, as raccoons, stray cats, and the occasional deer made their way toward the plants. Larry made sure the alarm made a different sound depending on which of the two patches had been violated. That way, he wouldn't waste time running to the wrong patch.

But he knew there was only so much he could do to protect the pumpkins. "No matter what, you're always at the mercy of the weather," he said. And so far in 2006, weather had not been on their side. It had started out cool and wet, with frosts hanging on until the middle of June. Then the temperatures began to swing wildly, from hot to cool.

Despite the erratic weather, both of Gerry's pumpkins were fast out of the gate, estimated at more than 300 pounds apiece. One revved up to gain a brisk 34 pounds a day until the weather turned and a two-day cold snap stopped it in its tracks. By the end of July it had started growing again, but it was only putting on about 24 pounds a day. Gerry was worried it wouldn't pick up its former pace. "I've been doing the up-and-down thing, and I don't like that. I like consistency," she said.

Neither of Larry's pumpkins was growing quite as well as Gerry's. One plant had developed a genetic defect, growing tendrils in places tendrils shouldn't grow. And then the main vine stopped growing. Larry trained a side vine to take its place, but that had set him back two weeks. His second pumpkin was just not growing as fast as he wanted. So far it didn't look like his year.

That was okay. Larry was still busy being world champion. Officially, he was the world's best giant-pumpkin grower, and he was in demand. His phone rang several times a day with questions from other growers around the country. E-mails filled his in-box. Larry knew he had a bull's-eye on his back this year. Everyone in the world was aiming to beat his record. But he was still willing to share anything he knew. In their early growing years, Larry and Gerry had leaned on other pumpkin growers to find out how to grow the giants. They were grateful for the time their mentors spent with them, and they were determined to do the same for other rookies.

Early Monday, July 31, in Massachusetts, Steve Connolly had made his usual dawn inspection of his pumpkins and then turned the sprinklers on in his patch to give the plants a drink before he left for work. The pumpkins all looked good and were growing steadily. At more than 600 pounds, the 1068 was still his runaway star. Steve stepped back and admired his garden in its midsummer glory. It was blanketed in a solid canopy of leaves floating two to three feet above the dirt. The curving tops of yellow and ivory pumpkins peeked above the leaves, accented by bright-blue shade tarps. Sprays of water from the sprinkler caught the sun and arched in shimmering gold through the air. Steve left for work with that idyllic picture still in his head. His garden looked better than it ever had. His 1068 was well on its way to a world record.

That evening, when Steve got home from work, it was cracked open.

Not a big crack. Just a thin, dark line, about two inches long, starting at the base of the stem and running into the shell. It probably would have gone unnoticed by the casual observer. Steve's first hope, his only hope, was that the crack didn't go all the way through to the hollow seed cavity inside the pumpkin. If it did, then air would already have seeped into the sterile, closed internal environment of the pumpkin, introducing microbes, fungi, bacteria, and rot. But if the crack was only skin-deep, there was a chance it would heal over. Steve didn't kid himself. He had feared this exact thing. The 1068 had been growing too fast. It was still growing fast, and as it grew, the crack would just get bigger.

By Tuesday, the crack was longer, wider. By early Wednesday morning, Steve knew it was over. He poked a stick into the black depths of the crevice, now several inches long, and it went all the way through the meat to the void in the center. In the summer heat, it wasn't going to take long for the 1068 to start stinking. So before he left for the office, Steve got his shovel, lifted it high over the pale-orange sphere, and plunged it down with grim resolve. At least this part, ramming the shovel down to crack open the pumpkin, then chopping it up into smaller pieces, was a way of venting frustration. The vine, whose every leaf he had sweated over for three months, was trampled into the soft dirt as he worked. There was no need to be careful anymore. The plant was officially 2006 history. Steve buried the pumpkin pieces in the garden soil as food for next year's plants.

He was deep in thought as he worked. This was no time to whine about what might have been. It was time to start thinking about what he might do to solve the problem next year. This was the exact same place in the garden where a pumpkin had grown like crazy and then blown up last year. There was something about that area of land that was making them grow rampant, he realized. "Next year, I might go in with a different attitude," he said. "I'll water less. Fertilize this spot less. Try to slow down the growth."

Steve finished the job and left for work. Last year he'd lost his largest pumpkin about this same time, and he still finished the season with three pumpkins, weighing 855 pounds, 1,214.5 pounds, and 1,333 pounds. The biggest one had fetched him second place at the Frerich's Farm weigh-off, beaten only by Scott Palmer's 1,443-pounder. This year he still had four other plants that needed his care and attention to make it to weigh-off time. "Four others with great potential," he reminded himself. He needed to be thinking about those.

Steve had already pulled off one miracle in his patch. Earlier in July, he'd noticed a foamy, slimy liquid, like half-whipped egg whites, pooling at the base of one of his plants. It was leaking from the stump, soaking into the ground leaving a muddy, foam-flecked goo on top. Steve had treated it with fungicide and set up a fan to blow across the stump, trying to dry it out. And then he had let the main vine grow and keep growing, as long as it wanted. The base of the vine eventually rotted out, but by then Steve had 30 feet of vine growing out beyond the bad spot, providing plenty more roots to feed the pumpkin.

Steve's pumpkin, it turned out, had been among the first to come down with the foaming stump slime that now was beginning to take a heavy toll on the plants of nearly every top grower along the East Coast. The fast-spreading scourge was shaping up to be the 2006 season's dream-killer. For those plants that had survived the flooding rains of spring, the wet year had set up ideal conditions for disease. Fungal spores and bacteria flourished in the water-logged soil, humid air, and warm temperatures. And once a disease got started in a pumpkin patch, it was tough to root it out before all hopes for a world-champion season were destroyed. That had been the Wallaces' perennial sad story. And this year, grower after grower in the soggy eastern United States was coming down with the same mysterious disease.

Jerry Rose and Quinn Werner, two of the Ohio Valley's finest growers, with formidable records of producing 1,000-plus-pound pumpkins, were fighting the slime in their patches. Of Werner's 14 plants, 12 were infected. The problem usually started near the base of the vine, and unless it was stopped, it would creep farther along the vine, rotting the plant from the inside out, slowing the pumpkin's growth and eventually infecting the fruit itself.

Werner's infected plants were still growing a respectable 20 to 30 pounds a day. "But I think they would be doing a little more," he said. "It could be costing me two to eight pounds a day, and that adds up like crazy." His fear was that the problem would get worse.

No one knew what the disease was, though there were many guesses. Some growers believed it was caused by *Fusarium* or *Pythium,* two of the notorious plant-rotting fungi that pumpkin growers fought every year. So they hit the infected plants with an assortment of fungicides. Jerry Rose thought it was a bacterial problem, so he'd been using alcohol to try to disinfect the plant. Otherwise, all that growers could do was drain and clean the infected spot, then set up fans to blow air over the stump to dry it up and try to stop the rot.

It was no cure, but they hoped to slow down the infection long enough to get their pumpkins through the season without too much damage. As a last resort, growers would cut the main vine off the stump to keep the rot from spreading to the rest of the plant. The trend of growing larger plants meant the plants had more-extensive root systems. As Steve Connolly had found out in Massachusetts, the plant could still thrive without its stump, and the pumpkin could still grow. But a damaged plant without a stump seemed to have a poor chance of producing a world-record specimen.

Mother Nature can be heartless, but she's not the only one doling out misfortune in the pumpkin patch. Growers also have to worry about their fellow man. In early

August 2005, Randy and Debbie Sundstrom had had four big, beautiful pumpkins growing in their New York pumpkin patch. A couple of them had prizewinning potential. But as they checked on their pumpkins one evening, they noticed the water tank next to the patch, which had been full just that morning, was drained dry. There was a large wet spot on the ground beneath the tank, as if the spigot had been left open. "We knew somebody had been there," recalled Randy.

Then he looked more closely at the plants. The leaves looked wrong. They were a little droopy and were starting to pucker up. "I thought, 'Oh no, something isn't right,' " he said. The Sundstroms suspected someone had poisoned their plants, and they quickly washed them off as well as they could. But it was too late. By the next morning, the plants were lying flat on the ground, as if a tractor had rolled across them.

The murder of a pumpkin isn't something a grower takes lightly. It gave Randy insight into the phenomenon of temporary insanity. "I wanted to kill pretty bad," he said. The couple called the police to report the crime, to no avail. "Pumpkins?" the police officer said. "You gotta be kidding me!"

Every competition has its scoundrels and

cheaters, and giant-pumpkin growing is no exception. Pumpkins are uniquely vulnerable, as they are often left unattended and unprotected in wide-open fields or yards where anyone, under the cover of night or while growers are away at work, can slip in and end a season with a few whacks of a hammer.

Winning is a powerful tonic. Overnight, a world-champion grower becomes a pumpkin maharishi, with other growers reaching out to tap their skills and wisdom. Congratulatory e-mails and phone calls pour in from pumpkin peers around the world. Television and newspaper reporters request pictures and interviews with the person who has just grown the biggest pumpkin in the world. Even television talk shows come calling — past winners have traveled to New York to appear (or have their pumpkins appear) on *Live with Regis and Kathie Lee, The Martha Stewart Show,* and the *Late Show with David Letterman.*

After the first rush of attention dies down, the world champion gets a yearlong victory lap to revel in the crown. The official presentation of the orange jacket is made in March at the annual growers' conference in Niagara Falls. The champion is invited to speak at grower seminars and pumpkin events. They're asked again and again to — just one more time — tell the story of how they did it. And even after the baton is passed to a new champion, winning growers get to claim the title for life, their name forever coupled with their world title.

Even at the local level, where growers compete in front of friends and family, egos are on the line and the desire to beat a neighbor can sometimes overtake good sense.

The Sundstroms had only been growing a few years, but they'd been extraordinarily successful, winning local weigh-offs and unseating other past champions. The couple had no room for a giant-pumpkin patch at their home at the foot of the Catskill Mountains, west of New York City. So they made a patch on a vacant lot owned by Debbie's parents about 15 minutes away. The lot had no utilities, so they kept a 3,800-gallon water tank in a trailer, filled it with water each week, and parked it at the patch to water their plants.

After the sabotage incident, the Sundstroms sent in plant samples to a laboratory for testing. The lab confirmed that weed killer had been sprayed on their pumpkins. They could never prove it, but they suspected a jealous grower of trying to knock them out of the year's competition — though Randy didn't like to dignify the vandal by calling him a grower. "If he was a true pumpkin grower, he would know how hard you work to get that pumpkin success-fully to the weigh-off," Randy said, noting that a true grower "would never do some-thing like that."

Later in the year, the house across the street from their patch went up for sale, and the Sundstroms bought it and moved in so they could keep a closer eye on their pump-kins. They installed lights and surveillance cameras on the lot's driveway and along the pathways of the garden. And they recruited spies from the neighborhood to keep an eye on things while they were at work during the day. "We have everybody driving by our garden watching out for us," Randy said.

Sabotage isn't the only way to cheat. With weight being the determining factor, the pumpkin's hollow core presents a tantaliz-ing opportunity to bulk up a pumpkin from the inside out. Growers often joke about filling their pumpkin with sand or some other heavy substance to increase its weight. They laugh over the notion of pumpkins filled with cement. They call them "white dwarfs," like the collapsed stars that are among the densest objects in the universe.

But the jokes aren't that far away from reality. Years ago, a grower on the East Coast cut a small hole in his pumpkin, filled it with water, and then plugged the hole so that it was nearly invisible. The trick was discovered after the pumpkin sloshed as it was carried to the scale and suspicious judges cut a hole in it. As Dick Wallace tells it, "The water gushed out like diarrhea out of a cow's behind."

The trick inspired the rule disqualifying damaged pumpkins from competition. Bruises and scars and even some soft spots are allowed, but there can be no holes or cracks, no matter how tiny, that penetrate through the shell to the seed cavity. Through the growing season, competitors are given tremendous leeway in their pursuit of the biggest, heaviest pumpkin. There is no limit to the kinds of fertilizers or additives that can be tried, and no restrictions on the growing techniques that can be used. But once the pumpkin is cut from the vine, it's got to be 100 percent pure fruit; no foreign substances are allowed anywhere near it, not even vegetable oil to give the skin a shine.

That decree has caused much heartbreak among honest growers who have had a pumpkin disqualified when it developed a minuscule fracture right before a weigh-off. But it's also led to a new dedication to good sportsmanship in the hobby.

Ohio Valley pumpkin grower Dave Stelts was watching broadcasts of the 2004 Winter Olympics when television commentators reminded viewers of the story of the bobsledders in the 1964 games in Innsbruck, Austria. British bobsledders Tony Nash and Robin Dixon had broken an axle bolt on their two-man bobsled before their final run. Their Italian rivals loaned them the part. The British team fixed their sled and went on to win the gold medal, while the Italian team that had helped them came in third. The incident went down in history as one of the most inspiring moments ever in sports competition.

"That's the kind of generosity you find in the pumpkin world," Dave recalled thinking to himself. "We'll give you all the tips and all the information. And then if you beat me, you beat me. But if I beat you, I know I'm beating you at your best."

It hadn't always been that way. When the sporting aspect of the hobby was gaining momentum in the 1980s, thanks to Howard Dill's Atlantic Giant seed, most growers striving to grow the Big One jealously guarded both their seeds and information. Few were willing to share anything that might give another grower an advantage. Bad blood boiled up frequently among growers, who were then more adversaries than colleagues.

The constant backbiting and petty rivalries led to a fracturing of the competitive-growing community. At one point in 1993, rival groups bickered over who could claim the world record — each group claimed the other group's top grower had broken the rules and should be disqualified. Finally, the leader of the group with the smaller pumpkin succeeded in registering with the Guinness Book of World Records.

The move was viewed as the ultimate in competitive nastiness, and support consolidated around the group that felt cheated, the Great Pumpkin Commonwealth. In recent years, the GPC has been the ruling organization over most weigh-offs around the country, save for some West Coast growers who have stuck with the rival International Pumpkin Association. Today, the GPC recognizes its own grower, Donald Black, as the 1993 world-record holder for his 884-pound pumpkin.

The secretiveness that had ruled over the hobby early on gradually faded away as the

Internet came along. There are few secrets on the World Wide Web. Growers began posting Internet pages with tips and instructions on how to grow the giants. Web sites devoted to pumpkins and giant pumpkins began appearing, complete with pictures and records of all the world champions. Growers soon realized the wealth of information publicly available to any newcomer was actually helping the hobby, not hurting it. The shorter learning curve meant a new grower could easily produce a 300- or 500-pound pumpkin the first year. Those speedy results encouraged even more people to try, and as more people tried it, more became addicted.

Competition got stiffer as people were able to quickly gain growing expertise and produce world-class pumpkins in just a few years, instead of the dozen or more years it used to take to figure it all out. Naturally, some of the old-timers resented that a little. But they also saw the benefits of bringing more people into the fold. New growing clubs were formed to accommodate the influx of growers, even in places like the Deep South, Arizona, and Alaska, where the miracle of growing a gigantic pumpkin was even more wondrous because of the cold or the heat or the humidity or the dryness. The more the clubs expanded, the more members there were to pay dues, bringing in more money for bigger prizes, which made the weigh-offs more exciting and attracted more people.

And so a new attitude was born among pumpkin growers — a Muskateerish one-for-all-and-all-for-one kind of creed where sharing information was applauded and stinginess and secrecy and dishonesty condemned. Except that pumpkin growers were still human beings with human foibles, and so every year there were still plenty of people whining and bellyaching. Sniping and gossiping about other growers' techniques or habits was a common and even popular pastime. And in the comfortable anonymity of the Internet, it could get quite vicious. Especially when growers were antsy and cranky and bored.

The desire to plant the best and "hottest" seeds each year came from the desire to win. And the stakes had only gotten higher in recent years as the prizes awarded at weigh-offs climbed into the realm of real money. A championship pumpkin could easily win $3,000 to $5,000 at just one weigh-off, and the amount could be doubled or tripled if it set a new world record.

Meanwhile, the plant-variety protection

— the botanical world's version of a patent — expired on Howard Dill's Atlantic Giant seeds in 2005, meaning anyone could sell or market giant-pumpkin seeds. Anyone at all. Which was a worry. Pumpkin seeds don't have fingerprints; there are no unique marks that can prove any given seed is authentic. So a dishonest seller could claim his seed was anything he wanted, and no one would be the wiser. Even among growers who swapped seeds, some of that had undoubtedly been going on. No one had kept a strict count, but growers noted hundreds of plants had been represented as 723 Bobiers over the years — many more than could possibly have existed. A reputation for honesty and integrity was a competitive pumpkin grower's only guarantee of authenticity. So those who prized championship genetics over everything else could not risk obtaining a seed from an unknown grower. They planted a seed only if they had bred it themselves, or if they knew it came from a trusted competitor with the same high standards. This is why a doctored photograph of a pumpkin grown in Germany ignited a raging controversy early in 2006. The pumpkin was proclaimed by its grower to have set a new European record at 1233.5 pounds. Not only that, but it was a gorgeous, round, orangey-red fruit. The young grower, a college student, posted pictures of his champion on his BigPumpkins.com diary. It was both beast and beauty, and the pumpkin world buzzed with admiration. "This really has a good chance to be a landmark seed . . . imagine the flood of new orange genetics that will be produced next year all coming from that one pumpkin," wrote one grower on BigPumpkins.com.

Sure enough, the young grower was bombarded with requests for seeds. Then someone noticed that the picture he'd posted was a fake. It was a crude digital cut-and-paste job. If the photo was a fake, was the pumpkin a fraud, too? The prospect of a questionable seed entering competitive bloodlines in a big way was a disturbing prospect to many serious growers. Debate raged in the cyber hallways of BigPumpkins.com over whether the seed should be accepted or boycotted.

The young grower defended himself. He said his camera had broken and he hadn't been able to get a picture of his pumpkin as it was weighed. He admitted the photo he'd posted was doctored, but he insisted the pumpkin was genuine. In the end, each grower had to make up his own mind whether to plant the seed. Some stood behind it. But many wouldn't touch it. "Too many questions for me," said one veteran grower.

As the summer heat wave wore on, air conditioners were turned on high and the nation's power grid continued to strain with the unprecedented demand for electricity. The air, still packed with moisture from the heavy rains, created smothering, saunalike conditions. As summer's furnace heated up the air, black thunderclouds boiled up in the sky each afternoon, exploding with violent blasts of rain and wind and lightning. And Southern New England pumpkin growers seemed to have a bull's-eye on them.

Another violent thunderstorm swept across Massachusetts and into Rhode Island the first week of August. Part of Steve Connolly's patch was flattened, sending him to the hardware store for bamboo to prop up his leaves. "I think God invented bamboo for us pumpkin growers," he said.

Peter Rondeau had just arrived home from work when the same storm reared up and sent him running into his backyard to batten down the hatches. "It was really lightning," Peter said. "The dogs were barking, the wind was blowing. Everything was going crazy. I'm running out there with the hail hitting me in the head, and I'm wondering, 'What am I doing?' "

Peter's small yard turned out to be an advantage, as his house and trees provided good wind protection from the storm's fury. The Wallaces suffered a few rolled vines and some broken leaves. Ron was at work when the storm hit, so he woke up at 5 the next morning to repair the damage before the sun came out in full force.

Ron and his dad had measured their pumpkins a few days before the end of July, and Ron was afraid to let himself believe the numbers. Despite his vow to stay calm, he couldn't help it; hope bubbled in his chest. They had several strong growers. The biggest was the 500 Wallace, measuring an estimated 416 pounds and gaining 31 pounds a day. But there was a 1068 estimated at 407 pounds, even though it was three days younger and it was gaining a whopping 38 pounds a day. That one made Ron's stomach do a flip-flop — it was a world-record pace. And there was another 1068 closing in on 400 with gains of 37 pounds a day.

Now was not the time to be knocked out of commission by a storm. Ron worked three hours, rolling the vines back into position, trimming off broken leaves and propping up bent ones. He hoped he wouldn't suffer too much of a setback, but the storm wasn't his main worry. His main worry was the foaming stump slime that had made its appearance in the Wallace patch a few days before.

The first sign of the disease had appeared on a plant that already was having problems. It had never grown as well as the other plants, so when the stump began to foam, Ron and his dad decided to rip it out rather than try to save it. That way, they hoped to keep the disease from spreading to the other plants. But it was too late. A couple days later, Ron and his dad found one of their 1068s oozing foamy slime. They'd cleaned out the stump, applied fungicide, and set up a fan to blow on it. Then they started pampering the plants, hand-watering underneath the leaves like the Checkons, and pulling weeds that were competing for nutrients. Ron spent $250 for a gallon of commercial-grade fungicide used to fight disease on golf courses. He drenched his patch and shared the fungicide with other club members.

The weather refused to cooperate. Ron described it as "swampy and nasty," like he'd never felt it before. Just as things started to dry out, another thunderstorm would roll up and dump another inch or two of rain. The garden never got a chance to dry out. No wonder disease was showing up. Ron and Dick finally decided to remove the stump from the diseased 1068 to keep the infection from killing the whole plant. Ron cut the main vine a few feet from its base, then pulled up the stump and threw it away. He still had a big plant left, with a huge root system from the buried vines. This would be the real test of the mycorrhizae program he'd been following. Had it built enough of a root system to keep the plant alive and the pumpkin growing? Apparently so. The stumpless 1068 continued to grow, though it had slowed from gaining 26 pounds a day to 20, based on the measurements Ron and Dick were taking more frequently now. Ron found that interesting: "Maybe this time of year, the stump doesn't matter as much as we think."

The Wallaces stepped up their fertilizing program, so Ron was spraying the plants with compost tea every week. He was feeling good, despite the stump rot. "We're down to eight competition plants," he said. "If we can still get four or five to the scale, then you can't ask for anything more."

On his morning patrol later that week, Ron discovered a third plant with its stump foaming. It was the second 1068 to get it. Now he was rattled. Is this how it was going to be? He'd heard the horror stories from the other growers that year. He knew some had seen their entire patch ravaged by the disease, with one plant after another going down. Not another year like that, he prayed. Other problems were cropping up. The spider mites had returned and done more damage. The hot weather had meant more-frequent watering and Ron's shallow well couldn't keep up. Then around dusk one evening, Ron was in the patch working when he heard something rustling. He looked up and saw a baby deer frolicking through the pumpkins. It jumped over two plants, then ran back out through the cheap plastic netting he'd used as a deer fence. The deer hadn't hurt the pumpkins, but Ron found several holes ripped in the fence. Obviously, his budget solution wasn't working so well. A bigger deer might do some real damage.

Meanwhile, several other growers in the club were worried. Their pumpkins had started growing more slowly in recent days, stressed by the extreme heat. Peter Rondeau had seen his pumpkins' daily weight gains drop by 10 pounds. They were starting to pick up again, but now the forecast was predicting a cool front, with temperatures dropping into the low 50s or high 40s. That was bad. Hot weather followed by cold was the perfect prescription for splitting a pumpkin. The cold tightened up the pumpkin's skin just as it needed to stretch the most. Last year, the Wallaces lost two pumpkins after temperatures dipped into the 50s one summer night. So out came the blankets, even thought it was only the first week of August. Growers would layer the blankets on top of the pumpkins at night and not take them off until the sun was high the next morning. Ron held off watering his patch, just in case. That would help slow the growth and hopefully put less strain on the pumpkins. After that, it was just a matter of luck. And luck had never favored the Wallaces.

Over the next few days, the foaming stump slime on the second 1068 got worse, so Ron cut the stump off that plant too. That was a real disappointment, since it was one of their better pumpkins. But the other pumpkin he was growing on a stumpless

1068 plant was still gaining weight, so he hoped for the best. "If we can just make it to the middle of August, if my other plants can stay upright, I think we can ride it home," he said.

Now they were down to seven healthy plants, all with the potential to go over 1,300 pounds. Maybe there were even a couple of contest winners. Maybe even — why not? — a world record. If they could just hold it together. That was Ron's mantra now, every hour of every day. Just hold it together.

"You only need one pumpkin," he said. "One is all it takes to win."

And the Wallaces still had nine. Nine giant pumpkins growing in what six months ago had been a field of pine trees. Ron and Dick could see all the flaws with their expert eyes, but visitors saw a 7,500-square-foot garden bursting with lush, green pumpkin plants. Above the surface of the tall leaves, like boats bobbing on a sea of green, the half-moon shapes of pumpkins were rising higher every day. Now they were easily visible from the road, and attracting the attention of passersby.

One night, as Dick sat on his front porch reading over the day's measurements, a car drove up to the house and parked on the shoulder of the road. A man jumped out and ran over to the pumpkin patch, furtively snapping a picture with his camera.

"Then he ran like hell back to his car," Dick said, laughing. "All he had to do was ask."

12
Humpty Dumpty

On August 3, plant pathologist Olaf Ribeiro received a box packed with pieces of rotting pumpkin vines from Ohio grower Jerry Rose. Ribeiro ran a private laboratory at his home on Bainbridge Island, Washington, near Seattle. He was an expert in diagnosing plant diseases, and pumpkin growers hoped he would be able to figure out what was causing the foaming stump slime that was putting so many of them out of business that summer. Ribeiro had talked to Jerry and other growers on the phone in recent days and was expecting the package. "Oh my God, does my lab smell of rotting pumpkins," he complained after it arrived. In his business, though, he'd smelled worse. His lab assistant now refused to touch any package that was labeled "garlic."

Ribeiro's work with pumpkins was the tiniest of sidelines, one that he really didn't have time for, but also that he couldn't resist. He respected the growers' novice efforts to understand complex plant science, and he was impressed by the time and effort they spent trying to get their pumpkins to grow ever larger. He'd been sucked in to the giant-pumpkin world a few years earlier by Washington grower Geneva Emmons. She'd been fighting disease in her pumpkin patch, and had heard that Ribeiro specialized in how the soil's microbial environment affected plant health. Ribeiro was skeptical about trying to help. Giant pumpkins? World records? "I hadn't ever heard of such a thing," he said.

Ribeiro spent his time hunting down crop-destroying pathogens to save commercial farmers from ruin. Major landscaping companies and West Coast billionaires hired him to solve problems with sick or dying plants. He had no time for backyard pumpkins. Politely, he put her off. But Emmons called back, and Ribeiro agreed to look at soil samples from her garden.

"It starts like anything else," he said. "You're curious, and then all of a sudden, you're in the middle of something that you never expected to be in the middle of." Ribeiro saw immediately that Emmons was doing several things wrong. After following his suggestions, Emmons went on to set the

2001 world record with a 1,262-pound pumpkin. She told Ribeiro that she'd spread the word that he had helped her.

"Oh," said Ribeiro. "Great."

Soon, the scientist's phone was ringing with pumpkin growers calling from all over the world: Europe, Japan, and South Africa, as well as North America. Ribeiro was taken aback. He had no idea there were so many people in the world interested in growing giant pumpkins. But he understood how a person could acquire a passion for something. Ribeiro's own passion was saving trees. He had a theory that trees could live virtually forever if they were provided with the right growing conditions. The key, he believed, was the microorganisms in the dirt, which had evolved in sync with trees for hundreds of millions of years, and which were destroyed by modern farming techniques and the spread of urban civilization. Fix the dirt, save the tree.

Ribeiro applied his philosophy about trees to giant pumpkins. "I figured if I could keep trees growing forever, why can't I help these pumpkins get to be one ton? The genetics are there. It's just a matter of doing it right."

He'd found that the pumpkin growers weren't so different from his commercial clients — both were seeking a competitive edge that would help them succeed. But Jerry Rose's giant-pumpkin stump samples couldn't have arrived at a worse time. The pumpkin growers were in the middle of the most crucial phase of their growing season, and so were a great many commercial farmers.

Every day, Ribeiro Plant Lab was receiving samples in the mail from farmers who were watching their tomato or potato crop succumb to some unnamed blight. Everyone, of course, needed immediate answers. He was stretched thin, working late into the night and every weekend to diagnose problems. The commercial farmers depended on getting an answer quick enough to solve the problem, save the crop, and escape financial ruin. The stakes were somewhat lower for giant-pumpkin growers. But Ribeiro could not bear to disappoint his friends in the pumpkin patch. "I'm buried with samples of citrus and chives right now, and in between I'm trying to figure out the giant pumpkins," he said, a little amazed at himself. "I guess I just like a challenge."

And the foaming stump slime was intriguing. He had received several calls from panicked East Coast growers, while none of the West Coast growers seemed to be having the problem. A few, including Rose and at least one other Ohio grower, had sent in samples for testing. Ribeiro concluded that the hot, wet weather in the East, combined with the supernatural growth of these giants, was straining the pumpkins' systems to the limit, putting the plants under so much stress that they were vulnerable to disease that they might ordinarily be able to fight off. "Disease is opportunistic," he explained to the growers when they called. "It attacks a plant that's weakened."

Ribeiro believed pumpkin growers were victims of their own enthusiasm. They watered too much and tilled too much and fertilized too much, upsetting the natural balance of the soil. Unwittingly, they wound up creating a microenvironment that inhibited the good kind of bacteria and fungi, and encouraged the growth of bad microbes that cause disease. Meanwhile, the plants already were under huge stress as they strained to grow unnaturally large fruit. When the plant began to show signs of a problem, the growers typically rushed in with a grab bag of fungicides and fertilizers and wound up killing off more of the good guys and feeding the bad guys. "They create a monster," Ribeiro said. It was just this kind of vicious cycle that had plagued the Wallaces' pumpkins through the years.

It frustrated Ribeiro, who had found that pumpkin growers would often discard his advice when they didn't see immediate results and go back to carpet-bombing the pumpkins with chemicals. "They don't understand that it's a patience game," he said. "This is science. You don't fly by the seat of your pants."

But Ribeiro also realized the pumpkin growers' panic was driven by the fact that there was only a limited amount of time in the season. One lost week of growth could put an end to a whole year's worth of hard work and dreams. So when Jerry Rose's diseased pumpkin samples arrived, Ribeiro set aside his other jobs and worked until midnight preparing tests that would help him isolate any bacteria or fungi growing in the plant.

Within a couple of days, he'd identified several nasty actors at work on the vines, which were teeming with a combination of harmful fungus and bacteria. Among other things, he isolated *Colletotrichum,* a fungus that usually causes black splotches on leaves. In Rose's sample, Ribeiro found that "fruiting bodies of this fungus were profuse up and down the stem." He also detected the bacterium *Pseudomonas* at work. "This has caused the stems to turn mushy." And in a sample from another Ohio grower, Ribeiro detected the notorious *Fusarium*.

All of these were made worse with an excess of nitrogen or moisture in the soil, he noted. He reported his findings to the growers and recommended a combination of fungicide treatments, as well as some organic controls.

"Let's hope we can turn it around in time," he said.

The disease, meanwhile, continued to boil up in other growers' patches. Dave Stelts walked into his Pennsylvania garden one morning to find three of his plants foaming, including the star of his patch, his 1068. To try to save them, he amputated the stumps and ripped out the diseased part of the vines, leaving about half the plant to support the pumpkins. They were still growing, though more slowly.

In Rhode Island, Peter Rondeau was battling the slime too. He'd had his wife and daughters e-mail him pictures of his plants while he was out of town for four days working in New York. They'd reported that he had a few leaves wilting on one of his plants. Not good, he thought, but he wasn't too worried. When he got home, though, he found the stump and part of the vine had rotted through. It was "mush mush mush

mush mush," he said. At least it was his little orange pumpkin plant that was infected, not his 1068. The 1068 had measured an estimated 500 pounds at the beginning of August, then had slowed down after the heat wave, but was still growing more than 20 pounds a day in mid-August.

"This is not a sport for the weak of heart," Peter said. "You never know what can happen at any given time — it could be a storm, it could be hail, it could be a disease. Who the hell knows?"

Early on Saturday, August 19, Steve Connolly and Joe Jutras made the three-hour drive north from Rhode Island for the New Hampshire Giant Pumpkin Growers Association patch tour and picnic. It was a neighborly gesture of support, but also a chance to see how one of their archrivals was measuring up so far that year. The 100 or so tour members traveled on two rented school buses, which pulled to a stop in the parking lot of His Mansion Ministries in Hillsboro about 10:30 a.m. Joe and Steve descended from their bus to the fairy-tale spectacle of 20 enormous pumpkins in shades of cream and orange rising above a field of spreading green leaves. This was Jim Ford's patch. It covered an acre of ground amid a complex of sheds and barns and auxiliary buildings at the residential Christian rehabilitation center where he worked as the agricultural supervisor. Ford oversaw the vegetable and fruit gardens that provided therapy for the center's residents and food for their table. And while he was at it, he grew a lot of giant pumpkins.

As the guests spread out to survey the patch, classical melodies streamed from two speakers attached to a barn flanking one side. The music wasn't for the guests. "Everything's for the pumpkins," Ford said. He'd heard that plants do better when accompanied by music. In fact, a lot of growers liked to broadcast to their pumpkin patches, including the Wallaces. But while most favored soothing symphonic tones, the Wallace pumpkins grew to the sounds of Van Morrison, Billy Joel, and the Rolling Stones.

Steve strolled the perimeter of Ford's garden, his tan Southern New England Giant Pumpkin Growers T-shirt tucked into a pair of white cargo shorts, a small digital camera slung over his shoulder. He studied the signs noting the pollination dates and estimated weight of each pumpkin. Ford's pumpkin patch was doing exceptionally well. There were some definite world-record

305

contenders there; pumpkins that, if they kept going, had the potential to reach 1,500 pounds and beyond. There was one that already had topped 900 pounds and another at 850 pounds that was still growing 30 pounds a day, when most growers were lucky to see 20. Steve pulled a small notebook out of his pocket — his portable record of all his pumpkins' vital statistics. His best contender was growing about 23 pounds a day. That wasn't as good as Ford's, but still not bad. At that time of year, with summer waning, growers were losing about three minutes of sun a day. "That's about half an hour a week, which, of course, is less growing time," Steve explained.

Ford was having his own problems, though. In the past week he had dug out more than 200 squash vine borers from the plants, using a pocketknife to slice into the vines, harpoon the fat grubs, and pull them out. Steve preferred to go after the borers with one of his wife's sewing needles. He'd sterilize it with alcohol, then poke it into the vine where the larvae were feasting, piercing them through. "I just let them die right inside the vine," Steve said. It was less traumatic for the plant that way, he believed. He called the technique "MIS" — minimally invasive surgery.

All growers attend patch tours with their own pumpkins in the back of their mind. It is a pumpkin growers' fate to worry. And perhaps the toughest worry to come to terms with is that they may not be doing something as well as another grower; that it wouldn't be rotten luck or Mother Nature that beat them, but their own bad judgment. Now, as Steve studied Ford's pumpkins and listened to Ford talk, doubts were creeping in. Steve had been watering his pumpkins every other day. He wanted to give the pumpkins plenty of water, but he feared getting them too wet and contributing to more disease. Here at the Ford patch, he heard something different. Ford watered every day — hundreds of gallons of water, *every day.* And it was working well for him. Steve was staring at the proof. Ford's pumpkins were growing bigger and faster than his.

Steve climbed back aboard the yellow school bus and took a seat next to the window. As the diesel engine roared to life and the bus pulled out of the parking lot, Steve made small talk with the other passengers, raising his soft voice to be heard above the sound of tires crunching across the gravel. But in a few minutes he fell silent and stared out the window, his mind a hundred miles away back at his own patch. His hand twitched at his side, reaching for the cell phone clipped to his belt. He unclipped the phone and held it in his hand, turning it over and staring at it, thinking. He opened the clamshell. Closed it. He bounced the phone gently in his hand as if weighing it, weighing his decision. "No," he said quietly to himself. And then more firmly: "No."

Steve clipped the phone back on his belt and suddenly seemed quite sure of himself. "You know," he said, "The biggest mistake a grower can make is changing course in the middle of the season. They'll go to someone's house, see someone's pumpkins that seem to be doing well, and hear that they're doing something different that seems to be working. So then they'll rush home and try it. And it'll shock the plant. And the next thing they know, their pumpkin has split or something else has gone wrong."

He delivered this speech with the conviction of a man who knew that particular demon well. Steve had just come this close — *this close* — to urgently calling home to ask his wife to start the sprinklers, even though the plants weren't due to be watered until the next day.

He'd managed to stop himself from making the call, but the thought nagged him for the rest of the tour, and he was still thinking about it as the bus headed back to New Hampshire grower Jim Beauchemin's house for a barbecue lunch. Beauchemin owned a landscaping company, and his house sat at the top of a hill surrounded by lushly landscaped grounds. Near the bottom, next to a pond, was Jim's pumpkin patch. He was hosting the tour picnic, as usual. The centerpiece of the meal was a whole pig roasted over coals in a giant barbecue pit. Tour members lined up to fill their plates and find a seat beneath the white canvas canopies set up to deflect rain and sun.

One grower, Ed Hemphill, carried a paper plate laden with roast pork, potato salad, and coleslaw to one of the long plastic tables arranged across Beauchemin's front lawn. Steve Connolly sat down across from Hemphill. There had been whispers buzzing through the tour all day about the Hemphill pumpkin. Almost nobody had heard of Ed Hemphill before that day. But rumor had it that the man had a massive fruit growing back at his home in New Brunswick, Canada — one bigger than anything else anyone had heard about that season. Hemphill was a tall, lean, 69-year-old with a leathery brown face. Large ears jutted from a head full of bristling dark brown hair cut short and flat on top. Only a smudge of gray showed at his temples, but his brow and mouth were etched with the deeply carved lines of a man who had spent a lifetime outdoors.

This was Hemphill's first time at the New Hampshire patch tour. He'd come with his live-in partner, Joan Kent, and the couple had kept mostly to themselves, standing apart like awkward strangers in the crowd of growers. Hemphill had the eager shyness of a man who finally had something to brag about, yet didn't want to make too much of it. He didn't even like saying how big his pumpkin had grown. But when Steve pressed him as they sat across from each other at lunch, he opened up. "More than eleven hundred pounds. I taped it just this morning," Hemphill said with a curt little nod of satisfaction. "And it's still growing twenty-three pounds a day."

Hemphill was as excited as a youngster. He'd tried something new that year, and it seemed to be working out. Since weight was all that counted at the end of the season, Ed had decided to weigh his baby pumpkins when they were a couple of weeks old to help him decide which one to keep on the plant. He put them on a scale right on the vine, then he compared the estimated weight to the actual weight, and kept the pumpkin on each vine that weighed the heaviest compared to its OTT measurements. "I'm an old man. I don't have time to grow 'em big, so I've got to grow 'em heavy," he said, his words rising and falling in a lilting Canadian cadence.

"I'd like to grow the world champion," Hemphill said, chuckling at what he knew must sound like an old man's pie-in-the-sky dream. "I was told I was in too cold a country to do it. But I'm on my way." Undoubtedly, he was, if his measurements were accurate. The weigh-off was still seven weeks away, plenty of time to get to 1,500 pounds, especially if the pumpkin was still growing more than 20 pounds a day.

Hemphill had started growing giant pumpkins after he was diagnosed with cancer in 1995. His doctor told him to put his affairs in order. He wasn't expected to live for long. "I've always said, 'You're going to die one way or another, so there's no use sitting and worrying about it,' " Hemphill said.

He'd looked around for something useful to do to keep his mind off his troubles, and he decided to grow potatoes. When the first

311

crop of potatoes were ready to harvest, he loaded them into the trunk of his car and delivered them around to people he knew. He developed a weekly route. "Every Tuesday evening, they knew I was coming. It took all evening to deliver them, because I like to talk."

Hemphill confounded his doctors that year by not dying. Not that year and not the next. During his 2006 checkup in February, his doctor told him, "I don't know why you're still living, but the cancer isn't going to kill you now."

Hemphill thinks the potatoes saved his life. "I've seen people, as soon as they heard they had cancer, they faded right away just like a rotten pumpkin," he said. But when he was working in the garden, "I couldn't care less if I was going to live six months or six years," he said. "Every day is a plus for me now."

The year after he grew his potatoes, he decided to try giant pumpkins. He got hooked, and he'd been growing them ever since. In 2005, he'd taken third place with an 1,171-pounder at a weigh-off in Windsor, Nova Scotia. That put him on the map of big Canadian growers, but he was still a nobody in the United States. He had trouble getting the top seeds he wanted. "The

Americans never e-mail me or call me back," he said. He'd asked the Wallaces for a 1068 seed over the winter — "I almost begged them for one" — but Ron had turned him down. Then, just before planting time that spring, the seed had arrived in the mail. Hemphill had a decent pumpkin growing on his 1068, but that wasn't his big one. His big one was growing on a seed he'd gotten from Jim Beauchemin.

One of the reasons Hemphill had come down to New Hampshire was to talk to growers and get their advice. His main strategy now was to keep the pumpkins heavily watered. Steve Connolly paid extra attention when Hemphill talked about that. "You gotta have lots of water to grow these beasts," Hemphill said. "I'd rather weigh a wet pumpkin. It's heavier than a dry one."

Steve excused himself from the table and joined a group talking with Larry and Gerry Checkon. The Checkons had been invited as special guests at the tour. All day Larry had been surrounded by growers seeking the wisdom of the world champion. Now someone asked, "How often do you water?"

"Every day," Larry said. "We water every day."

That did it for Steve. He backed away and grabbed his cell phone and dialed home.

No one answered, but Steve wasn't about to let that stop him. Now that he'd made up his mind, he wanted to get the sprinklers going on his pumpkins and to get them going *now*. He called his next-door neighbor, who was Pakistani and had a weak command of English. "You want me to do *what?*" the puzzled man asked. Finally, Steve was able to explain what he needed, and the neighbor agreed to take care of it. Steve snapped his cell phone shut with a sheepish grin.

As the days of August unfolded, as thousands of giant pumpkins in backyards across the world gorged on nutrient-fat soils and siphoned up thousands of gallons of water, as shells creaked and groaned and bulged and swelled with unnatural swiftness, a wail of anguish rose. The pumpkins were beginning to blow.

"These pumpkins, they really know how to hurt us," a grower wrote on BigPump kins.com. The ones you love most are the ones that can hurt you worst — and that was no less true in the pumpkin patch. In early August, world-record contenders were a dime a dozen. But it was the biggest and fastest-growing pumpkins, the ones that inspired dreams of glory, that were usually the first to go.

Every competitive grower has a story of the one that got away. Some stories were more painful than others. In 2003, New Hampshire grower Bruce Whittier had a pumpkin estimated to be 1,250 pounds when it blew a small hole in its blossom end, on August 23. The hole went all the way through to the cavity, so it disqualified the pumpkin from competition. But growers sometimes have a hard time letting go. Whittier patched the hole with grafting wax to see if the pumpkin would keep growing. When it split again on September 7, he took it off the vine and weighed it on an official scale — it was 1,458 pounds. It was the biggest pumpkin ever grown at that point, far bigger than the 1,385-pound pumpkin that set the official new world record that year. In fact, it would have beaten the 2004 world record of 1,446 too. But the rules say a damaged pumpkin doesn't count.

Growers console each other with misery-loves-company bravado. "If you're not blowin' 'em, you're not growin' 'em," they say. There was a certain prestige in suffering heartbreak in the garden and then coming back for more the next year. One of Jim Beauchemin's pumpkins had split just days before he hosted the New Hampshire tour.

315

He left it on the vine as a reminder of the odds facing anyone who tried to grow the giants. Growers filed past, nodding in somber recognition at the yellow carcass still sheltered under its plastic hoop tent. The pumpkin looked perfect from every angle except one: the blossom end gaped open with a split 10 inches long and nearly 3 inches wide.

Cracks can show up anywhere on a pumpkin, but the most vulnerable places are the blossom end, where the flower once grew atop the baby fruit, and the stem end, where it is attached to the vine. Giant pumpkins also have a peculiar habit of forming "sag lines" — cracks that split their internal walls but don't always break through the skin. Sag lines were thought to be a legacy of the genetic tinkering that produced Howard Dill's Atlantic Giant, so the defects were also referred to as "Dill rings." But most growers now called them sag lines, which was more descriptive of the deep crevices that would develop across the pumpkin where it was splitting internally. From the outside it looks as if a belt has been cinched around the pumpkin, squeezing it in. These indentations were greatly feared among growers, as they indicated a weak point where a pumpkin might split — and many often did.

August was the peak time for growing and the peak time for blowing. Pumpkins literally cracked under the strain of putting on 30 to 50 pounds a day while adjusting to changes in temperature and water. Growers ventured into their patches each morning with their hearts in their throats, checking over their pumpkins like paramedics examining an accident victim. Every grower knew the odds — more than half wouldn't make it through the season. But every grower hoped the bad luck would pass him by.

As the pumpkins popped, growers retreated to BigPumpkins.com to lick their wounds. "This very morning she blew a dime-sized hole at a segment dead center on the Dill ring," wrote "docgipe" of Mountoursville, Pennsylvania. "Dadgum it anyhow . . . I finally had a good grow going."

"We now have a split into the cavity on our 560lb LaRue," said "Creekside" of Santa Cruz, California.

"My 898 gave way today to a small 1/2 inch split," said "Pennsylvania Rock."

Matt, of New Hampshire, posted a disconsolate note in his grower's diary: "Things look bleak. I am just about done. The 1081 has a deep stem split and the 953 has slowed to a crawl. It has been a very unpleasant season for me and I am quite certain that I will be taking next year off in favor of a vacation."

On August 12, Don Young of Des Moines, Iowa, had proudly recorded the championship pace of his 1068 in his grower's diary: "1068 day 47: 1,002 pounds."

On August 20, he reported, "1068 split in sag line = real sad day."

Ron Wallace was in his element. With a long white apron snugged around his waist, he hovered over a six-foot-long gas grill set up outside the Pumpkin Shack, adding water to a simmering pot, giving something in a pan a stir, peeking under a tinfoil lid to check the progress of another dish warming on the burner. Behind him, a hubbub of voices arose as growers arrived with their families and the booze and banter began to flow. The Wallaces were hosting the Southern New England Giant Pumpkin Growers' summer picnic. Ron had scaled the usual patch tour back to a simple social gathering this year as part of his campaign to reduce his workload.

Just as the guests began to arrive for the 2 p.m. picnic, though, black clouds darkened the horizon. Within a few minutes, the wind picked up, whipping the white tablecloths off the picnic tables, and then the skies opened and the rain poured down. The picnic guests huddled under the porch and inside the Pumpkin Shack waiting for the storm to pass. Water gushed from the sky in a downpour so heavy it was difficult to see 10 feet beyond the edge of the porch. The storm moved fast, passing by in only 15 minutes. The tables and chairs were dried off, and Ron went back to his cooking as the guests continued to arrive. By now everyone was used to the afternoon thunderstorms.

As he manned the grill, Ron nursed a frozen mudslide, a potent concoction of Kahlúa and Baileys Irish Cream. Children played in a red and blue bounce-house set up on the lawn, and guests wandered back and forth across the wet grass from the Pumpkin Shack to the pumpkin patch. The Wallace plants looked good. Their pumpkins look good. But word of the impressive fruit seen at the previous day's New Hampshire patch tour already had reached Ron, stirring up his competitive juices. When a guest commented on how good the Wallace pumpkins looked, Ron couldn't resist a little chest-puffing. "That'll give those fellas in New Hampshire a run for their money, eh?" he said. But he immediately dropped the bluster. "Nawwww, just kidding. You know I'm just kidding," he said.

Ron and his dad were both working hard to contain their excitement. This was partly out of superstition — Ron was afraid that bragging at this point would put the jinx on him for sure. But it was also to protect their sanity. If they thought they had a potential world-record pumpkin out there, if they thought they really had a shot, they probably wouldn't be able to sleep again until the October 7 weigh-off.

For the picnic, Dick had put up signs in front of each pumpkin with the pollination date and the parentage, but without the estimated weights many growers displayed. Instead, Dick had scrawled names and captions for the different pumpkins. "Hard charger," he called one promising 1068. "Blockhead," he named a squarish pumpkin. The 500 Wallace, which had the same genetics as the 1068, except the mother and father were reversed, was the biggest pumpkin in the patch so far, and Dick named that one "Pap's Pride." For another 1068 that had been crossed with the 1354 Checkon seed, he scrawled, "Could be?" in a corner of the sign.

One of the 1068s that had lost its base to the foaming slime had stopped growing shy of 500 pounds. The sign on that one said, "Deer Food. Eat me."

Dick was having more fun than usual this year. He wasn't as tied up in knots as he usually was at this point in the season, trying to calculate and recalculate their odds of success with every shifting breeze. Maybe he'd finally learned to chill out. Maybe he was just tired. Maybe it was because he was hoping this would be Ron's year, and that took a little pressure off Pap.

"This is the first year I've gone to bed at night and not laid there thinking about and wondering about how well the pumpkins are going to do. When we had some good ones going in years past, every night I'd lay there thinking about, 'Gee, if this thing does another thirty pounds a day, and thirty times seven is' . . . and like that. But this year I don't even go out to the patch as much. When I go out there, I go out there to work. I don't go out there and keep walking around just lookin' at 'em. I don't really give a shit what anybody else has. Or if I win or don't win. I just want to get something to the scales."

When it rained so heavily on the Southern New England club's picnic, Ron had given his dad a baleful look. "This is trouble," he'd said. Pumpkins were notorious for splitting after a burst of heavy rain prompted a burst of growth. So Ron knew what he was looking for when he went out to the patch the day after the picnic to pull the blankets off the pumpkins for their morning inspection. He looked for it, and he found it. Pap's Pride was split open at the blossom end.

Not much — just an inch — but that's all it took. "As soon as I uncovered it, it was looking at me," Ron said. Dick grabbed a roll of duct tape and slapped a makeshift bandage across the split. That would keep out the air and stave off rot so that they could try to keep the pumpkin growing a little longer. Dick wanted to get another 100 pounds or so on the pumpkin, just to see if he could. And if the seeds had a little longer to mature, they could at least salvage the genetics. Wait too long, though, and the pumpkin could rot, ruining the seeds. It was a gamble, like everything else in the hobby.

Either way, they'd lost another pumpkin. That made four that had run into trouble. Strangely enough, though, one of the 1068s that had lost its stump to the foaming slime was still growing strong. So really the Wallaces were down only three plants, which left them with seven good pumpkins. Out of those, they figured four were real contenders, including the stumpless wonder. And with four shots at a world record, Ron didn't want to take any more chances. If they got another heavy rainstorm, he figured he might be out in the patch cutting vines off the plants. That would reduce the water sucked up by the plant, and hopefully prevent the pumpkin from splitting. But then again, it might slow down growth for the rest of the season. "If we get a big rain, we'll have a decision to make," he said.

Dick was disappointed at losing the 500 Wallace. "Pap's Pride was taping 1,104 and still doing 25 pounds a day," he said. "Now we'll never know what she could have been." But he was already looking on the bright side. "We have several others doing well and a possible late-season surprise from the 1068 growing second from the end on the north side of the patch. Stay tuned as the drama of September unfolds."

When Ed Hemphill got home from the New Hampshire patch tour, he found his big pumpkin split wide open. He and Joan pulled in the driveway about midnight, and he was up at dawn the next day checking on the pumpkins. "It had split open at the top," he said. Right away, he saw where he'd gone wrong. Early in the season, he'd put a one-inch-thick piece of Styrofoam underneath the baby pumpkin to cushion it. The Styrofoam was 20 inches square, and when the pumpkin got bigger, it created a kind of overhang. Hemphill figured that had put the pumpkin shell under extra strain, leading to the split. He beat himself up over it. He should have done something to brace it. Better yet, he should have put a bigger piece of Styrofoam under there from the start, or nothing at all. "So that was quite a lesson to me," he said.

Another of his big ones had split the same weekend. After starting the season with six, he was down to just one pumpkin. But Hemphill wasn't afraid of long odds, and he liked the looks of his last chance. This pumpkin had been one of the slower growers in the patch, but it had made some impressive gains lately. And he figured it had a lot of promise. It certainly had a good pedigree. It was his 1068. The one that had arrived in the mail so unexpectedly right before planting time, the one Ron Wallace had sent on a sudden impulse of generosity.

Dave Stelts woke up Sunday morning, August 27, feeling nervous. Another heavy thunderstorm had moved through Ohio and western Pennsylvania overnight. He checked the rain gauge — an inch and a half. No matter how much well water or city water you pump onto your pumpkin, there's nothing like a good dose of rainwater to get it growing. The rain douses the plant with nitrogen-rich, chemical-free water, super-charging the growth. With just enough water, the pumpkin gets a good growth spurt. With too much, the pumpkin could split. "They just keep drinking until they blow," said Dave. "So anything over an inch and it's pretty much hold-your-breath time for the next two or three days."

Dave stepped into the rain-washed morning air and made his way down the hill to the patch. He scanned his plants. They looked okay. As usual, though, he could see a million things that needed doing. He began puttering around, pulling weeds, clipping vines. As he worked, Steve Razo, another top grower in the Ohio club, pulled into the driveway for a visit. As the work eases up in the patch in late summer, growers have more time to step out and survey the competition. It's a friendly ritual, with growers offering each other encouragement and exchanging advice — but also a good-natured let's-see-what-you've-got visit.

And Dave Stelts was at the top of the to-visit list. He had six pumpkins left, and five were going strong. Even his ugliest pumpkin, one of the smaller ones he called Elephant Boy, was doing well, "getting gnarlier and uglier every day," Dave said. "He's covered in little cracks in his skin, with big ol' wartlike things growing."

His 1068 was a comeback story. It had been the first of Dave's plants to come down with foaming stump slime. He'd had to cut off the stump and about nine feet of the main vine. But the pumpkin was still growing 15 pounds a day and estimated at 883 pounds the third week in August. Half the plant was gone, but it was, as Dave marveled, "still a machine."

He had decided to harvest his 1068 for the Canfield Fair, an agricultural expo in northeastern Ohio. He figured it would be over 1,000 pounds by then, and he didn't expect many other 1,000 pounders to show up this early. Dave and Steve Razo made the rounds of the patch, making the morning pumpkin checks. Dave had his own system: First he checked the stem for any sign of cracking, leaking, or softness. Then he checked the blossom end. Then he scanned the sag lines along the pumpkin shell. If a pumpkin is going to go bad, those are the places it usually happens.

They arrived at the 1068. Razo bent low over the pumpkin, running his eyes expertly over its pale, rough skin, slapping it firmly to test for the solid feeling that marks a heavyweight. Dave was yammering away about the 1068's comeback, how he thought it was a goner, how it had kept growing, amazingly, even after losing half its vine. Steve Razo interrupted him. "Uh oh," Razo said.

Those two syllables sent a blast of adrenaline coursing through Dave Stelts's veins. His heart leaped. His brow furrowed. "What?" he asked. "What is it?"

Razo pointed to the top of the 1068. And there it was: a tiny crack, about half an inch long and maybe an eighth of an inch wide, running perpendicular between two ribs. One glance and Dave knew it went all the way through. It was tiny, but it was black and bottomless. Just to check, he reached down and snapped off a blade of grass, then carefully threaded it through the crack. It went all the way through to the cavity. His 1068 was finished.

Now Dave was even more nervous. He and Razo started making the rounds again, checking over each pumpkin a second time, even more carefully. Dave inspected his 1023, his second-biggest pumpkin, especially closely. This pumpkin was a beautiful, deep orange, but it had a sag line that he feared was a split waiting to happen. He ran his eyes over the sag line. Nothing. It was fine. Dave moved on to inspect the next pumpkin. Razo lingered. "Oh no," Razo said.

Dave snapped. *"What?"*

"This doesn't look good," said Razo, pointing to the blossom end of the 1023, where a black line had appeared. Dave had looked at the blossom end on their first rounds just 10 minutes before. But he'd only checked the sag line the second time. And in the time it took for Dave and Razo to walk around the pumpkin patch, the blossom end had split. "That's how quick they go," Dave said despondently.

The loss of the two pumpkins in one day — within 15 minutes — hit Dave hard. Not only that, but they were two of his biggest. "The 1068, I could have gotten over that," he said. "But the 1023 hurt bad. It hurt real bad."

There was nothing he could do now except reconsider his weigh-off plans. He decided to harvest both split pumpkins and take them to the Canfield Fair. He was pretty sure there wouldn't be many pump-kins — if any — as big as those at the weigh-off. When he drove up with those giants, heads would turn. Hopefully, no one would notice the cracks before he got them to the scales. Not that he was thinking about cheating. He would fess up to the judges, accept their disqualification due to damage, and at least walk away with an official weight. But in the meantime, maybe he could make a few growers sweat. Just for fun.

"I want to freak everybody out when I bring 'em in there," Dave said. "Give 'em a little shortness of breath."

Early on Thursday morning, August 10, right before they'd left for a short trip to Oregon, Jack and Sherry LaRue went out to measure their pumpkins and found two had split overnight, one of Sherry's and one of Jack's. A cool front had moved through the day before, so they suspected the change in weather was behind the splits. They chopped up the pumpkins and heaved them down the "pumpkin chute," the hillside next to the patch where they dispatched all their rejects and failures. It was starting to get crowded at the bottom.

"This time of year, you hate to even go out there and lift the blankets," Jack said. "They're dropping right and left."

July's weather had been a roller coaster for the West Coast growers. They'd had a cool spell early on that dropped temperatures into the 40s at night, and two weeks later they were broiling in the high 90s. The LaRues had already had a number of casualties, including Jack's 1420 LaRue — a seed from the biggest pumpkin he ever grew — whose blossom end split the first week in August.

It was shaping up to be the Year of the Splits. By the end of August, the LaRues had cracked seven pumpkins — all but one were blossom splits. And that got Jack to thinking. Splits along sag lines or next to the pumpkin stem were generally considered to be caused by genetic defects. But splits at the blossom end were thought to be the result of environmental factors: sudden growth spurts caused by overfertilizing or a hard rain, or a cold spell that made the shell more brittle. Jack was having second thoughts about this theory though. "We're just getting too many of them this year," he said.

Most growers liked to keep the seeds from their biggest split pumpkins and grow them in later seasons. But Jack wondered if those splitters might be starting to contaminate the genetic pool, making ensuing generations more susceptible to cracking. If you salvaged seeds from pumpkins after they split, Jack believed, you were perpetuating survival of the weakest. "Just wash it out of the genetic pool and go with the ones that didn't split," he said. "The ones that make it, make it for a reason."

Despite their losses, the LaRues still had more than a dozen pumpkins going strong, some measuring close to 1,000 pounds as they turned the corner to September. That was well behind the best East Coast growers, but Jack wasn't worried. East Coast pumpkins put on most of their weight in August, then slowed way down in September. But the West Coast had steady growth right through September. It wasn't unheard of for pumpkins to gain 400 pounds in September and keep growing right up until the October weigh-offs.

Sherry was down to one good pumpkin, her 1068, and it was one of the biggest in the patch. She'd given up on her 1370 Rose, christened "Problem Child," when it lost all its leaves. Her 1354 Checkon was so misshapen that she called it "BU," for Butt Ugly, and now it had some kind of white fungus growing on it.

On August 26, Jack had lost one of his favorites, a nice orange pumpkin grown from his own seed. It was another blossom split. "I saw that thing, and I thought, 'You rotten kid.' I just wanted to haul off and kick it. That one really got to me. It was pretty depressing." On August 30, his second-biggest pumpkin split along a rib, and another of his biggest looked like it might be starting to split near a stem.

"It's hard to understand why so many growers get caught up in this sport," Jack said. "The frustration level runs very high. Especially this season."

13
THE RECKONING

August ended, as it always ended, in a colli-
sion of hope and fear and envy and disappointment. Those who lost their best pumpkins to disease or splits resigned themselves
for a while to the misery of defeat, and then
turned their thoughts to next year. Those
who had managed to hang on to a potential
champion braced for a monthlong white-
knuckle ride.

Every day in September was a day of
reckoning. The growers with a big one still
on the vine tossed restlessly in bed at night,
dreaming of what it would feel like to set a
world record, wondering if it could really
happen to them this time, worrying about
whether their best shot would still be in one
piece in the morning. They checked on their
pumpkins at the first light of dawn, in the
afternoon, in the fading light of evening,
and sometimes in the middle of the night.
They spent hours poring over growth charts,

comparing their fruit to past champions, and recalculating what it would take to make it into the record books. They had survived nature's gauntlet of floods and storms and ravenous animals and insidious microbes. They'd made it through the pumpkin-popping growth spurts of August. They had come so far. They had gotten so close. But more would fall before the season was done.

Dick Wallace had talked a good game at the club picnic, but he wasn't nearly as sanguine as he was trying to appear. True, years of disappointment had dulled the intensity of hope and leached away some of the excitement he used to feel at this point in the season. But in other ways he was as anxious as ever. He felt it most keenly not for himself, but for his son. Dick, like most fathers, wanted his son to have more than he ever had. If the Wallace luck was going to turn, he wanted it to turn for Ron.

Dick had pulled out the charts in late August and crunched the numbers. He'd listed all the championship pumpkins from the East Coast and calculated how much weight they had gained, on average, from the middle of August until the weigh-off in the first week of October. The results were remarkably consistent. Winning pumpkins had typically gained 400 to 450 pounds from August 15 to weigh-off time. The Wallace patch had a few pumpkins weighing close to a thousand pounds by August 15, so if these pumpkins followed the norm, they could expect to take 1,300- to 1,400-pounders to the weigh-off. And Dick figured if they had a pumpkin measuring 1,400 pounds, then they had a shot at a world record. "Because, you never know," he said hopefully, "sometimes they weigh a little more."

But August had not cooperated. The month started with intense heat, then socked growers with a cool spell that sent their plants into a shock they never recovered from. The weather extremes had slowed down growth just as the pumpkins were getting revved up. Most of the club's pumpkins never reached the kind of 40-pounds-a-day peak growth rates that pushed a fruit into championship territory. The last two weeks of August were chilly and rainy. People were already digging into the back of their closets to pull out their sweaters. "It's no good," Ron said. "There's no sun."

Ron saw his club's chances of becoming repeat champion slipping away. "I don't know, I don't know. It'll be hard." He was worrying about his own odds too. On their Tuesday measuring day, August 22, Ron noticed his biggest pumpkin's growth rate had dropped from 30 pounds a day to 17 pounds. And he knew that in September, it would gradually decline to nil. If he could get 150 or 175 pounds more in September, he'd count the month a success.

The Wallace plants were beginning to show their age. Some of the older leaves were yellowing and dying. Others were looking ragged. Powdery mildew fungus and bacterial leaf spot were taking a toll. Ron and Dick amped up their applications of compost tea. "We're spraying like hell," Ron said. "I was spraying in the pouring rain today. The rain washes it down into the root system. It's the best time to put it down."

They'd weighed Pap's Pride using an in-line scale attached to the chain they used to lift the pumpkin. According to its measurements, they had estimated the pumpkin would weigh about 1,175 pounds when it split; its actual weight was 1,186 pounds. They had other pumpkins doing just as well. But Dick knew that it would be a fight to pile on much more weight in September. "The first twelve hundred pounds is sometimes the easy part," he said. "It's getting that last couple hundred that's a bitch."

Ron ran the numbers in his head every day. "Okay, I'm here now, we're doing this much a day, I know I'm always putting a hundred and fifty pounds on in September, I've got bigger plants . . . I think I've got four that could make a run at thirteen hundred. *Could.* Who the hell knows."

Ron was annoyed by anyone — well-meaning friends, even his dad — who looked at his pumpkins, looked at their measurements, and tried to pump up his hopes. He was having none of it. It was just more pressure — pressure that he didn't need. "People keep saying, 'Ronnie, you could do this; Ronnie, you could do that,' " he grumbled. "But who the hell knows? If my aunt had a package, she'd be my uncle."

"It's reality-check time," said Dave Stelts.

Stelts's best pumpkins in his western Pennsylvnia patch had stopped growing — just like that. "You sit and think you're doing real good," he said, "and all of a sudden Mother Nature rears her ugly head and lets you know she's still in control." By the end of the first week in September, Dave had one pumpkin measuring over 1,000 pounds. And he had two more he thought might "go heavy," weighing more than estimated. They had what Dave called good "thunkability."

Growers measure that by leaning down over a pumpkin, pressing their ear to the shell, wrapping their arms around it, and giving it a good slap. Experienced growers believe they can tell by the vibrations whether they have a thick, solid pumpkin that's likely to go heavy, or a hollow balloon that would go light and weigh less than it measured. Dave thought he had a total of three that might go over 1,000 pounds if they went heavy. Plus, he said, "There's an outside chance Elephant Boy might surprise me."

Dave was hoping at least one of his pumpkins would get to 1,200 pounds. But he'd be happy with even 1,141 pounds. That would give him a new personal best, beating his 2000 world record. "That was my baby," Dave said, his voice warming sentimentally. "I grew the biggest pumpkin of the twentieth century — no one can take that away from me. But I tell you what, the twenty-first century has been a real bummer for me."

This was the time of year when everyone finally had a little time to sit back and look around and start guessing who would bring in the heavy ones. It was a kind of pumpkin parlor game full of intrigue and secrecy and guesswork. Competitive pumpkin growers were proud of their willingness to share information about how to grow the giants, but they were less willing to show their hand toward the end of the season. There were a variety of reasons for this. Mainly, growers who believed they had a chance at a world record didn't want to endure the embarrassment of being wrong. As soon as word began to leak out that they had a potential bomb sitting in their patch, the phone would start to ring. Everyone would want to know what it looked like, what it was measuring. Many would even want to come by and take a look for themselves. And then the growers, of course, would gossip. Was the pumpkin measured correctly? Was it a cork? Did it look like it weighed heavier than X's pumpkin? Or Z's pumpkin?

Ron and Dick Wallace were among those who preferred to keep their measurements to themselves, except for a few trusted growers within their own club. "When people ask me what I'm taping, I don't like to lie to 'em," Dick said. "I just tell 'em we're doing very well and we've got a couple over a grand. But a lot of these guys don't like to tell nobody nuthin'. And I understand why, because if they don't make it to the weigh-off, you have to answer all those questions. People will say, 'What happened to that eleven-hundred-pounder you said you had?' "

By September, Larry and Gerry Checkon knew for sure that it was not going to be another world-record year in the Checkon patch. Their careful watering routine and minimal fertilizing had kept disease out of their patch. But the weather never gave them a chance. The nights had stayed too cool, regularly dipping down into the 40s. Two of their four pumpkins had stopped growing early in the summer. When they'd arrived home after three days away attending the New Hampshire patch tour, they'd both gone straight out into the patch to measure their pumpkins in the dark. "You get to find out how they've been doing while you've been gone. It's so exciting!" Gerry said. Both of their remaining pumpkins had gained about 100 pounds each.

But on September 5, Larry's pumpkin had split along a sag line. That shut him out of the season and left the Checkon fortunes in Gerry's hands. Her orange 1225 Jutras was growing well despite all the drawbacks of the season, but not at a world-record pace. With a little coaxing, Gerry thought she might be able to get it to 1,200 pounds — big enough, she hoped, to win her local weigh-off. "At this point," she said, "you're trying to think of anything you can do. If I knew any voodoo dances that would work, I would do them."

The Checkons measured the fruit and watered it, and Gerry gave it a little lovin' every day. "I run my hands all over it and I say, 'You're so beautiful.' "

Local agricultural fairs were beginning to be held around the region. The fairs were a chance to spend a day immersed in rural culture, with pie-eating and pig races and bubble-gum-blowing contests, swine shows and sheep shows and llama shows, corn dogs and fried Twinkies. Farmers and garden hobbyists brought the best of their summer crops to be judged as tastiest or biggest or most beautiful. This was the traditional venue for pumpkin weigh-off contests.

But the giant pumpkins were sometimes lost in the blizzard of other events at these fairs. So over the years, as the hobby became more popular, growing clubs organized their own weigh-off contests. The Ohio Valley growers weighed off at a local nursery and garden center owned by Tim Parks, one of the founders of the Ohio club. The Southern New England growers weighed off at Frerich's Farm, a small commercial farm and garden center in Rhode Island.

Growers, ideally, saved their biggest pumpkin for their own club's weigh-off, to add to the club's reputation. But growers lucky enough to end the season with several pumpkins intact wanted to make the most of their year of hard work. It was against the rules of the Great Pumpkin Commonwealth to take the same pumpkin to more than one weigh-off, or for one grower to enter more than one pumpkin at the same weigh-off. Not all weigh-offs were GPC-sanctioned, and only fruit weighed at GPC sites counted for the GPC's awards. But non-GPC weigh-offs still provided an opportunity for a grower to at least get an official weight and perhaps even win a prize. And since there were usually fewer, smaller pumpkins at the fairs early in September, even a 500- or 600-pound fruit could win.

After another week of rain and chill at the start of September, Ron was growing despondent. There were only three weeks before the big weigh-off at Topsfield Fair, and four weeks before the Southern New England club's weigh-off at Frerich's Farm. The pumpkins were only growing a few pounds a day. Now he would be glad to get just another 100 pounds on his best pumpkins. He figured he and his dad still had five really nice ones. And if they could get five entries weighing over 1,200 pounds apiece to the scale, that would be nothing to sneeze at. "I don't know if anybody's ever done that before," Ron said.

At this point, Ron and Dick still had seven pumpkins on the vine. One was on the 1068 plant that had lost its stump to disease earlier in the summer. Even without the stump, the pumpkin had steamrolled along, slow, but still strong. Now it was one of their biggest. Several of the other plants that had escaped disease were doing better than anything else Dick or Ron had ever grown. A couple of the 1068s were measuring more than 1,200 pounds, another was in the 1,100s, another was over 1,000. As the weigh-offs began, Ron and Dick would have to begin deciding which pumpkins they would each enter at the different contests. They were ending the season with enough good pumpkins that they would each have one to enter at the biggest weigh-offs, though that would mean they'd compete with each other. With the best of their crop, Ron hoped to have a shot at winning his club's weigh-off at Frerich's Farm, and maybe even winning Topsfield. The rest he and his father would take to other local weigh-offs.

On September 6, the Wallaces cut their first pumpkin from the vine. As of that week, their 1354 Checkon was the runt of the crop, measuring just 790 pounds. It had been pollinated later than the others and had never really taken off. So when the Bethlehem Fair arrived on the calendar, Dick decided to take their Checkon pumpkin there. Joe Jutras took a pumpkin from his patch and went along. It would be a trial run for the season's upcoming weigh-offs.

Ron and Dick were trying to tune out the hubbub over who had what and to focus on their own pumpkins, but they did want to keep track of how the 1068s planted by other growers were doing. Though a great many had bitten the dust, at the end of August, J. D. Megchelsen had set a new record at the Alaska State Fair with a 1068. He'd met his goal to grow the first 1,000-pounder in Alaska, winning the top prize at the fair with a 1,019-pound pumpkin.

Dick and Ron had heard from a grower named Buddy Conley in southern Ohio who had a big 1068 going in his patch. And word was filtering out about Ed Hemphill's 1068 in Canada. It was a monster, people said. The pumpkin was huge and high and round, but looked solid as concrete, with the cantalouping veins that usually signaled a heavy pumpkin. The ribs had forked along one side, giving it the asymmetrical look of two pumpkins that had been welded together. Ed Hemphill wasn't wired into the digital age, so another Canadian grower had snapped a picture and e-mailed it to Dick and Ron. "That's the most impressive thing I've ever seen," said Ron. A flash of envy rippled through him, and something else. That was the seed he'd sent at the last minute last spring. What if it was *the* seed — the seed out of all others destined to grow the next world record? The seed destined to break 1,500 pounds. And he'd given it away at the last minute.

But Ron couldn't let himself think that way. He and his dad had had five shots at the 1068 that year. If that wasn't enough, so be it. Ron was happy for Hemphill. "I'm excited for him, and I'm excited for Buddy Conley; I'm excited for Peter Rondeau; I'm excited for *me.* I'm excited for anybody who's going to grow a personal best this year."

Besides, it wasn't just the 1068 that might pop a world record. They'd started to hear about some other monsters coming on. There was one in New York estimated at 1,500 pounds, one in Washington and one in Oregon. There were at least two in Ohio, including Conley's, with potential. And they still had another month before the big weigh-offs. Who knew what would happen in a month.

"Everybody can talk — who's got this and who's got that," Ron said. "It's the ones that aren't talking you have to worry about."

It had taken Ed Hemphill about a week to snap out of his funk when he lost his best pumpkin after the New Hampshire tour. "That was a big letdown," he said. But as soon as he took a better look at the one pumpkin left in his patch, his 1068, his spirits rallied. "It was a very backward plant," Hemphill said. "I had no hopes for it in the world. It was the poorest plant I'd ever had. Slow, slow. It was riding two weeks behind all the other plants putting on foliage. I only kept it because I had lots of room there for it and nothing else to take its place." By the time the New Hampshire tour had rolled around, it was measuring less than 900 pounds, compared to the 1,100 pounds of his big one.

Then the 1068 took off running. For seven days, it averaged 49 pounds a day. Hemphill looked at it with new eyes. It was getting really big, he realized. It was a pumpkin with potential. But then he started to worry himself sick it was going to split like the others. He woke up each morning in early September and hustled out to the patch beside his house at first light. The weather was chilly, but that 1068 had an uncanny ability to keep growing even when it was cool. He had it swathed in wool blankets — two sewn together and another one across the top of those. He pulled the blankets away each morning with his heart in his throat. But so far, the pumpkin had held together.

The OTT measurements on Hemphill's 1068 now totaled 403 inches, which put it at 1,367 pounds. Lately, the growth had slowed way down. It was nearly done, but still moving. Hemphill was banking on it going at least 10 percent heavier than the estimate. "That's just my own thinking," he said. "You talk to most pumpkin growers and they think I'm a little bit out to lunch. But we're going to find out, if it holds together until October 7."

If. That was the word that haunted every giant-pumpkin grower at this time of year, and it was haunting Hemphill in a big way. At night, he lay there thinking about it. "Sometimes the damn thing wakes me up," he confessed. "It's a lot of stress when you know you could possibly have the best one. It's going to be a long four weeks."

Hemphill was sure he was going to break the 1,500-pound barrier. With a whopper like that, he decided he would make the 18-hour drive on October 7 to the Port Elgin Pumpkinfest weigh-off, the biggest, most prestigious weigh-off in Canada. That was where Canadian Al Eaton had weighed his 1,446-pound world-record winner in 2004.

"Yup, I'm going to Port Elgin," Hemphill said. "I'm going up where the lights are bright. If it holds together."

The Wallaces' 1354 Checkon had shocked everyone by weighing 23 percent heavier than expected at the Bethlehem Fair on September 8. The pumpkin's estimated weight was 790 pounds, but it racked up 977 pounds on the scale. The Wallaces had won first place, beating the old fair record by 200 pounds. Joe's pumpkin had done well too, coming in second at 901 pounds.

It was just a small fair, but the heavier-than-expected weights seemed like a good omen. "It's always nice to get a win," said Ron. "I don't care if it's a 4-H fair."

The days were ticking by with no further disasters in the Wallace patch. The peak season at the country club was winding down. Banquet business remained brisk, but golf course traffic was lighter and the pool had closed after Labor Day — that was a big headache out of the way for Ron. Work had slowed way down in the pumpkin patch too. Ron and his dad watered when it wasn't raining, sprayed on compost tea and fungicide from time to time, covered the pumpkins at night, and uncovered them in the morning. Other than that, it was watching and waiting and praying that nothing went wrong.

The weather had been crazy again in the past week, but in a good way. With the cool start to the month, Ron and Dick had resigned themselves to getting, at best, another 100 pounds in September. But then the weather had turned unusually warm and sunny. The pumpkins had revved back up a little for another growth spurt, putting on 50 pounds with the sunny days, and then slowing back down to a steady 5 or so pounds a day. "If I can put another fifty pounds on the pumpkins, I'll be happy," Ron said.

But with the days getting shorter, every pound was harder to come by. In fact, it was difficult to tell if the pumpkins were growing at all. They were so huge and lumpy and irregularly shaped now, that just a small shift in where the measuring tape ran over the pumpkin could mean losing an inch instead of gaining an inch. The plants continued to look ragged, so Ron was allowing some new vines to grow out a little to give the plants some fresh leaves to work with. He and his dad were worried about a couple of stems that looked like they might be starting to rot. So they set up fans on them every day to keep them dry.

Though the Wallaces had some monsters in their patch, Ron was trying to be realistic. Their pumpkins were big, but others were bigger. From the most recent pictures he'd seen, he thought Ed Hemphill's 1068 could go 1,600 pounds. It just had the look of a heavy pumpkin, and there were no sag lines at all.

"The world record isn't going to happen for us this year," Ron said. "Our soil just isn't balanced. It's not where I wanted to be. You're not supposed to take a field of pine trees, work on it in November, and plant it six months later."

Dick consoled him. "I told Ronnie the other night that the next best thing to us setting the world record ourselves is for somebody else to set it on the 1068."

The Wallaces didn't have much hope that the Southern New England growers would be repeat world champions. There had been too many slow starts, too much disease. Ron figured the lousy weather alone had trimmed as much as 150 pounds off most of the club's pumpkins. The Rhode Island mafia would deliver some nice fruit, and he hoped for a solid top 10 of 1,000-plus-pounders. But they would be missing the heavyweights they had last year, when Scott Palmer brought his 1,443-pounder and they had three others over 1,300 pounds, with Joe's 1,228-pounder rounding out the top five. The Wallaces knew from conversations with Dave Stelts that the Ohio growers were heavy and deep at the top, with several growers estimating their pumpkins to be over 1,300 pounds, including some potential world-record winners.

Those who'd had a less-than-stellar season already were busy planning for next year. Steve Connolly, who still had some nice pumpkins, but nothing that matched last year's 1,333-pounder, was spending his weekends hauling in fresh compost. Steve Sperry was planning to cut down some trees and rip up part of his yard to put in a new patch. Scott Palmer, who hadn't come close to his miraculous 1,443-pound winner, was thinking about expanding too.

Starting September 23, the Wallaces would

be taking pumpkins to a weigh-off every weekend for three weeks. First there was the Durham Fair in Connecticut. Ron had picked out the smallest 1068 for that event; its measurements put it at 1,040 pounds.

Then there was Topsfield on Saturday, September 30. Ron would enter a 1068, and his dad would enter the 1370 Rose, which had turned out to be a beautiful red-orange fruit with deep, wide ribs — a pumpkin right out of the pages of a fairy tale. Topsfield was the most prestigious weigh-off in New England, and it would be the place where some dark horses could emerge — the big ones that had been kept under cover. "There's always a surprise or two at the scales," Ron said.

The following Sunday, Ron would take their 1228 Jutras to the Connecticut club's weigh-off at Pennfield Beach, right on the ocean. Some people thought the 1228 looked like the biggest pumpkin in the Wallace patch. But Ron and his dad thought it would be light — it sounded hollow when they thumped it.

And then, finally, there would be the club's Frerich Farm weigh-off on October 7. The day was shaping up to be the Final Four of giant pumpkins. The Ohio Valley club would weigh-off that morning, and so would Port Elgin and Altoona in Pennsylvania, as well as several other clubs across the country.

So just three more weeks. "We're heading down the final stretch," Ron said. "Everybody just wants to get on with it."

Buddy Conley was sweating it, and his friend Tony Vanderpool was fielding phone calls and running interference. "It's as big as a freakin' king-size bed," Vanderpool panted to one caller. "It's huge."

The biggest pumpkin Conley had ever grown was 955 pounds. But this year he'd gotten hold of a 1068 seed, and it had outrun everything else in his pumpkin patch. "It's unlike anything I've ever had or anything I've ever seen before," Conley said.

Conley, 52 years old, was a member of the Southern Ohio Giant Pumpkin Growers, friendly rivals to Dave Stelts's Ohio Valley group farther north. He'd been growing giant pumpkins since 1997, and now leased a little piece of land from his brother-in-law to grow four plants. The property was seven miles away from his house, and during the summer, Conley traveled back and forth at least three times a day to tend to his pumpkins. He spent an average of six hours a day in his patch from May to October. "It's a full-time job," he said.

He'd noticed right away that the 1068 was special. "From day one, I've called it 'the Freak.' " It was growing so fast, he worried it would blow up. One day after a heavy rainstorm, it put on 60 pounds in a single night. "That scared the hell out of me," he said. "But then it slowed back down to about forty pounds a day."

Conley's 1068 pumpkin was nearly six feet wide, five feet long, and three feet tall. It was a creamy salmon color, with a rough skin covered in heavy cantaloupe veining. The pumpkin was round, but lopsided, with a large hump on one side and a deep rib line on the other. "It's not pretty by any stretch of the imagination," he said. Mice had been nibbling around the pumpkin lately, so Conley had surrounded it with traps. A few years ago a mouse had chewed all the way through his pumpkin and made a nest inside. "So I definitely know they will take one down and it won't take them long to do it." He'd trapped at least 30 of the small rodents in the past month.

As word had gotten around that he had a big 1068 growing, his phone had started ringing and growers started e-mailing. The pumpkin's OTT measurements put it at a little over 1,300 pounds, but other growers kept saying, *if* it weighed more and *if* he could keep it together, then he might have a shot at a world record. It was an intoxicating thought, but one Conley was resisting. "Everybody's saying I've got this world-record potential out there, but it's not measuring world record," he said, holding on tight to his good sense.

The last thing Conley wanted was to grow the biggest pumpkin of his life and end up disappointed. If his 1068 hit the scales at 1,300 pounds, it would be the biggest pumpkin he'd ever grown, the biggest anyone in his club had ever grown. That should be plenty to make him happy. But the thought of what might be or what might happen tormented him. "The past couple days my stomach has been killing me," he said. "My other half is telling me it's an ulcer. She said, 'You've got more white hair than you did a month ago.'

"I go to bed and for two hours I'll toss and turn and think. Is it going to be okay in the morning? Which weigh-off do I take it to? Do I go to the Southern Ohio Growers weigh-off? Or do I let it grow another ten days and take it to Circleville? That's a long time to have to hold one together."

Conley had learned his lesson. He told his friend Vanderpool, "Next year, if it looks like I'm going to have a big nice one, I'm not going to tell anyone. It's just too stressful."

Another Ohio grower, Tim Parks, was flying under the radar with an even bigger giant. Parks realized what he had in early August, when his pumpkin gained 226 pounds in five days. By late September, it measured an estimated 1,568 pounds. But almost no one knew about it. "There's probably only one, two, maybe four growers who truly know how big my pumpkin is," Parks said. And he wanted to keep it that way until the weigh-off. "You've got this pumpkin growing and you want to go out and scream it to the world," he said. "But it's just easier. You don't have to deal with all the questions and gossip."

About the middle of September, Ed Hemphill's 1068 pumpkin stopped growing. That worried him a little bit, but other growers had reassured him. Maybe it was just the cool weather. Maybe it had just grown all it was going to grow. Nevertheless, Hemphill started checking extra carefully each morning for signs of trouble. He'd slide the blankets off and stand back and give his pumpkin a quick once-over. Then he'd step closer to examine every inch for cracks and soft spots. He'd run his hands gently over the shell, fingers spread, feeling the bumpy-smooth coolness of the pumpkin skin beneath his palms. And then one day his fingers paused. Something was different. He laid both hands on the spot. It was warm, as if a lightbulb were burning underneath, heating it up. Warm, like horse manure steaming in the winter air. Warm, like a pumpkin going bad from the inside out.

Hemphill knew with the certainty of sore experience that it was over. "I said, 'Yup. It's rotting.' "

He went back inside his house and slumped in his favorite chair. He stared at the wall for half an hour, slowly, painfully, letting go of all his dreams and hopes. He was in shock. "I was looking for trouble, but I wasn't ready for trouble," he realized. "I knew it could happen, but I didn't think it would. Especially since it was the first time I ever grew a big one."

Hemphill roused himself from his sulk and went to fetch his tractor with the front-end loader. The pumpkin still looked perfect, so he figured the problem was where he couldn't see it — on the bottom. He maneuvered the edge of the scoop under the pumpkin and lifted it slightly. There it was. A crack in the bottom of the fruit ran right along the edge of that Styrofoam square he'd placed under all his baby pumpkins months before. The Styrofoam had done it again. The 1068 had sagged over the edge of the plastic, creating a pressure point along the bottom where he couldn't see it. For all their girth and weight, giant pumpkins are really fragile. No matter what the cause, Hemphill blamed himself. And that was the hardest part. "I had great plans," he said. "But it all came to an end. I'm a little disappointed, I tell you what."

Hemphill's season was over. He had started with six prospects and ended with nothing. He walked next door to ask his neighbor to take some last digital pictures of the pumpkin before he said his final good-bye. He salvaged the seeds, then broke it to pieces with the tractor, loaded it into the bucket he used to move manure, hauled it to the edge of the woods that bordered his property, and dumped it. "Bye, bye, pumpkin," he said mournfully.

Ed moped a few more days. He could hardly bear to think about it, much less tell anyone that he'd lost his sure-thing world-record pumpkin. So for nearly a week, he sat on the news. Then he told another grower and asked him to spread the word.

After that, there was only one thing

Hemphill had to do. "There's no point going around feeling sorry for yourself," he said. The next week he started back to work on his patch. He hauled manure from the local mink farm, spread out some compost and potato waste from his potato garden, and then tilled it all in. "Come May, I'll be ready," he said. "Next year I'm going to prove I can grow a fifteen-hundred-pounder, and I'll keep it together this time. I hope Mr. Wallace will let me have another seed."

As Ed Hemphill was grappling with his misfortune, Ron and Dick were feeling more hopeful. After the bad weather at the start of the month, September had turned out to be one of the warmest and sunniest in memory. The pumpkins had continued growing, and the Wallaces estimated each one had gained at least 200 pounds during the month. They'd gotten more encouragement at the Durham Fair, where their 1068 entry had weighed 12 percent heavier than estimated and won the contest at 1,174 pounds.

So now Ron was considerably more upbeat. "This has been the best September we've ever had," he said. His dad's spirits had perked up too. By September 26, the two pumpkins they had picked to take to their club's October 7 weigh-off were an estimated 1,350 pounds. Dick was hoping for another few pounds before the pumpkins hit the scales. He was beginning to think they had a lock on finally winning their own weigh-off, unless a ringer showed up with a surprise. "There's even an outside possibility, if you're a dreamer, that with the over-the-chart weights our patch and 1068 seed has put out this year, that even a world-record weight could happen," he said. Although he hadn't forgotten the other big pumpkins out there. "Only to be broken again the same day," he added.

Dick was deliberately keeping the volume turned down on his enthusiasm. Ron was still nervous and didn't want to advertise that they thought they had a shot at the record. Even after Hemphill's 1068 went down, there was still a pumpkin estimated at more than 1,500 pounds in New York and another in the mid-1,300s in Michigan. Who knew what might turn up along the West Coast. Nobody ever counted out Jack LaRue. There were Conley and Parks in Ohio, and now whispers were growing about Quinn Werner's pumpkin. Word was that despite his battles with foaming stump slime over the summer, one of his plants had escaped the disease and was growing a pumpkin that might blow everyone out of the water.

Ron's hopes were still pinned on going heavy. The Wallace pumpkins weren't measuring as big as some of the others, but he knew he had some solid fruit in his garden. "You start putting 10 percent on top of these numbers and you're talking about something pretty special," Ron said.

But that's as far as he'd go. Ron was still afraid of the jinx. Dick couldn't even get him to talk about his hopes of winning Grower of the Year, a new award offered by the national GPC organization. The person with the largest three pumpkins weighed at GPC sites would win the title, so even if he didn't have the single biggest fruit in the world, he could still reap honors.

"A few nights ago I said to him, 'Ya know, Ron, you've got a good chance to get Grower of the Year honors from the GPC,' " said Dick. "And he said, 'Aaahh, Dad, I don't want to talk about that.' "

Dick laughed. He knew his son. "I bet he thinks about it every night before going to bed," he said.

There'd been more bad news for the Rhodies. Steve Sperry had lost everything in his patch. And in the past few days, Scott

Palmer had lost his 1225 — his second pumpkin to go down. That left him just one, the pumpkin growing on his 1443, and he was getting nervous that he might lose that one too. He didn't want to risk holding on until October 7, so he'd decided to take his last pumpkin to Topsfield that weekend and skip the club's weigh-off at Frerich's Farm. "As the grower, you gotta do what you gotta do," Ron said. "People will tell you they're sorry and they feel bad for you, but until you've lost one of your own that you've put a year's worth of work into, you can't know what it feels like. So I told Scotty, 'Scotty, I know how you feel.' "

The Wallace pumpkins were so big now that they were easily seen from the road looming above the bedraggled leaves in the patch. The pumpkins were attracting 25 to 30 people a day. Some stopped and gawked from the road; others walked right up to the patch to take pictures and ask questions, as if the Wallace garden were a tourist attraction. Even a motorcycle gang stopped by one day. One guy actually drove his car across the grass right up next to the patch, ogled the pumpkins a few moments, and then drove off.

Ron had set some traps for a mouse that had been nibbling on one of his pumpkins at night. There were tiny scrape marks in the skin a few inches above the ground. And he was still worried about the deer doing some damage. They'd torn his makeshift fence to shreds and were making regular appearances in the patch. Ron tried to fight off a feeling of foreboding. In the Wallaces' bitter tradition, this last week in September had been the worst week of the year. "I've lost so many pumpkins between now and the weigh-off," he said, his voice trailing off, unwilling to finish the thought.

"But hey. They're still growing. The stems look good. I'm already happy with what I did this year. I just want to finish up and get them to the scales."

Every night now when he got home from work, Ron would grab a flashlight and walk out along the edge of the pumpkin patch to have a look around. The air was chilly now, every breath a frosty puff of white. Autumn had arrived in New England. One night that week the stars had seemed extra bright in the sky, and there was a full moon. "I saw a shooting star right over the middle of the patch," Ron marveled.

That was a rare moment of serenity. Another year of grinding it out was nearly over. In just eight days, the 2006 season would come to an end one way or another.

14
TOPSFIELD

Heavy and pregnant with their cargo of giant pumpkins, the pickup trucks began lining up outside the cattle arena at the Topsfield fairgrounds long before the morning air had shaken off its nighttime chill. Brake lights blinked on and off in the gray morning light as the trucks inched forward one at a time through the great barn doors of the arena. Growers rolled down their truck windows to hang an elbow out as they waited patiently for their turn to unload. Some got out to stretch their legs and shake off the torpor of a long drive across New England in the predawn hours. They wandered up and down the line to visit with friends and rivals, warming their hands around plastic cups of steaming coffee, their eyes sliding to the back of each truck in furtive appraisal.

It was a sleepy, quiet start to a momentous day. The Rhode Island mafia joined the procession about 6:30 a.m., bringing up the rear of the line. Joe Jutras led the pack in his tall, white company van, loaded with both his own pumpkin and Dick Wallace's entry for the weigh-off. Ron followed in his red Ford 4×4 pickup, followed by Steve Sperry and Peter Rondeau. Scott Palmer wasn't there. The day before, when they were loading their trucks for the fair, they'd picked up Scott's pumpkin and the bottom had fallen out of it — rotten. So that was Scott's story for 2006: from glory to heart-break in 12 months. He'd finished the season zero for three.

Ron's pumpkin was noticeably bigger than any other pumpkin in the line, though that didn't necessarily mean much. Plenty of huge pumpkins had come to the scales only to be smacked down by smaller, heavier rivals. But Ron was attracting the attention of the other growers, who already were beginning to lay odds on the day's winner. Ron and Dick had surveyed the fruit in their patch carefully, measuring and thumping and ranking them according to which ones they thought were heaviest. They had five competitive pumpkins left, and they wanted to save the heaviest two for their own weigh-off the following week.

Dick had settled on the 1370 Rose, the

most perfectly shaped orange pumpkin in their patch. He wanted to walk into Topsfield with style. Ron wanted to win, plain and simple. What a vindication that would be, to finally win the top prize at the most prestigious weigh-off in New England. So he'd brought what he and his dad figured was their third-heaviest pumpkin, one of his 1068s, and he hoped it would be enough to do the job. He'd packed it in securely for the two-and-half-hour drive from the patch to Topsfield. The tremendous fruit sat on a wooden pallet, cushioned by a six-inch-thick foam rubber mattress. He'd braced it all around with hay bales and quilts wedged firmly against the walls of the truck bed. Given the pumpkin was more than half a ton, Ron figured he didn't need ropes to hold it down.

Sitting in the crawling line, Ron craned his neck to see how many trucks were ahead of him. He'd made this trip so many times over the years, sat in the same line, engine idling and hopes percolating. But always he had left disappointed. Three times he'd made it into the top 10. He'd thought he had a winner in 2000, only to settle for second place after Steve Connolly rolled in with a bigger pumpkin. Ron hoped today would be different, but in the back of his mind he was remembering how he'd hoped that before. There were a lot of top growers in New England, any one of them capable of showing up with a world-record contender that day.

If someone outside of Rhode Island was going to set a New England record, this was the most likely place for it to happen. There wasn't another weigh-off in the nation, much less New England, that boasted the kind of pedigree attached to Topsfield, an old-fashioned county agricultural fair attended by tens of thousands of people each fall. The event originated in the woodlands north of Boston in 1820, when farmers began gathering each year during the first week in October to exchange information about raising cattle and swine and growing crops such as potatoes and corn.

Giant pumpkins were latecomers to Topsfield. The fair held its first weigh-off in 1984 with 16 growers from Massachusetts and Connecticut. The winner that year weighed 433 pounds. By 2005, Jim Beauchemin led a field of more than 80 entries with his 1,315-pounder. Two things propelled the Topsfield pumpkin weigh-off to the top of the heap: money and the promise of celebrity. The prizes were among the best offered anywhere: $3,500 for the heaviest pumpkin,

$1,000 for second place, and $750 for third. But the main allure of winning Topsfield was status. The weigh-off is held on the morning of the fair's opening day, and the winning grower enjoys minor celebrity as the focus of newspaper, radio, and television stories, pushed by the fair's public-relations muscle. The winning pumpkin becomes a star attraction of the fair, displayed in a climate-controlled glass case in the center of the huge Fruit and Vegetable Barn, where visitors ogle other prizewinning fruits and vegetables, decorative gourds, vegetable-themed scarecrows, and painted jack-o'-lanterns. A sign painted above the building entrance exhorts visitors to "Come In & See New England's Largest Pumpkin" — even though that wasn't necessarily true any-more.

A slow-burning rivalry had emerged in recent years between the Rhode Island growers, now operating under the Southern New England Giant Pumpkin Growers banner, and the larger New England Pumpkin Growers Association, which held the Topsfield weigh-off. The ascendancy of the Rhode Island weigh-off, which claimed the bragging rights to New England's biggest pumpkin in 2005 with Scott Palmer's bright-orange 1,443-pound fruit, had taken a little of the shine off the Topsfield weigh-off. But only a little. Reigning Topsfield champion Jim Beauchemin said it loud and often: Topsfield was "New England's premieeeeeeer weigh-off site."

The 2006 season had been a rough one for all New England growers. So many of them had lost pumpkins that only 45 had registered entries — half the number expected. Only the hardiest pumpkins and luckiest growers had made it to weigh-off time. And here were the Wallaces, among the survivors, bringing not just one pumpkin, but two. That alone was gratifying to the father and son. Whether they came home with a prize or not, these were still the biggest pumpkins they'd ever managed to get to a weigh-off.

About 7 a.m., it was finally Ron's turn to pull his truck inside the cavernous metal-paneled building, where already the day was kicking into high gear. Weigh-off volunteers and fair workers bustled across the arena, kicking up the deep, orange sand that covered the floor as they directed the pumpkin unloading with the urgent efficiency of traffic cops at a busy intersection. Aluminum bleachers on opposite sides of the rectangular arena were designated for spectators. In front of one set of bleachers, weigh-off officials had drawn two rows of white chalk lines in the sand, marking off neat squares where the pumpkins would be parked to await their turn at the scale. Forklifts crisscrossed the arena, spearing the wood pallets beneath the pumpkins in the pickups, then roaring away with the monster fruit suspended high in the air — a harrowing sight for the growers. The growling engines and incessant warning beeps from the forklifts drowned out most conversation as the growers went about seeing their pumpkins safely to the floor of the arena.

Weigh-off coordinator Jim Kuhn, a veteran grower from New Hampshire, eyed each entry as it came in and directed the pumpkin to a spot on the floor based on how heavy he judged it to be. The heavier it looked, the closer it went to the front of the line near the stage and scale. The smallest pumpkins would be weighed first, and the biggest saved for last. Kuhn waved pumpkins he judged to be under 1,000 pounds — the noncontenders — to an area on the other side of the arena. Competitive growers cringed a little when their pumpkins landed in what they called the "kiddie patch," though most everyone had been there at one time or another. Kuhn took one look at Ron's pumpkin and directed it to the front of the arena — the very first spot.

As their pumpkins were unloaded, the growers were freed to roam about, gossip with each other, and assess the competition. Lined up in a double row in the sand, the massive fruits looked like alien pods in the cargo bay of a spaceship. Most were pale orange, though they ranged from nearly white to the bright reddish-orange of Dick's pumpkin. Most of the shapes were not what anyone would readily describe as pumpkin-like. Joe Jutras had brought a long, flat fruit that looked more like a giant, orange jalapeño pepper. Some pumpkins were broad and low, some high and round. Most were covered with the rough brown cantaloupe veins that competitive growers loved.

The growers prowled around the biggest pumpkins, like dogs sniffing an adversary. They were generous with praise, and gracious with mutual respect, but occasionally, fangs were exposed. "Look at that one," Dick said of an especially huge, round pumpkin riding high and proud on its wooden pallet, attracting many admiring looks. "It's a balloon," he whispered. "Stick it with a pin and it'd probably blow up."

A bright sun was quickly warming the day

outside, but growers and spectators still huddled in sweaters and jackets inside the unheated arena, a place usually reserved for horse shows and livestock auctions. Ron paced nervously, occasionally stopping to talk with rivals, but mainly sticking with the Rhode Island crew, huddling now and then to consult with Joe Jutras or Steve Sperry in a hushed voice while taking sidelong glances at the rows of competing pumpkins.

"Hey, buddy, nice to see you," Dick called to New Hampshire grower Bruce Whittier, a trim, handsome man in his 50s who had walked up to admire Dick's orange entry. "I didn't bring a big one, but I brought a pretty one," Dick said. He was hoping he'd have a shot at winning the fair's prettiest pumpkin award. "Ah, well, you never know," Dick said, his gaze wandering over to the kiddie patch, where he'd spotted another bright-orange pumpkin with an appealing apple shape. "That's a pretty one over there too."

"Well, mine ain't pretty," Whittier said, pointing to a tire-shaped pumpkin that looked as if it had just rolled off a giant dump truck and crashed against the curb. It leaned crazily on top of its pallet, one side high in the air, stem angling downward, blossom end up.

"That's yours? What are you talking about?" said Dick, trying to be polite.

"I don't have a clue what it weighs yet," Whittier said. "You know . . . how do you *tape* that?" he asked, his voice rising in puzzlement. "I taped it at eight-something."

Dick lifted an eyebrow. The pumpkin looked a lot bigger than 800 pounds. As these giants matured, growing lumpy and crooked on the vine, getting an accurate measurement could be a challenge. But Whittier, a veteran who knew his way around a pumpkin as well as anybody, had a bumbling-professor-like penchant for acting a little extra perplexed. He had looked just as mystified that summer when visitors to his patch, one of the stops on the New Hampshire tour, asked him how much his pumpkins were taping. He claimed to have no idea. But he hadn't objected, and in fact seemed tickled when several of the growers pulled out a measuring tape and made their own calculations on the spot. The same thing happened now. As Whittier discussed with Dick the proper way to estimate the wheel-shaped pumpkin's weight, another grower pulled a measuring tape out of his pocket and set to work.

"I taped it from stem to blossom," Whittier explained.

"Well, that would make it a lot smaller then," Dick said. "The right way to tape these is this way," he said, running a finger around the edge of the largest part of the pumpkin.

"Right around the whole bottom?" Whittier said skeptically.

"Absolutely. You've got to tape it like the ass end was up in the air. That's the way we always taped ours."

"You know," said Whittier, much amused by watching his rivals take their own measurements of his pumpkin, "they say the more you tape it, the bigger it gets."

Indeed. When Whittier's pumpkin was measured Dick's way, it tallied 378 inches, or 1,130 pounds.

Ron's pumpkin was the star attraction. This one was the Wallace's 1068 that they had crossed with the 1370 Rose. It was shaped something like an avocado — with a high, rounded top sloping down to a long, thick snout at one end — punctuated by a stem as thick and gnarled as the trunk of a small tree. The pumpkin blushed orange at the top, but faded to a mottled cream color with salmon undertones along the sides. The longer you looked at it, the bigger it looked. Based on its measurements, it was supposed to weigh right at 1,300 pounds.

But there were other contenders, nearly as big, that would make this weigh-off a real contest. Jim Ford's big one was parked right next to Ron's. Mark Breznick from Vermont had a beautiful, high, round pumpkin that might hold a surprise. That was enough to put the Wallaces on edge. Then, after the other entries already had been settled into their places, a dump truck rolled into the arena with a gargantuan, plastic-wrapped blob filling its bed. Ron spotted it immediately, jolting to attention. "That looks like a big pumpkin," he said, his eyes narrowing. "Who is that? I think I'll take a look." He walked briskly across the arena, dodging beeping forklifts, to get a better view of the gigantic fruit that had been mummified in shiny plastic wrap. Some growers wrapped their pumpkins after cutting them from the vine to keep them from losing weight through evaporation.

Ron stopped several yards away from the truck. He didn't want to get too close, or make it too obvious that he was scoping it out, but his eyes were glued to the new challenger. He could tell it was big. How big, though? Another grower walked by. Ron acted nonchalant. "That's a nice pumpkin in the dump truck," he said to the grower, who walked on by without responding.

Ron steadied his nerves, calmed his face, and tried to shrug off his worry. The pumpkin's owner, Joe Goetze, from Pittsfield, Massachusetts, jumped up into the bed of the truck and quickly stripped away the plastic wrap. The forklift speared the pallet, backed up, turned, and began rumbling across the arena. The forklift driver stopped briefly to consult with Jim Kuhn, who had been looking the pumpkin over as it rolled across the sandy floor. Kuhn pointed to the front row, right next to Ron's pumpkin. Ron walked over to Joe Jutras and leaned in to speak quietly.

"I don't know, Joe. It's going to be close," he said.

"I know," said Joe. "It's going to be close."

Dick was concerned, but he was determined to stay upbeat. "It's hard to tell," he said, looking over the Goetze entry. The cream-colored pumpkin was low and wide and looked like solid rock. "That's a nice pumpkin. If Ronnie wins it, it probably won't be by more than twenty pounds. But you know, when you get here, they all look just as big as yours."

Ron had on his game face. "Would I like to win? Sure I would. But you can only have one person win these things. You can make the top ten at this weigh-off and you've done your job. It's very difficult, you know. It's very difficult . . ." The beeping of a passing forklift punctuated his words. The bleachers now were filled with spectators. Jim Beauchemin climbed onto the 18-inch-high wood platform that was to serve as the announcer's podium, grabbed the microphone, and asked the crowd to stand for "The Star-Spangled Banner." The weigh-off had begun.

The pumpkins were weighed on two industrial scales installed on either side of the podium. The scales were four-foot-by-four-foot metal plates set on the ground and wired to a digital display mounted high on the wall of the arena behind the scales. Several volunteers designated as "pumpkin lifters" carried the smaller entries to the scales on a tarp. The larger ones were carried over on pallets by a forklift. Beauchemin called out the name of each entry's grower, filled in the waiting time with microphone chit-chat, and then announced the official weight for each pumpkin. Ron paced the arena alone, sometimes staring down at his feet as he walked, sometimes snapping open his cell phone to make a call. "He knows there's a couple here that could beat him," Dick said, watching his son pace.

The weigh-off sped along, starting with the kiddie patch pumpkins that climbed steadily from 343 pounds into the 400s and 500s and on up into the 800s. Steve Sperry, who had won at Topsfield in 2004, was the first of the Rhode Island crew to have a pumpkin weighed: 891 pounds. Then, Steve Connolly weighed 923.5 pounds. "Are we going to see the first thousand-pounder of the day?" Beauchemin had teased the crowd when Peter Rondeau's entry was brought to the scale. Peter had been taping it at about 950 and was hoping it would go heavy. But as the weight blinked onto the screen, Beauchemin broke the bad news; "No! Nine hundred and fifty pounds!"

As more pumpkins were weighed, more disappointments piled up. Everything seemed to be weighing in lighter than expected, and it was taking an embarrassingly long time to get to the half-ton mark. Topsfield was beginning to look like the junior league. Only 15 pumpkins remained to be weighed. "Okay," Beauchemin said, reassuring the crowd. "We haven't seen a thousand pounds yet, but we will."

It was Joe Jutras who finally broke the barrier. His jalepeño-shaped pumpkin was 10th to the last to be weighed, starting the top-10 countdown with the first 1,000-pounder of the contest. But even his pumpkin was unexpectedly light, weighing 1,054 pounds when it was estimated to be 1,100. Dick's bright-orange pumpkin was the first to go heavy, weighing 1,110 pounds, nearly 8 percent more than expected.

Jim Ford, one of Ron's main challengers and third to last to go to the scale, weighed in a pumpkin at just 1,062 pounds. With only Ron and Goetze left, Dick still had the heaviest pumpkin of the day. Already, he was assured of third place, along with prize money and a ribbon. He'd never expected that. "Third is the highest I've ever done," Dick marveled. "Almost got a tear outta me," he wisecracked. "But nawwwwwt quite."

As the forklift maneuvered Goetze's pumpkin into place, Dick walked over to the grower, a small, wiry middle-aged man with a bushy gray mustache, and shook his hand with a grin. "May the best man win," Dick told him.

"Do we have a leader?" Beauchemin shouted into his microphone as the weight blinked on the display. "Do we have a leader? One thousand . . . two hundred . . . eighty-three pounds!"

At 1,283 pounds, Goetze was in first place, but his pumpkin hadn't weighed as heavy as it looked. And now it was Ron's turn. As the forklift rumbled across the sand with his pumpkin held high, the last of the day to be weighed, Ron stepped into a clearing in the middle of the arena. He stood with his hands buried in the front pockets of his jeans, his body tense, his eyes fixed on the digital display at the top of the wall. Dick stood next to him, his arms folded across his chest, eyes on the display too.

"Ron Wallace is from Rhode Island . . ." Beauchemin told the crowd. "This is one big pumpkin, folks. One big pumpkin!"

Ron's fruit settled to the scale. "Allllll-righty . . ." Beauchemin said. "The leader is one thousand two hundred and eighty-three pounds. Are we going to get a new record for Topsfield? Are you witnessing the biggest?" The forklift backed away. The scale jumped from zero and zoomed through the hundreds. "Allllllright . . . one thousand . . ."

The red digital numbers clicked rapidly higher, then stopped. "One thousand . . . three hundred and eighty-seven pounds!" shouted Beauchemin. "Thirteen hundred eight-seven pounds! The heaviest pumpkin ever to be weighed at Topsfield Fair!"

The crowd roared its approval. So did Ron. He cocked his arm, leaned back, and pumped his fist in the air. "WooooHaaaaaa!"

he hollered. Then his dad grabbed him in a bear hug. Then Joe and Peter and Steve Sperry, grins splitting their faces ear to ear, pulled him away and lifted him high on their shoulders. Ron again shook his fist in the air. The applause and shouts of congratulations thundered in his ears. Dick stepped back, his eyes red and brimming, watching his son get something they'd both wanted for a long, long time.

The initial frenzy over, Ron and Dick mingled in the crowd of growers, accepting congratulations.

"I didn't know father and son were going to take first and third," said old-timer Jim Kuhn in his woodsy New Hampshire drawl.

"I didn't either, to tell you the truth," said Dick, looking a little dazed. He'd not only won third, but also he was taking home the prettiest-pumpkin award, just like he'd hoped. "You had a lot of pumpkins that didn't weigh what I thought they would weigh," Dick said.

"Yup. They all went light," agreed Kuhn. "That one pumpkin shocked me."

"Where's the treasurer?" Dick said, glancing around. "I want to get paid *now*."

"Your check'll be in the mail," Kuhn grinned.

"You start doubting yourself," Ron was

telling Whittier. He'd been mobbed by well-wishers and was about to be whisked off by Topsfield Fair officials to take care of some paperwork and public relations duties. His victory was just beginning to sink in. "I've always questioned myself," he told Whittier, who had walked over to add his own congratulations. "Are people going to think I don't know what I'm talking about? I'm always preaching and researching and everything, and are people saying, 'Gee, if you know so much, how come you haven't grown the biggest pumpkin?' You get sick of hearing stupid stuff. You start doubting your own abilities."

Whittier nodded sympathetically. His wheel-shaped pumpkin had weighed 1,058 pounds — enough for fifth place, and a lot more than the 800 pounds he expected. But he was a little let down about it not weighing the 1,100-plus pounds Dick's measuring technique had suggested.

"Heyyyyy, Ronnie!" Dick yelled, waving his son over. It was time for pictures with the winning pumpkins. Ron took up position behind his 1068, now adorned with a jumbo-sized blue ribbon. His lips stretched stiffly into a grimacelike smile. His jaw was sore from all the teeth-grinding he'd been doing lately in his sleep. "Hey, Ronnie!"

Now it was George Hoomis, one of the directors of the New England Pumpkin Growers Association. "You know what they say," Hoomis shouted at him, "Rhode Island: the smallest state, the biggest pumpkins!"

Ron's face relaxed into a happy grin as the cameras flashed. "Yeah, that's what they can say now, baby!" he crowed. "It's about time."

When the furor had died down and the championship pumpkin was safely ensconced on its climate-controlled throne in the Topsfield Fruit and Vegetable Barn, Ron had driven straight to the office. "Club members don't care about pumpkin weigh-offs," he said. "I've got to stay on top of things. I was out half of Friday and most of Saturday and I'll be out most of Sunday. I had to return phone calls, set stuff up — the maintenance guy was out this week, carpet cleaning needed to be scheduled. I was excited and happy about winning, but I wasn't going to stand there and talk about it all day. I had to get to work."

Winning first place at Topsfield had been a rare taste of triumph, but that wasn't the prize Ron was really after. He hadn't come close to a world-record weight at Topsfield.

He hadn't even broken the New England record, which was still held by Scott Palmer. The fact was, Topsfield was a local weigh-off, and there were lots of local weigh-offs — hundreds, actually. Topsfield wouldn't get him the orange jacket. And it wouldn't get him into the record books. Everyone would forget the Topsfield winner as soon as a new winner was crowned the next year. Ron wanted to be a world champion. He wouldn't rest until that happened.

And the season was far from over. Ron was still hoping to win Grower of the Year, which meant he had to get three really big pumpkins to the scales at three GPC-certified weigh-offs. Topsfield was the first. He needed two more. The next chance would be at Pennfield Beach in Connecticut the very next day. Then he'd have a six-day break — six more days that the Wallaces' last two, biggest pumpkins had to hold together — before the final weigh-off. If there was going to be a new world record that year, it was probably going to happen October 7. But who knew? Already, one of the pumpkins that had been taping over 1,500 pounds in New York had proved to be a dramatic disappointment. Growers with the New York club had gathered for their weigh-off the same Saturday as Topsfield's, fully expecting to see a new world record set and the fall of the 1,500-pound barrier. But the pumpkin had been a balloon — a hot-air balloon — floating on the scale at just 1,091 pounds. It hadn't even won the weigh-off, placing third behind a 1,225-pounder.

Everyone felt bad for the grower, but also secretly happy that the game remained wide open. So Ron was up at dawn again the Sunday after Topsfield, loading another pumpkin for the Connecticut weigh-off. Joe Jutras was competing too, and this time they were joined by club members Mike Oliver and Fred Macari. A storm front had moved through overnight, bringing in black clouds and heavy rain. The friends rendezvoused at the Wallace house at 9 a.m., their pumpkins already loaded in their trucks. Then they set off in the pouring rain for the two-hour drive along the southern New England coast.

There are few things in this world as strange as the sight of a caravan of pickups carrying giant pumpkins down the freeway. As the procession zoomed down the road in the rain at 70 mph, the creamy-orange pumpkins glowed like beacons through the gray haze. Joe Jutras led the way in his white van. He drove in the slow lane to stay out of the way of faster drivers, but the pumpkins still clogged traffic. Drivers in passing cars hit their brakes and gaped at the fascinating deformity of the gargantuan fruit. Despite the slippery roads and driving rain, some drivers fumbled for cell phone cameras at 70 mph, risking their lives to snap pictures of a sight they knew they would never be able to describe in words.

The weigh-off proceeded despite the rain. It was a much smaller affair than Topsfield, not much more than a gathering of local enthusiasts in the parking lot of a beachside community center in Fairfield. Connecticut growers had suffered as much as anyone, and only a dozen pumpkins were registered for the weigh-off, five of them from Rhode Island.

If Ron's Topsfield entry was considered big, his Pennfield one was certifiably huge. Grown on a 1228 Jutras seed, it was the only pumpkin that season (after the 500 Wallace blew up) to rival the 1068s in size. Several people told Ron they thought it was the biggest in the patch. It was another one of the cream-colored fruits that boasted more heavy-fleshed squash genetics. It was broad and deep, with a high hump in the middle. But the 1228 was actually measuring a bit smaller than the Wallace's three biggest 1068s, including the Topsfield winner, and it thumped hollow — "like a drum," Ron said.

Joe Jutras had brought a pumpkin he'd grown with the 1354 Checkon seed. It was noticeably smaller than Ron's, measuring an estimated 1,064 pounds, while Ron's pumpkin was measuring close to 1,300. Joe had a fondness for orange, but his pumpkin that day was lumpy and pale, with roughly veined skin. He'd named it Winky, because it had bulged and sagged over itself on the blossom end, the way a fat man's belly overlaps his trousers. The crease gave it a "winking" effect, for those who had a lot of imagination.

Vermont grower Mark Breznick had brought what he thought was a 1,000-plus pounder, and Ed Giarrusso, a newer grower from Providence, Rhode Island, was hoping to cross the 1,000-pound mark for the first time.

Anyone eyeballing these pumpkins would have placed their bets on Ron's, and his was again slated to go to the scale last. Giarrusso got his 1,000-pounder, and Breznick's weighed 1,023 pounds. Joe's was 1,169 pounds — a whopping 10 percent more than its estimate. But Ron's pumpkin, just as he and his dad had thought, went light, coming in at 1,140 pounds.

It was Joe's turn to be on top. "This is my first win," he told a local television news crew that was covering the weigh-off. "I've been traveling with the Wallace boys, and it's been kind of hard to beat 'em."

"This pumpkin doesn't look nearly as big as the other one," Joe acknowledged. "So you can't go by size. You go by genetics and —" he banged his palm on the side of the pumpkin — "by the thump. If you bang these things and they're hard, you know it's going heavy."

Ron and Dick weren't too disappointed. Ron still racked up an 1,140-pound pumpkin to go with his 1,347-pounder, which gave him a respectable 1,243 average so far in his bid to win Grower of the Year. And the Wallaces were pleased for Joe, who had put just as much time and effort into his garden as they had into theirs.

With Pennfield over, the focus shifted to October 7. "There's only one question people are asking now," Ron said. "Who's going to have the biggest pumpkin?"

Meanwhile in the Ohio Valley, Dave Stelts was talking trash. "I'm not worried about Rhode Island," Dave boasted. "As Paulie said to Rocky, 'I don't sweat you.' "

Dave's own attempt at a champion season had imploded, but that didn't stop him from beating the drum for his club. "The boys from R.I. are going down to the big guns from the Ohio Valley," he wrote in an October 3 message titled "Let's talk some SMACK!" on BigPumpkins.com. Now that most of the growers who had set out to grow a competitive pumpkin had resigned themselves to watching from the sidelines, the whole of giant-pumpkin land was waiting to see if a new world record would emerge on October 7, not to mention the world's first 1,500-pound pumpkin. The two Ohio clubs and Port Elgin would hold weigh-offs that morning, and the Rhode Island club's would start at 1 p.m. Everyone expected the year's champion to be decided by the end of the weekend, even though a handful of other weigh-offs would be held over coming weeks, most on the West Coast. On Columbus Day, Monday, October 9, Sherry LaRue was taking her 1068 to Half Moon Bay, California, the biggest weigh-off on the West Coast.

Word was everywhere now that Ohio had two pumpkins likely to be over 1,500 pounds, and another one that could get there if it was lucky. Growers knew, too, that the Wallaces had been holding their best for last — two pumpkins that were supposed to be bigger than the 1,347-pounder Ron weighed at Topsfield. But most believed it would take a small miracle for Dick or Ron to sail past the armada of Ohio giants. And no one saw the Southern New England club delivering the kind of big numbers it had the year before. The Ohio Valley, instead, was predicted to step in and claim bragging rights as the best giant-pumpkin growing club in the world. Ohio's Quinn Werner, who was thought to have at least two pumpkins over 1,300 pounds, might pull ahead of Ron for Grower of the Year.

Ron kept his own counsel, as usual. But Dick waded in to the smack talk with relish. "It's about time Ohio got back into the hunt," he answered Dave on the Internet message board. "I just hope all those 13 and 1400 pounders don't turn out to be balloons. It would be a shame for little Rhody to spank your butts — AGAIN."

After all, if there was one thing that Dick had learned from 16 years of disappointment, it was that anything could happen once the pumpkins hit the scales.

15
It Is What It Is

Donald Salisbury, a skinny, 60ish man with a baseball cap perched on his head and a frizzy gray beard sticking out from his chin, worked the controls of his tractor like a conductor directing a symphony. The tractor bumped into gear and headed straight for Ron Wallace's giant pumpkin with its bucket scoop lifted high in the air. The old engine grumbled and growled, belching white smoke from a narrow steam pipe that rose from its rusty chassis. The tractor lurched, the bucket wobbled, something, somewhere, groaned.

"Whooaaaa! Oh! Oh!" hollered Jeff Blais, trying to make himself heard over the roar of the tractor and waving his hands back and forth in a stop signal. "You gotta go up and tip it forward . . . Come up a little bit. Okay . . . okay . . . now, let it come forward." Salisbury, the farmer from down the street who always seemed ready to answer the Wallaces' calls for assistance, sat calmly atop the tractor, ignoring Blais's urgent shouts and gestures with the unruffled confidence of a man who knew his tractor better than he knew his wife. There was a rattle and a bang as the bucket moved into position in front of the pumpkin resting on its wooden pallet. Salisbury had fitted the front of his loading bucket with a forklift attachment, and with surgical precision, he maneuvered the shaking, jerking fork tines into the narrow spaces beneath the pallet, then lifted the whole thing toward the sky.

All this wasn't especially good for Dick's heart. He watched anxiously as the giant pumpkin wobbled into the air on top of the pallet at the end of the fork tines attached to the bucket connected to the old tractor driven by Mr. Salisbury. Dick's forehead was creased in a deep frown of concentration, his eyes narrowed. Every grower knew the potential horrors of pumpkin-picking time. An Australian grower and poet, Tony Hickman, even wrote a poem about it:

I'll never forget Blossom
She Met with Bad Luck
On the way to the weigh-off
She rolled off the truck.

Ron was at work, so Dick was overseeing the pumpkin loading by himself that evening, with the help of Salisbury and Jeff Blais, who had donned one of his favorite T-shirts for the event, one of Dick's Pumpkin Toons: MY LIFE IS GIANT PUMPKINS — JUST ASK MY X-WIFE, it said.

The next day, Friday, a half-dozen Rhodies were in line to have their pumpkins picked and loaded for Saturday's weigh-off. Several growers would team up and make the rounds from patch to patch. That would take all day, so the Wallaces had decided to get their pumpkins out of the way Thursday night. They had borrowed a flatbed trailer that was big enough to carry both the pumpkins together. Dick and Blais would load them up in the evening, and then Dick would drive them to the weigh-off site the next day while Ron helped the other growers load.

Harvesting and loading a giant pumpkin into a truck is not so different from the task ancient Egyptians faced when moving great blocks of stone to build the pyramids. Growers usually use a tall tripod fitted with a block and tackle, which they position directly over the pumpkin in the garden. The chain running down from the pulley is hooked to a two-tier metal lifting ring that sits atop the pumpkin like a hat. Straps attached to the ring run down along the sides of the pumpkin, gripping it like an octopus. A rope is strung through loops on the bottom of the straps, encircling the pumpkin's base and cinching tight to secure it. Then, slowly, the pumpkin is winched into the air so that a pickup truck can back up between the tripod legs beneath it. The pumpkin is lowered onto a pallet in the back of the pickup and voilà: It's loaded and ready for the trip to the weigh-off, where a forklift will take care of the unloading.

Dick and Jeff used a tripod and winch to lift each of the Wallace pumpkins onto a pallet in the garden. But then, since they were loading the pumpkins on a trailer instead of into a pickup, Salisbury and his tractor took over. It took a tedious, nerve-racking hour to pick and load both the fruits. Dick and Jeff sprawled on their bellies in the soft garden dirt, fastening the lifting harness to the pumpkins, which had been cut from the vine with one swift slice of a small knife. Then Salisbury used his tractor to lift the pumpkins onto wooden pallets padded with old sofa cushions right there in the patch. Finally, he loaded both pumpkin and pallet onto the trailer.

About a foot of vine was left on each side

of the stems. Later, Dick would attach bags of water to these whiskers to keep the pumpkin hydrated. The vine would siphon the water from the bag, helping prevent any weight loss. Or so the theory went.

Finished with the loading, Dick walked back to the barn to check on some equipment they would need the next day. He passed by the emptied pumpkin patch without a glance. There wasn't much to see. The vines were all trampled and torn. Weeds already were beginning to cover the dirt. In the middle of the mess there was one bright spot: the Cleome, spider flower, that Dick had asked Ron to leave earlier in the summer. Ron had never followed through with his vow to yank it, and it stood tall and proud, bursting with its pale purple flowers, now queen of the garden.

"Well," Dick said, "they're on the trailer. There's nothing wrong with them. I didn't have to pose for pictures with my saw on my shoulder."

But he didn't sound happy. He sounded tired. He sounded stressed. He sounded like he was ready for it all to be over.

Steve Daletas, the former world-record holder from Oregon, was a guest of honor for the Rhode Island mafia's "Phat Friday"

— the name they'd given their day of pumpkin picking and loading before their weigh-off. The name was inspired by the Mardi Gras day of revelry, and usually it was an occasion of much beer drinking and good fun, with all the growers in a cheerful state of anticipation. This year, though, no one was in a partying mood.

It had been a bad year for too many of them. In a reversal of fortune, Ron and Dick were the only ones in the club, except for maybe Peter Rondeau, who believed they had managed to grow a personal best. Steve Sperry had nothing to bring to the weigh-off at all. Neither did Scott Palmer. But both men had still taken the day off work to help pick and load the other growers' pumpkins.

"It's the thrill of victory and the agony of defeat," Scott deadpanned, making light of his misfortune. But really, it had hurt more than that. After he had lost his 1225 a couple of weeks before, Scott had been worried about losing his 1443 too. "I went out there to tape it and I bumped into it and it felt like it moved, and I thought, 'That's not right.' That pumpkin is taping over eleven hundred pounds. How can it move with me just bumping into it? It shouldn't be moving."

Scott's wife, Shelley, was in denial. "Oh, there's nothing wrong with it," she had assured him. But the next night Scott had gone out for his evening pumpkin check and it seemed to be moving a little more. "I figure, that's gotta be bad. Nothing's leaking or anything, but it seemed like it just wasn't right."

Sure enough, when the crew arrived to lift the pumpkin to load it for Topsfield, its bottom fell out. "We picked it up, and *bllllpp-ppt!*" Scott said. "Ahhh well. Next year we'll get 'em."

The Phat Friday lifting team met at Ron's house at 10 a.m., and set out from there for Joe Jutras's house, the first stop of the day. Joe greeted the growers as they arrived in his driveway, then led the way to the back of the house through his empty garden to his last, best pumpkin. It was grown from the same seed, the 1228 Jutras, as the pumpkin that Ron had taken to the Pennfield weigh-off — the one that had weighed so much lighter than expected. That was worrying Joe. He pointed to one, bulky end of the cream-colored pumpkin. "It's very thick right there," he said hopefully. "That sounds good there."

Ron leaned over Joe's pumpkin, encircling it with his arms in a bear hug, then gave it a smart slap. "Oh, yeah. That sounds great," Ron agreed. "What are you taping on this?"

Joe told him it was 1,125 pounds.

"I think you can come close to twelve hundred pounds out of this, Joe."

The tripod was hauled out of Ron's pickup truck and set up over the pumpkin. With the plants crushed and trampled, the patch bristled with the remains of bamboo sticks that had been propping up the leaves. The growers worked swiftly to wrap the pumpkin in its harness and hook it to the chain. Mike Oliver began hauling on the chain, which rattled and clanked as it began slowly lifting the pumpkin from its bed of dirt.

As the fruit cleared the ground, Ron dropped to his hands and knees to peer beneath it. What a grower wants to see is a flat bottom. Sometimes the underside of a pumpkin grew curved, like an upside-down bowl, which could trim 20 or 30 pounds off the final weight. "You're in good shape, Joe," Ron announced. "Nice bottom."

"You've always had a nice bottom, Joe," Mike Oliver added. Somebody had to say it.

Joe had not had such a great year in his pumpkin patch. The storm that had leveled his plants in July had been a major setback. But he'd had more success with something new. Joe had decided this year to try his hand at growing long gourds — baseball-bat-shaped fruit that grow from climbing vines. Growers competed to see how long they could grow these. The world record stood at 116 5/8 inches — more than 9 feet.

Joe built a 12-foot-tall trellis to support the vines and give the gourds plenty of room to hang. And he'd grown a gourd 126 1/2 inches long, beating the old world record his first year trying. Joe had cut the gourd from the vine and taped it to a long board to stabilize it for transport. At the Frerich's Farm weigh-off, he'd have the gourd's length measured and officially certified. His giant pumpkins weren't much to crow about, but if nobody had grown a longer gourd that year, he'd have a shot at his own world record after all.

The Rhode Island team drove from patch to patch that Friday, loading pumpkins. It was slow work, and fraught with unexpected difficulties. At Norm Gansert's house, the loading crew found that he'd grown his pumpkins on the side of a steep hill. There was no way to set up the tripod or back in a truck. They had no choice but to use a tarp to manually haul an 800-pound pumpkin up the hill to the truck.

Backs were aching by the time the lifters

arrived at Peter Rondeau's house. Peter was bringing his 1068 to the weigh-off, but he'd been fighting a problem with the stem the past few days. The skin around the stem was cracking and curling like old paint. But it wasn't rotting, and the pumpkin was still in good-enough shape to be weighed.

It was after 4 p.m. by the time all the pumpkins had been loaded and 5 p.m. by the time they arrived at Frerich's Farm to unload. David Frerich, the farm's owner, had decided to hold the weigh-off in the parking lot instead of in the grassy field next to the farm, which was still soggy from rain. Frerich ran the 200-acre farm and nursery with the help of his wife, Barbara. The couple hoped the weigh-off would be good publicity for their nursery business, which needed a boost after its worst year ever. The Frerichs specialized in decorative fall crops, growing squash, gourds, chrysanthemums, and 15 acres of field pumpkins — the jack-o'-lantern kind. Their mum business had done well — they had started the year with 30,000 pots of the colorful flowers and were down to just 4,000. "That's the only high-light to the whole season," Frerich said. The rains had delayed planting, so they'd been able to bring in only one good hay crop, instead of two. Disease ruined their tomato and cucumber crops. And the summer heat wave had stopped the pumpkin plants from setting fruit, decimating that year's yield. The Frerichs weren't alone — pumpkin crops all up and down the East Coast had been ruined, making it a lean fall for jack-o'-lanterns.

"I've talked to seventy-five-year-old guys and they say this is the worst year they've ever seen in their entire career," Frerich noted.

The Rhode Island pumpkins were unloaded and set in a line on the grass along the edge of the parking lot, just down from the pumpkin catapult Dick had made one winter for David Frerich. The Frerichs entertained schoolchildren on field trips by loading little pumpkins into the catapult and launching them across an open field, where they landed with a splatter.

The Rhodies hovered protectively over their pumpkins, getting their first good look at the fruit off the vine. Peter leaned over his 1068 and slapped it hard with his open palm. Then he laughed self-consciously. He hadn't the faintest idea what he was listening for. "That's an art I haven't learned yet," he confessed to Joe. Joe gave the pumpkin a confident thump, more with the heel of his hand than with his palm. "Put your ear on that," Joe told him. "Feel that?" *Thump thump thump.* The pumpkin vibrated dully under his pounding. Peter's face looked blank.

"Slap it harder," Peter said.

THUMP THUMP THUMP.

"Can you tell any difference?" Joe asked.

"Not really," said Peter.

Ron was fussing over his pumpkin, concerned that the water bags were still full, which meant the pumpkin wasn't sucking up much moisture. He stood back, looking first at his own pumpkin, then at his dad's, then at his own again. The two 1068s were set side by side, just a few feet apart. It was the first time he'd been able to really compare them that way. To the eye, Dick's pumpkin looked slightly larger, but the tape measure showed Ron's to be bigger by a few inches. Both were pale orange and roughly the same shape — though they had distinctly different personalities. Ron's pumpkin was a sumo wrestler sitting back on fat haunches, muscled ribs bulging with veins, powerful shoulders surging forward around the stem. Dick's pumpkin was rounder, softer, nicer-looking, reclining on its blossom end like Great-Aunt Nellie resting in her favorite chair. Dick had named his pumpkin Mrs. Calabash. Ron had suggested calling it Durante, because of a slight hump on top reminiscent of comedian Jimmy Durante's famous big nose. Dick was a traditionalist, though. Pumpkins are females, the womb of the plant. So he'd borrowed from Durante's nightly sign-off, "Good night, Mrs. Calabash, wherever you are."

"I think these two pumpkins could be within twenty-five pounds of each other," Ron concluded. "You never know. This one" — he ran his hands across the rough surface of his pumpkin — "on the blossom end and the stem end is solid meat. Now, like I've been saying, all I need is 3 percent heavy to hit fourteen hundred pounds."

That was Ron "the numbers man" talking. He had, of course, calculated the estimated weight of his pumpkin based on its OTT measurements: 1,367 pounds. And how much more it would have to weigh to break over 1,400 pounds: 3 percent more. And how much more it would need to break 1,500 pounds: almost 10 percent.

The problem with that, as Ron well knew, was that the bigger a pumpkin was, the less likely it was to go heavy, as recent history had proven. In fact, odds were far greater that it would go light. Witness Larry Checkon's estimated 1,700-plus pumpkin, which actually weighed 1,469, and the rumored 1,500-plus pumpkin from New York, which just the previous week had weighed less than 1,100. But neither had been grown from a 1068 seed.

"You know what," Ron said, snapping back to reality, "just to finish out the season, to get one to the scale — whatever it weighs, it weighs. But I've got a good shot going into tomorrow." Ron was swinging wildly now between the Dr. Jekyl of cautious optimism and the Mr. Hyde of crazy hope. "If I do what I did at Topsfield or better, then I have a good shot at Grower of the Year. And if it happens, it happens. But this was really just about me, proving to everybody that I can do this thing."

The daylight was fading fast, and the temperature was dropping. Ron fetched an armful of blankets and comforters from his truck and started tucking them around both his pumpkin and his dad's. None of the other growers bothered covering their pumpkins.

"It's going to get cold tonight," Ron explained.

"Mine is tough; it can take it," Joe cracked, getting a laugh out of the other growers. But Ron was dead serious. "You never know. Tonight is a harvest moon . . . You could get a frost."

"Naaah," Joe said. "Not with this wind. With a wind like this, you won't get a frost."

It was, indeed, very windy. And it was getting colder as night fell. The setting sun spackled the sky with a last gasp of electric blues and pinks. The Rhode Island mafia drifted together into a small circle, an instinctive gathering of the tribe. It was time to go, but they seemed to be having a hard time leaving their pumpkins. Dick was already thinking ahead to the next day's weigh-off. Ron would emcee the event, announcing the growers and the pumpkin weights. They had 45 pumpkins registered for the contest, and only one scale. Dick worried it would get tedious for the crowd, and he wanted to make sure Ron kept things interesting. One way to do that, he suggested, was to announce the awards for prettiest and ugliest pumpkin as the owners had their entries weighed. "Just tell them something like, 'Gee, that's an ugly pumpkin!' or however you want to ad-lib it, and then give them their award right then," he advised Ron.

Ron tucked his chin under and looked at his dad through his eyebrows with a son's patient skepticism. "Okay," he said. "I will."

405

Dick pressed on. "There has to be some excitement for the crowd," he insisted.

That got a rise out of the other growers. Excitement at a pumpkin weigh-off? "Oooooooooooooo!" the men all chorused breathily.

"And the crowd goes wild!" Peter said, cracking up everyone except Dick.

"Ah, come on," Dick said, throwing his hands in the air.

"Alright. Ready to get out of here?" Ron asked briskly, breaking it up. Nobody moved. Everyone fell silent. The mood shifted subtly. It was the end of the season. Finally. There was nothing to do now but wait for tomorrow. They didn't even have any pumpkins to go home to.

"Well, boys," Ron said after a short silence. "We've only got twelve more hours as GPC champions."

"Yeah," Dick said. "Ron is going to be laying in bed all night, saying, 'I hope my father doesn't beat me, I hope my father doesn't beat me.' " He paused while everyone laughed, then added with a grin, "And I'll be laying in bed thinking, 'I hope my son beats me, I hope my son beats me.' "

Pumpkin weigh-offs aren't your typical competition. Once the pumpkins are lined up at the scale, there's not a darn thing for the competitors to do. They can't run faster or jump higher or sing louder to improve their chances of winning. The race is already run. Their pumpkin will weigh what it weighs. It's just a matter of waiting to find out the number. Which makes pumpkin weigh-offs a little slow in terms of action and also torturously long and tension-filled for the growers who hope to win.

That may have been why Dick Wallace was more than a little cranky the morning of the weigh-off. His mood matched the long-sleeved black T-shirt he'd donned for weigh-off day, which was emblazoned with a picture of an evil-faced, flaming orange pumpkin against a background of crossed swords. No one blamed him for being out of sorts. By the end of the day, the Wallaces would either be winners or just a couple of schmucks who'd spent their whole year — *again* — trying to grow the world's biggest pumpkin.

The Rhode Island growers had arrived at Frerich's Farm before 9 in the morning to begin preparing for the 1 p.m. weigh-off. There was a lot of work to be done: setting up the scale, unloading pumpkins, decorating the podium, and erecting the magnificent new pumpkin-shaped scoreboard Joe

Jutras had made only a few days before. Every grower was assigned a job, and Dick's was to check in contestants and make sure they were registered and had paid their membership and entry fees. He sat at a white folding table next to the podium, silently flipping through a stack of papers, an unmistakably antisocial look on his face. A bottle of champagne was at his elbow, waiting for the winner of the day's weigh-off. At the end of the table, Ken Desrosiers, the BigPumpkins.com Webmaster and SNGPG director, was setting up his computer equipment. He would be entering all the growers' data and the weigh-off results as each pumpkin went to the scale, for posting later on the Web site.

Ken couldn't help but notice Dick's sour mood. "Dick, you're not your normal self." Without even looking up, Dick grumbled something unintelligible. But then his good nature got the better of him. "I haven't been sleeping well lately," he explained. "I wake up at two thirty, three a.m. And then that's it. Night's finished. I can't get back to sleep."

The farm's parking lot was bustling with activity. Growers had already begun trickling in, and Peter Rondeau was busy directing the forklifts as they unloaded the pumpkins and began setting them in line to be weighed, smallest to largest. Joe, Steve Sperry, and Scott Palmer were constructing a frame for the big scoreboard that would serve as the backdrop for the afternoon's action, if only they could figure out how to get it to stand up at the back of the flatbed truck they were using for the weigh-off stage.

Ron had the jitters big-time, but he coped by going into manager mode. Rectangular, mirrored sunglasses concealed his eyes. He paced around the parking lot with his lucky orange jack-o'-lantern T-shirt peeking out from beneath his long-sleeved denim SNGPG shirt, drifting from workstation to workstation to check on everyone's progress and then wandering away to make another call on his cell phone. He was worried the stage wouldn't be ready in time. He was worried the parking lot was too small and cramped for the weigh-off and the crowd. He was worried his pumpkin would go light — oops, no, scratch that. He refused to entertain the thought. He was actually more worried that the Ohio growers would have such a big pumpkin they'd be impossible to catch.

One mercy: The Ohio weigh-offs were starting in the morning. They should be finishing up about the time the Rhode Island weigh-off got underway. That meant Ron would know exactly what he was up against before his pumpkin went to the scale. Would he be trying to beat a new world record from Tim Parks? From Buddy Conley? From Quinn Werner? Someone had talked to somebody and the word was that Werner had arrived at the Ohio Valley weigh-off that morning with a giant bomb that could blow everybody away. And no one was counting out Port Elgin, Ontario. There could easily be a surprise waiting in Canada, which had claimed world records in 2004, 1998, and 1994.

By 11 a.m., a line of heavily laden pickup trucks had stacked up along the drive into farm, and two forklifts were humming and beeping nonstop as they ferried pumpkins to the parking lot. Growers from across New England were lined up in front of Dick's table as he paged through his lists, looking less cranky now, focusing on his task. He had some help from Ed Giarrusso's wife, Rose, a cheerful woman who seemed more unabashedly excited to be there than any of the growers that morning. She'd been delighted when her husband had weighed in his first 1,000-pound pumpkin at Pennfield Beach the week before, and she was hoping he would have an even bigger one today. She beamed from her chair in an orange corduroy shirt, greeting the growers with infectious good spirits. Dick left the check-in to her and got up to attend to his favorite part of the ceremony: the awards. He'd been assembling the collection of ribbons and trophies since last year's weigh-off, and they would finally be put to good use today.

Dick tacked the ribbons in a row across the front edge of the truck-stage. They were as big as homecoming corsages, four-inch buttons surrounded with ribbons of black and green and orange and purple. He lined up the trophies along the top. Dick and Joe had cooked up an assortment of trophies and plaques, all topped with a ceramic or glass or plastic pumpkin, including one sitting on top of a toilet — the "Ugliest" prize.

Dick's mood lightened as he concentrated on the awards. The scoreboard was finally up and looking good. The day was bright and sunny, though very windy and a little cool. Dick had purchased a collection of decorative flags to mount around the stage. Now they were flapping and snapping colorfully in the brisk wind. The U.S. flag flew high above the scoreboard, right in the middle. A crowd was gathering. A few hundred people already were milling around the parking lot, with more arriving every minute. Spectators wove in and out of the giant pumpkins lined up at the edge of the lot, posing for pictures in front of their favorites. Children were impressed, but the adults were incredulous. "Look at these!" one woman said to her companion. "They're all different colors. They look fake!"

At 12:30 p.m., Ron directed the crowd over to a field behind the parking lot where a crane was waiting to start the weigh-off with a splat. It had become a popular feature at pumpkin weigh-offs in recent years to find creative ways to smash the big fruit as entertainment. It made up, a little, for the tedium of the actual weighing. Most events simply dropped a pumpkin from a crane and let it splatter on the ground at the feet of the spectators. Some were more ambitious: the Terminator Weigh-off at the Chinook Winds Casino in Lincoln City, Oregon, climaxed with a 1,000-pound pumpkin dropped 85 feet onto a car.

The Frerichs had chosen the simple crane-to-ground drop, and the crowd, which had swelled to nearly 1,000, migrated obediently to the field to watch the spectacle. The people roared their approval as the pumpkin went into freefall, a bright orange spot against a blue sky, soaring through the air like Linus's mythic Great Pumpkin, except with more velocity. It shattered against the ground with a gratifyingly wet thunk, spreading gory chunks of pumpkin guts about and generating cheers, applause, and whistles from the delighted audience. Once the flying pumpkin was smashed, they quickly lost interest in it and drifted back to their spots in the bleachers. It was time for the weigh-off to begin.

Ron Wallace had never been what you would call a relaxed kind of guy, even on his calmest days. But that afternoon he was coiled so tight it seemed the slightest touch would send him springing like a jack-in-the-box. He picked up the microphone and stepped onto the podium his father had built. It was only about a foot tall and set right in front of the scale to keep Ron close to the action. Behind him loomed the stage, with Mike Oliver's two young daughters posted on either side of the scoreboard, like teenage Vanna Whites dressed in sweatshirts and jeans, with the youngest wearing a neon-orange wig.

Ron looked out over the parking lot to the crowd packing the bleachers at the opposite end. His sunglasses reflected the bumpy orange field of giant pumpkins stretched out before him. It was time to begin, and he had prepared a small speech. Ron did not have the zoom and zest of Jim Beauchemin, but he was perfectly comfortable in the spotlight.

"A few years ago people wouldn't have thought it was possible," he began. "They think of Rhode Island and they think of the 'Island State,' sailing — stuff like that. Giant pumpkins don't come to mind. But in the last few years a group of individuals has got together and we've fought and we're very proud of our accomplishments. Last year we were named the number-one weigh-off site for giant pumpkins in the world. We hope to retain our title today, but we're up against a tough task. We're up against a big-time group out of Ohio that claims they have several world records going to the scale today. But we are still site champions for a few more hours, and we hope to defend our title here today."

On cue, Joe Jutras, Fred Macari, Steve Sperry, and Peter Rondeau each lifted a corner of a blue tarp and carried forward the first pumpkin of the day. These early entries were small, but they were still treated with dignity. Their growers, usually beginners or children, had worked hard on them, and were proud and excited to find out what they weighed.

"Okay, Joe, what do we have here?" Ron asked.

"Philip Johnson of Bristol, Rhode Island, the first pumpkin to be weighed . . . and it is . . ." Ron peered down at the digital readout that had been set up on the ground in front of the podium. The sun was shining directly onto the readout, washing out the numbers. A makeshift shade they'd taped around it wasn't helping much. "And it is . . ." Ron said, barely making out the numbers, "One hundred sixty-two pounds! Congratulations, Philip!"

Fifteen-year-old Alex Noel, the club's youngest member, was put in charge of marking the weight on a small dry-erase board and presenting it to each grower. The grower would then hold up the sign and have his or her picture taken next to the officially weighed pumpkin. Philip Johnson knelt down, cameras clicked, and his pumpkin was quickly cleared off the scale to make way for the next one. It was a delicate balance, keeping the weigh-off moving so the crowd wouldn't get too restless, while also giving each grower a full measure of recognition. The smaller pumpkins were easy, though, and could be moved quickly. The scale had been calibrated to account for the weight of the tarp. So the pumpkins were simply lifted and carried to the scale, weighed, then carried away again.

Ron did what he could to pump up the action. "There are sites throughout the world weighing off today in competition to see who has the largest pumpkin," he noted. Indeed, it seemed that Ron's attention was bouncing back and forth between his duties as host and his interest in what was happening elsewhere. Last year he had been free to emcee without worrying about his own stakes in the contest. But it was a whole different ballgame this year. He and his dad had not only made it to the weigh-off with big pumpkins; they had brought the biggest pumpkins they had ever grown in their lives.

It was assumed by all the growers that one of the two Wallace pumpkins would win the weigh-off. But which one? And would it weigh enough to win the orange jacket? Everything depended on what was delivered to the scales in Ohio and Port Elgin. Several New England growers were keeping in touch by cell phone with the Ohio growers and friends at the other weigh-offs. Ohio and Port Elgin were posting their results live on the Internet. There wasn't a handy Internet connection at the Frerich's Farm weigh-off site, but it was easy to call up someone who had access to a computer.

Every once in a while, a grower would walk up to Ron at the podium and Ron would bend down to listen to some tidbit of intelligence being passed along. The news out of Ohio was interesting. At the Southern Ohio club's weigh-off, Buddy Conley had achieved his goal, but missed his dream. His pumpkin weighed 1,333 pounds, close to what it measured. Meanwhile, the Ohio Valley club's weigh-off was nearly finished, and many of their big pumpkins were coming in lighter than expected. Some that had been expected to weigh 1,300 pounds weren't even hitting the 1,200-pound mark. But the biggest pumpkins had yet to be weighed, and the story still could turn.

Ron didn't have long to wait. Shortly before 2 p.m., his phone rang. It was Dave Stelts calling with the results from Ohio. Tim Parks's pumpkin had come in light — just 1,327.5 pounds, well under the 1,500 he'd hoped for. Quinn Werner's pumpkin, at 1,446.5 pounds, had won the Ohio Valley weigh-off, but had fallen short of beating Larry Checkon's 1,469-pound world record.

That required a whole new set of calculations by Ron. He tried to keep up a good front on the podium. But he was distracted. The numbers were rattling through his head. Werner's pumpkin wasn't a new world record, but it was the biggest pumpkin weighed so far that year. As it stood, Quinn Werner would be wearing the orange jacket at Niagara Falls next March. His pumpkin was 3 pounds heavier than the biggest pumpkin ever grown in New England, Scott Palmer's 1,443-pounder. And it was 60 to 80 pounds heavier than the estimated weight of the Wallace pumpkins. Ron's only hope now was that at least one of the Wallace pumpkins was heavier than they'd estimated. It wasn't a baseless wish — both were "thumping" heavy. He and his dad had played down their chances, but they were confident they had two pumpkins that would weigh more than 1,400 pounds. The question was, how much more?

One small burden had been lifted off of Ron. No one yet had surpassed 1,500 pounds. That dream was still alive. He picked up his microphone patter as Peter Rondeau's neighbor came to the scale with the pumpkin Peter had helped her grow.

"Sally Sullivan, Coventry, Rhode Island. Sally, are you nervous?" Ron asked. Then he addressed the crowd: "She was hoping for six hundred pounds. The first time I grew a pumpkin with my father, it was nowhere near six hundred pounds. This is also a very pretty pumpkin," he said. "Okay, back away from the scales." Ron peered through the glare at the digital numbers. "Sally, your pumpkin weighs . . . five hundred sixty-two pounds! Congratulations to the rookie, Sally Sullivan, her first year growing Atlantic Giant pumpkins."

At 2:22 p.m., the first 1,000-pounder was weighed, and it was a shocker. It was Steve Connolly's biggest pumpkin that year, but it had taped only a little over 900 pounds. The official weight: 1,031 pounds. Steve held on to his lead for an hour while bigger pumpkins failed to break the 1,000-pound mark. Like everywhere else, most pumpkins in New England were going lighter than expected that year.

The Frerich's Farm weigh-off dragged on. The forklifts seemed to take an eternity at the scale, loading and unloading the big pumpkins, then moving them out of the way for the next contestant. Ron was vexed. "It's going too slow," he said. Eyeing the crowd, he noticed that a lot more people were beginning to move around. "I think I'm losing them," he fretted. To break up the monotony, Joe brought up his long gourd to be officially measured. Joe stood the gourd up beside him so that it towered over his head.

"Big gourd, huh?" Ron asked the crowd. "It got so big that at one point Joe had to dig a hole in the ground as the gourd started to touch down. Congratulations, Joe! First year growing long gourds and a new world record for Joe Jutras with his *realllllly* long gourd."

Dick was hanging out near the scales, talking with growers and keeping his hopes in check. "If mine weighs what it tapes, I'll be tickled pink," he said. "It may not hit fourteen hundred, but who knows? We'll see when it hits the scales."

Now the big players were rolling to the scale. Mike Oliver, who was hoping for his first 1,000-pounder, fell short, with 947 pounds. Ed Giarrusso scored his second 1,000-pounder of the year, with a 1,108-pound pumpkin, finally snatching the lead from Steve Connolly. Peter Rondeau's pumpkin weighed 1,046 pounds, less than his entry last year, and less than the 1,100 pounds he had wanted. "Well," Ron said, "it's not a personal best, but it's still a very impressive pumpkin at 1,046 pounds."

Jim Ford brought a fruit from his New Hampshire patch weighing 1,065 pounds — 3 pounds more than his fourth-place pumpkin at Topsfield.

At 3:45 p.m., only three entries were left, the three biggest, grown by Ron, Dick, and Joe Jutras. Ron wasn't even going to try to emcee his own pumpkins, so for the final three he turned the microphone over to his friend Don Langevin, the former president of the Rhode Island growers club and the author of three books about how to grow giant pumpkins. The forklifts shut down their motors so the crowd could hear Langevin's introduction. Langevin had spent years announcing the weigh-off, and he fell in comfortably behind the microphone. His deep voice and smooth delivery were as polished as a television news anchor's.

"It is indeed an honor to announce the last three pumpkins," he said, launching into a speech to recapture the crowd's attention and play up the drama of the moment. "The top ten pumpkins here averaged 1,178 pounds last year — the number-one weigh-off for giant pumpkins in the entire world. This little weigh-off site.

"I would love to see Joe Jutras go over 1,200 pounds, and I would love to see both Wallaces go over 1,400. So that's what I'm here for. Joe's record was 1,228 last year. He had a pumpkin four years ago, the 1225, that was one of the prettiest pumpkins I've ever seen in my life — perfect orange. And of course, the Wallaces are legendary for losing pumpkins. But this is their payback year. They finished one and three at Topsfield last week, and that was with their peanuts. The big ones are here today. So I'm hoping our average goes up. The work is cut out for us now, because I think the average is over 1,200 at a site in Ohio now. But maybe these pumpkins will go way heavy."

As he concluded, the forklift roared to life again. "The world record has not been broken yet today," Langevin reminded the crowd. "Fourteen hundred forty-six is the biggest pumpkin grown in the world so far this year."

Joe's pumpkin settled to the scale. It had been measuring 1,125 pounds. Don watched the digital numbers. "It went over!" he said. "Eleven hundred eighty! Joe Jutras from North Scituate, Rhode Island. And we have a new leader."

As the forklift rolled over to pull Dick's pumpkin from the line, Langevin kept working the microphone, pumping the crowd. "The next pumpkin going is Dick Wallace from Greene, Rhode Island. Dick is a perennial bridesmaid. He named his pumpkin this year Mrs. Calabash. She's not pretty, but this is not a beauty contest. Dick's personal best last week at Topsfield was 1,110 pounds. He's hoping this one is even heavier than that."

Dick stood to one side of the scale watching as his pumpkin advanced. He looked for Ron and spotted him across the parking lot, standing alone. "Ronnie! Come over here," he waved him over. "Ahhhh, I'm a back-of-the-crowd guy," Ron protested. But he came over anyway to stand next to his father. The two men stood shoulder to shoulder, their arms folded across their chests.

The forklift maneuvered Dick's pumpkin to the scale as Don filled the time with painful reminiscing about past Wallace disappointments.

"I remember one year they brought one to Topsfield and we thought they were going to win. Steve Connolly actually won that year. Steve grew the first one-thousand-pound pumpkin. Ronnie had one taping over a thousand. We thought it was going to weigh heavy. It weighed light. That was a tough ride home. So, Dick, you're due." The forklift backed away, and the lifting team scrambled to remove the harness.

"Just to remind you . . . the world record is 1,469 . . . The biggest one grown so far this year is 1,446, grown in Ohio," Langevin said. "I think one of these has a chance . . . My legs are shakin'."

Dick refused to look at his pumpkin on the scale. He wouldn't even look in that direction. He stared off over the crowd, his eyes hidden beneath the shadow of his SNGPG baseball cap.

"Okay, can't get excited now," Dick whispered to Ron, trying to make a joke. But his voice was thin and nervous. Don chattered away into the microphone.

"This really isn't that ugly of a pumpkin. But the key thing is, does it weigh what it measures? And we're hoping it weighs more than that."

Finally, the lifting team loosened the harness enough to pull it off. They stepped away. The pumpkin was free and clear. The crowd was quiet. Langevin crouched down a little to peer at the readout. "*Hooooool-y* crap!" he said. Dick's head snapped to look at him. He fixed Don with a glare, tense and impatient. He was a man ready for anything life was about to bring him, but he wanted to get on with it. Someone from the crowd shouted, "Dickieeeee!"

Langevin called out the weight: "One thousand *four* hundred . . . *fifty pounds!*"

Dick gave a little shudder. His hands reached up and grabbed the top of his head, crumpling his cap in one brawny fist. His knees buckled as if he were about to fall, but he staggered forward and Ron was there, throwing his arms around his father. Dick buried his face against Ron's shoulder as the other Rhodies rushed up and pounced on him, slapping his back, cheering.

"One thousand, four hundred and fifty pounds," repeated Langevin, as Dick was mobbed by grinning pumpkin growers. "What an achievement! It was a long time coming."

Dick had recovered himself and was grinning broadly, but was still speechless. He had just grown the biggest pumpkin in the world so far that year — he had beaten Quinn Werner by 4 pounds. It wasn't a world record, but it was the second-largest pumpkin ever grown, just 19 pounds lighter than Larry Checkon's world record, set the previous year.

"She weighed heavy," Langevin explained to the crowd. "She taped 1,340 and weighed 1,450. Who says big pumpkins don't weigh heavy? Congratulations, Dick. Mrs. Calabash is a beast!"

The furor gradually died down. No one had forgotten that the weigh-off had one more round to go. Ron's pumpkin, the one that had thumped just as heavy as his father's and actually measured a little larger, was on its way to the scale. And now the Wallaces were in that awkward position Dick had predicted the night before: father versus son.

"Fourteen-seventy, that's the number we need to see for a new world record," Langevin reminded the crowd.

"That would be a really tall order," Ron said. He was playing down his chances, and especially playing down the competition with his father. "I just wanted to beat the 1,347 I got at Topsfield. It didn't matter to me whether it was me or my father . . . So . . . how much of a surprise was that?" He beamed at Joe. "Huge, *huge!* The legend of the 1068 continues."

Dick had disappeared into the crowd.

"He's probably on the oxygen machine. I thought he was going down," Joe said, laughing. He eyed Ron's pumpkin as the forklift carried it to the scale. "I think this one's heavier," Joe said.

Fred Macari rushed over. "Ronnie, the forklift guy said it was the heaviest one for him to load so far."

"Twenty pounds, maybe," Ron said.

"You're going to be a happy man," Peter Rondeau predicted.

"After last week, after Topsfield, I think it's got a shot," Ron said. "We'll see what happens. If not, I'm not disappointed either way."

Dick walked up to wait beside Ron. He wanted to reassure his son. "It thumped a lot heavier," he reminded Ron. "And it taped about eighteen pounds more than mine." But Dick looked worried. The orange jacket had been his dream too, but the last thing he wanted was to beat his own son at the weigh-off. He wanted the world champion to be a Wallace, but he wanted it to be Ron Wallace.

"The truck driver says Ron's is heavier," Joe told him.

"It's heavier?" Dick said.

"Yeah, the guy over there said that punkin's heavier," Joe repeated, pointing to Ron's fruit.

"So, I had the heaviest pumpkin in the GPC for ten minutes," said Dick, relieved enough to feel a little disappointed.

The Wallaces waited impatiently as Ron's pumpkin was unharnessed at the scale. "This is not the time to go slow. This is the time to go full throttle," Dick griped.

Langevin picked up the microphone again. "The last entry is from Ron Wallace. He's the president of the Southern New England

Giant Pumpkin Growers Association." The crowd applauded politely. "The weight to beat is 1,450 . . . The world record is 1,469."

A voice called from the eerily silent crowd: "Come on, Ronnie! Let's go, Ronnie!"

It had been 17 agonizing minutes since they'd learned the weight of Dick's pumpkin. With mind-boggling slowness, the lifting team finished pulling the straps off the pumpkin and stepped away. The routine had been repeated at least 30 times that day. But now it was Ron's pumpkin on the scale, his fate being weighed. The digital numbers began flashing on the readout; they blinked and started to climb.

Don leaned over. The sun was going down behind him, shining straight on the readout. There was just too much glare. He couldn't get a clear view. He leaned closer. He forgot his manners. "You gotta be shittin' me," he blurted into the live microphone. "One thousand . . ."

And then he screamed it: "One thousand *five hundred and two pounds!*"

Ron jumped into the air as the crowd roared, applause and cheers filling his ears for the second time in a week.

"*Unbelievable!* You just saw history being made," Langevin shouted to the crowd.

Ron leaned back, both fists clenched and

raised in the air as he whooped his joy. "Oh yeahhhhh! Yeahhh! *Whooooooo!* Heeeeeeiiiiiaaaaaah!" Dick grabbed his son around the neck in a bear hug.

"Fifteen-oh-two! I think I'm gonna pass out here," Langevin said. "I mean, that's like a Volkswagen."

Dick still had a grip on Ron. "Fifteen-oh-two, fifteen-oh-two," he repeated to his son, tears welling in his eyes. "You deserve it!" Both men were mobbed by grinning, hollering pumpkin growers, who lifted Ron to their shoulders for a triumphant parade through the parking lot.

"No one has ever grown 1,500 pounds before, ever," Langevin reminded the crowd. "The world record was 1,469 pounds last year. Not only did he break 1,469, but he broke 1,500! 1,502 and 1,450 are the two biggest pumpkins grown in the world this year."

Ron's mom joined the mob surrounding her son. She looked happy, but a little stunned. Cathy had been feeling more and more exasperated and more and more neglected as the season wore on. A delicate gold-and-diamond bracelet sparkled around her wrist. Ron had surprised her with it out of the blue just a few days ago. No special occasion, just a gift to say thank you for being my mom, and maybe a little, thank you for putting up with the pumpkins. "I told him, 'I'll never take it off,' " Cathy said.

Now Joe walked over to her, took her face in his hands and leaned his nose down to hers. "How about that!" he said to her. "Now it was all worth it, eh?"

Mike Oliver complained good-naturedly, "Just when I get to where I can compete, the bar is raised."

Ron and Dick spent the next hour posing for pictures and giving interviews to local radio and television stations. Someone opened the bottle of champagne and Dick grabbed it and poured it over Ron's head. Neither of them had stopped grinning.

Ron called his mother over and she stood by his side, between him and his father, for a family portrait with the pumpkin. Ron's face was red and scrunched up with emotion. He was jubilant, and he was exhausted, and he was . . . relieved. God Almighty, he was relieved. There would be no disappointment to stomach today. No if-onlys. Just joy and celebration. And freedom.

Ron stood next to his pumpkin and his chin fell to his chest. He suddenly seemed overcome with the realization of what had happened. "I did it," he said. "The world record." Tears ran down his face.

"I sacrificed a lot for this," he said. "I sacrificed everything. I dreamed about it." He rested his fist on the pumpkin. Pounded it for emphasis. "Now I don't have to do it anymore. I don't have to win nuthin'. Now I can move on to something else."

The other growers — Joe, Peter, Steve — drifted over to him. Evening was settling over the weigh-off site. Most of the crowd had left. The pumpkins were throwing the long, rounded shadows of evening. It was time to think about dinner.

"I tell you what," Ron said to his friends. "I'm not going out tonight. I'm staying right here with this pumpkin."

EPILOGUE

Ron had to wait another couple of weeks before he could be sure he'd clinched the 2006 world record. There were still a few more weigh-offs to be held, most notably on the West Coast. And word had gone around that Jack LaRue was being mighty mysterious about a big pumpkin he had growing in his patch. In fact, when it came time for the October 9 weigh-off in Half Moon Bay, California, the most prestigious weigh-off on the West Coast, Jack decided to wait and let his pumpkin grow another week. Instead, Sherry LaRue entered her 1068, and placed fourth with a 1,116-pounder. Jack finally cut his biggest pumpkin off the vine and took first place at the Uesugi Farms weigh-off south of San Francisco. His pumpkin weighed 1,315 pounds — the largest pumpkin west of the Mississippi.

Once again, Jack and Sherry came in short

of a world record, but the LaRues grew nine pumpkins weighing more than 1,000 pounds in 2006. With that, Jack retained his title as the most successful pumpkin grower in the world, based on the combined weights of his ten biggest efforts that year.

In Pennsylvania, Gerry Checkon wasn't complaining about her and Larry's less-than-stellar year. Gerry's 1,125.5-pound pumpkin was lighter than its measurements indicated, but it was still good enough to win first place at the state weigh-off in Altoona. She later sold her pumpkin for $1,100 to a farmers' market, where it was carved and put on display. Because of the lousy weather, Larry Checkon labeled 2006 as one of their worst-ever years in the garden. "Even our watermelon and tomatoes were small," he said. For 2007, the Checkons were thinking about growing five plants, up from their usual four. "I might even grow a 1068," Larry said.

Dave Stelts came in ninth at the Ohio Valley weigh-off with a 1,062.5-pound pumpkin — still well shy of his 2000 world record. Looking back, he could see all the mistakes he'd made. The foaming stump slime hit him hard. But he wasn't making excuses. "I don't sit here crying," he said. "I've never given up in my life and I won't

433

give up now. Six years of setbacks is kind of hard, but I'll figure it out."

For the second year in a row, Steve Connolly gave his biggest pumpkin to David Letterman, who packed it with explosives and blew it up on his *Late Night* show.

Ron Wallace appeared with his 1,502-pound pumpkin on *The Martha Stewart Show* October 18, along with Joe Jutras, who brought his 10-foot, 6.5-inch-long gourd. A representative from the Guinness Book of World Records appeared to officially certify Ron and Joe as new world-record holders.

"I've always said, you need a little luck along the way. And the Wallaces finally got some luck," Ron said. After appearing on Martha's show, the 1,502-pounder was carved and put on display for a week in New York City's Central Park. Ron harvested the seeds — about 700 of them.

On November 18, the Southern New England Giant Pumpkin Growers Association held its seed auction to raise money for the 2007 season. There was the usual roster of royal pumpkin blood: Calai and Bobier and Jutras and Pukos and Daletas. But the seeds most in demand carried the Wallace name. A 1502 Wallace fetched $205 — more than respectable for a brand-new, unproven seed. And a 1068 fetched an astounding $850 — yet another record for the most money ever paid for a single seed.

Ron got his Grower of the Year award; his top three pumpkins weighed at GPC sites totaled 3,989.5 pounds. The Wallaces went down in history as the number-one and number-two giant-pumpkin growers in the 2006 season, the first father and son to win that distinction. Both men reveled in their new status as champions. Ron made it a point to respond to every congratulatory e-mail he received. Before October was over, he had 15 soil reports sitting on his desk from pumpkin growers seeking his advice. With newspaper and television reports chronicling his win, Ron became something of a local celebrity.

"Everybody loves a pumpkin," Ron noted with satisfaction.

The Wallaces quickly forgot their resolution to cut back to just five plants in 2007. By Christmas, Ron was laying plans to grow eight.

"I heard somebody say, 'He'll never be able to repeat that kind of success.' So now I'm going to come back next year and I'm going to be the first person to grow sixteen hundred pounds," Ron said. "I'm coming back. I'm coming back hard."

ACKNOWLEDGMENTS

Thanks are due to the uncountable many who endured my endless questions and pumpkin prattle for the year and a half I spent learning about enormous fruit and the people who grow them. The Wallaces opened their lives to me, smoothed my way with other growers, and were gracious and helpful even after they were thoroughly sick of me; I am indebted to them for that. J. D. Megchelsen amazed me with tales of growing giants in Alaska's snowbanks; Bennett Buchsieb shared the details of his experiments in the Arizona desert. Though these and other stories did not find space in the book, their spirit fills every chapter.

Randy Maniloff and David G. Hunter gave me encouragement and guidance when I needed it most. Colin Dickerman provided clear vision. Nick Trautwein scoured these pages with graceful precision and a ruthless intolerance for mixed metaphors. My agent,

Joe Veltre, first saw the potential in this story of ordinary people doing extraordinary things.

Thank you, Christina and Amy, for your enthusiasm, and Tony, for all the burdens you took on to make mine lighter.

SELECTED BIBLIOGRAPHY

This account of a season in the life of giant-pumpkin growers is based primarily on hundreds of hours of interviews, garden tours, e-mails, and phone calls with growers throughout the year. I have cited many of my sources within the body of the text. However, I also relied on other written works as I researched the background, history, and science of pumpkins and competitive gardening. The following books and articles provided me with information and inspiration.

Beauchemin, Jim. *The Secrets of Growing Champion Giant Pumpkins,* DVD. New Hampshire: Custom Flix, 2006.

Black & Decker, *Vegetable Gardening: Your Ultimate Guide.* Minnetonka, MN: Creative Publishing International, 2000.

Connolly, Steve. "Dill's AG Giant Pumpkin Roots: Is the Mammoth Really Extinct?"

Southern New England Giant Pumpkin Growers Newsletter, April 2006.

Csikszentmihalyi, Mihaly. *Finding Flow: The Psychology of Engagement with Everyday Life.* New York: Basic Books, 1997.

Damerow, Gail. *The Perfect Pumpkin: Growing, Cooking, Carving.* Pownal, VT: Storey Publishing, 1997.

Dempsey, D'Maris Amick, Jyoti Shah, and Daniel F. Klessig. "Salicylic Acid and Disease Resistance in Plants." *Critical Reviews in Plant Sciences,* vol. 18, no. 4. Waksman Institute and Department of Molecular Biology and Biochemistry, Rutgers, 1999.

Deppe, Carol. *Breed Your Own Vegetable Varieties: The Gardener's and Farmer's Guide to Plant Breeding and Seed Saving.* White River Junction, VT: Chelsea Green Publishing, 2000.

Fairbairn, Neil. *A Brief History of Gardening.* Emmaus, PA: Rodale Books, 2001.

Goldman, Amy. *The Compleat Squash: A Passionate Grower's Guide to Pumpkins, Squash, and Gourds.* New York: Artisan Books, 2004.

Heiser, Charles B. Jr. *Seed to Civilization: The Story of Food.* Cambridge, MA: Harvard University Press, 1990.

Kingsbury, Al. *The Pumpkin King: Four-Time World Champion Howard Dill and the Atlantic Giant.* Kentville, Nova Scotia: Atlantic Giant Book Distributing, 1992.

Langevin, Don. *How-to-Grow World Class Giant Pumpkins,* 3 vols. Norton, MA: Annedawn Publishing, 1993–2003.

Lavery, Bernard. *How to Grow Giant Vegetables.* Hampton, Middlesex, UK: HarperPerennial, 1995.

Opperman, Chris. *Allotment Folk.* UK: New Holland Publishers, 2004.

The Ortho Home Gardener's Problem Solver. San Ramon, CA: Ortho Books, the Solaris Group, 1993.

Royte, Elizabeth. "Pumpkin v. Pumpkin." *Outside Magazine,* February 1997.

Smith, Edward C. *The Vegetable Gardener's Bible.* North Adams, MA: Storey Publishing, 2000.

Storl, Wolf D. *Culture and Horticulture: A Philosophy of Gardening.* San Francisco: Bio-Dynamic Farming and Gardening Association, 1979, 2000.

Sucher, Dorothy. *The Invisible Garden: A Meditation on the Essence of Memory and the Healing Grace a Garden Can Bestow.* New York: Counterpoint, 2001.

SUNY College of Environmental Science

and Forestry. "Soil pH: What it Means." Prepared by Donald Bickelhaupt, Instructional Support Specialist. www.esf.edu/pubprog/brochure/soilph/soilph.htm.

University of Massachusetts Amherst, UMass Extension Vegetable Program, Soils and Nutrient Management Fact Sheet. www.umassvegetable.org/soil_crop_pest_mgt/soil_nutrient_mgt/soil_basics_I.html.

Uglow, Jenny. *A Little History of British Gardening.* London: Pimlico, 2005.

Vitez, Michael. "1,000 Pounds or Pie." *Philadelphia Inquirer Magazine,* October 29, 1995.

Whaley, Emily. *Mrs. Whaley and Her Charleston Garden: Emily Whaley in Conversation with William Baldwin.* Chapel Hill, NC: Algonquin Books of Chapel Hill, 1997.

Zabar, Abbie. *A Growing Gardener.* New York: Universe Publishing, 1996.

A NOTE ON THE AUTHOR

Susan Warren is the deputy bureau chief for the *Wall Street Journal* in Dallas, Texas. A native Texan, she lives with her husband and two daughters in Arlington, where she first got hooked on backyard gardening. Her biggest pumpkin so far is 240 pounds. This is her first book.

The employees of Thorndike Press hope you have enjoyed this Large Print book. All our Thorndike and Wheeler Large Print titles are designed for easy reading, and all our books are made to last. Other Thorndike Press Large Print books are available at your library, through selected bookstores, or directly from us.

For information about titles, please call:
(800) 223-1244

or visit our Web site at:
www.gale.com/thorndike
www.gale.com/wheeler

To share your comments, please write:
Publisher
Thorndike Press
295 Kennedy Memorial Drive
Waterville, ME 04901